Advance praise for Language in Literature

"This book will no doubt become yet another of Geoff Leech's classic works in stylistics. It demonstrates that what he was writing in the 1960s remains central to the study of literary language, and that he remains at the cutting edge of the subject nearly forty years later.

Geoff Leech writes so clearly and engagingly about stylistic topics that reading this book is pure pleasure. He resolves the dispute between literary criticism and stylistics in one chapter, clarifies the difference between aesthetic response and analysis in another and amongst other things deals with recent developments in corpus stylistics and applications of pragmatics to literature in others. This book is replete with theoretical debate, detailed analysis of literary texts and common-sense pronouncements on stylistic conundrums. It establishes once and for all that stylistics has a valuable place at the heart of literary studies and in the pantheon of linguistic approaches to meaning.

This will be a book to treasure!"

Lesley Jeffries, Professor of English Language and chair of PALA (the Poetics and Linguistics Association), University of Huddersfield, Author of *The Language of Twentieth Century Poetry* (1993 Palgrave) and *Textual Construction of the Female Body* (2007 Palgrave)

"I have been waiting expectantly for some years for this promised collection of Geoffrey Leech's Stylistics papers to be published. We now have a convenient location for all those influential Leechian papers scattered through journals and book collections as well as some fascinating new work. Leech has supplemented those papers we all read avidly when they first appeared (and still recommend regularly to our students) with some fascinating new work. We have a new two-chapter account of Virginia Woolf's short story 'The Mark on the Wall,' which nicely combines more traditional stylistic analysis with the new corpus-stylistic approach, as well as two chapters on the nature and philosophy of Stylistics and its relation to Literary Criticism. The analysis of 'The Mark on the Wall' has that remarkable combination of clarity, sensitivity and sureness of critical touch that Geoffrey Leech is so well-known for, and the philosophical discussions are full of his usual acute observation and balanced good sense. The Master has returned and we are all the better for it!"

Mick Short, Professor of English Language and Literature, Lancaster University

"This volume, by a founder of British stylistics, is long overdue. His articles, now usefully 'refreshed', mark the development of the discipline over forty years, from formalist functionalism to corpus stylistics. Always sensitive and sensible, they confirm the perennial value of close engagement with the text as a basis for critical judgements."

Katie Wales, Research Professor in English, University of Sheffield; author of the 'Dictionary of Stylistics' (2001 revised 2nd edn) (Pearson Education)

LANGUAGE IN LITERATURE

Style and Foregrounding

GEOFFREY LEECH

PEARSON
Longman

Harlow, England • London • New York • Boston • San Francisco • Toronto
Sydney • Tokyo • Singapore • Hong Kong • Seoul • Taipei • New Delhi
Cape Town • Madrid • Mexico City • Amsterdam • Munich • Paris • Milan

PEARSON EDUCATION LIMITED

Edinburgh Gate
Harlow CM20 2JE
United Kingdom
Tel: +44 (0)1279 623623
Fax: +44 (0)1279 431059
Website: www.pearsoned.co.uk

First edition published in Great Britain in 2008

© Pearson Education Limited 2008

The right of Geoffrey Leech to be identified as author
of this work has been asserted by him in accordance
with the Copyright, Designs and Patents Act 1988.

ISBN: 978-0-582-05109-6

British Library Cataloguing in Publication Data
A CIP catalogue record for this book can be obtained from the British Library

Library of Congress Cataloguing in Publication Data

Leech, Geoffrey N.
    Language in literature : style and foregrounding / Geoffrey Leech.
        p. cm.
    Includes bibliographical references and index.
    ISBN 978-0-582-05109-6
    1. English language–Style.   2. English literature–History and criticism–
Theory, etc.   3. English literature–Explication.   4. Style, Literary.   I. Title.
    PE1421.L37 2008
    808′.042–dc22

                                                                    2008016971

10   9   8   7   6   5   4   3   2   1
12   11   10   09   08

Set by 35 in 9/11.5 pt Palatino
Printed and bound in Malaysia (CTP-VVP)

The Publisher's policy is to use paper manufactured from sustainable forests.

Contents

Preface

This book has been a long time a-coming. Towards the end of the 1980s I found I had built up a small collection of articles on 'practical stylistics' – how to analyse the language of poems, passages of prose, and so on – and that these had presented somewhat different facets of a consistent approach, with emphasis on the concept of foregrounding. During the period that I wrote these papers, I was intimately involved in the teaching of stylistics as a 'link course' between language and literature, at first at University College London, and then in our School of English at Lancaster University.

From the 1970s, I went through a period of being distracted, and sometimes overwhelmed, with other non-literary interests and preoccupations. In particular, I was engaged in the swiftly developing field of pragmatics (applied to stylistic topics in Chapters 7 and 9 of this book) and in the equally swiftly developing field of corpus linguistics. These took me away from literary studies, but I never lost my interest and joy in examining literary texts closely, to see how they work in terms of language and its interpretation. When I look back on more than forty years of research and publication, it is working on language in English literature that has given me most enduring pleasure. Recently, I was engaged with my colleague Mick Short, with preparing a second edition of our book *Style in Fiction* (1981; second edition 2007), and this was the chief impetus for getting involved again in reading, thinking and publishing in stylistics.

During the fallow period (roughly 1990 to 2005) whenever I was invited to give a lecture on stylistics, I trotted out my ideas on a fascinating text of Virginia Woolf's, 'The Mark on the Wall', which never ceased to puzzle and engage me. This lecture, duly reworked and elaborated, has become Chapter 10 of this book, one of the three final chapters not previously published.

Although most of my research since the 1980s has been related to corpus linguistics in some way or other, I have never managed to bring together these two fields of interest – the power of corpus linguistics and the fascination of literary stylistics – until very recently, although my colleagues Mick Short, Elena Semino and Jonathan Culpeper were among the very first to engage in the budding field now known as 'corpus stylistics'. I have attempted my own debut in this field in Chapter 11, where I look at the same work examined in Chapter 10, 'The Mark on the Wall', from a different angle – the angle provided by the objective eye of the computer – to see whether this new viewpoint confirms my previous analysis (in Chapter 10) or provides new insights. In the final chapter, Chapter 12, I attempt something quite different: a rationale for the whole approach to literary style presented in the book. This chapter is retrospective in two ways. It looks back on the preceding chapters, and tries to justify the consistency and continuity of approach that I discern there. Also, it looks back on a half century when revolutions of thought in both linguistic and literary studies have taken place, often driving the two fields in different directions. I still believe, after fifty years of studying both language and literature, that there has to be, not a battle, but, a bond between them. This book is my attempt to show that bond.

As already mentioned, Chapters 2–9 of this book have been published before – mostly in collections of papers and in journal articles where they are unlikely to be come across today. In addition, four previously unpublished chapters (Chapters 1 and 10–12) have been added. The details of previous publication are given overleaf.

Only minor changes have been made to the chapters as originally published. The odd word has been changed, and references have been updated in minor ways. Sometimes, I deleted repetitions or added some cross-references to other chapters where there was further discussion of a topic. To make it clear that these footnote additions are new, they are printed in boldface. At other times, when a piece of text was glaringly out of date or needed explanation, I added some new information or some new references in a footnote.

I have also introduced consistency in the way chapters are divided into subsections. In their original form, some chapters had no subdivisions; others had numbered subdivisions but without titles. I decided to adopt the practice of giving sections of chapters a section number (e.g. 5.2) and a title. This should help readers to find their way around the book. Similarly, I adopted a consistent style of referencing publications, using the Harvard system throughout.

The following are original publication details of chapters 2–9 in this book:

Chapter 2

Geoffrey Leech, 'Linguistics and the Figures of Rhetoric', in Roger G. Fowler (ed.) *Essays in Style and Language*, London: Routledge and Kegan Paul, 1966, pp. 135–56.

Chapter 3

Geoffrey Leech, '*This Bread I Break*: Language and Interpretation, *Review of English Literature*, 6.2 (1965) pp. 66–75. London: Longmans, Green.

Chapter 4

Geoffrey Leech, 'Literary Criticism and Linguistic Description', *DQR* (*Dutch Quarterly Review of Anglo-American Letters*), 7.1 (1977), pp. 2–22.

Chapter 5

Geoffrey Leech, 'Stylistics', in Teun van Dijk (ed.), *Discourse and Literature: New Approaches to the Analysis of Literary Genres*, Amsterdam: Benjamins, 1985, pp. 39–57.

Chapter 6

Geoffrey Leech, 'Music in Metre: "Sprung Rhythm" in Victorian and Georgian Poetry', *DQR* (*Dutch Quarterly Review of Anglo-American Letters*), 14.3 (1984), pp. 200–213. Reprinted, with additions, in Theo D'Haen (ed.), *Linguistics and the Study of Literature*, Amsterdam: Rodopi, 1986, pp. 111–127.

Chapter 7

Geoffrey Leech, 'Pragmatics, Discourse Analysis, Stylistics and "the Celebrated Letter"', *Prose Studies*, 6.2 (1983), pp. 141–57.

Chapter 8

Geoffrey Leech, 'Stylistics and Functionalism', in Nigel Fabb, Derek Attridge, Alan Durant and Colin MacCabe (eds.) *The Linguistics of Writing: Arguments between Language and Literature*, Manchester: Manchester University Press, pp. 76–88.

Chapter 9

Geoffrey Leech, 'Pragmatic Principles in Shaw's *You Never Can Tell*, in Michael Toolan (ed.), *Language, Text and Context: Essays in Stylistics*, London: Routledge, pp. 259–79.

Acknowledgements

I should like to express my thanks to all those who helped me with this book, both by comment and advice on the content, and by preparing the manuscript for publication: particularly Diana Hudspith, Elena Semino, Mick Short and Brian Walker. Acknowledgements are also due for those who helped me on individual chapters at the time of their original publication. These are added as a note at the end of relevant chapters.

In thanking my sympathetic editor, Philip Langeskov, I give both thanks and apologies, through him, to the generations of Longman commissioning editors who have generously allowed me more time to finish this work.

Geoffrey Leech
Lancaster University
October 2007

Publisher's Acknowledgements

We are grateful to the following for permission to reproduce copyright material:

Chapter 2 from Roger G Fowler(ed) *Essays in Style and Language*, London, Routledge and Kegan Paul, 1966, pp. 135–56; Chapter 4 from DQR (Dutch Quarterly Review of Anglo-American Letters) 7.1 (1977), pp. 2–22, by permission of Editions Rodopi BV, Amsterdam; Chapter 5 from Teun van Dijk (ed) *Discourse and Literature: New Approaches to the Analysis of Literary Genres*, pp. 39–57. With kind permission by John Benjamins Publishing Company, Amsterdam/Philadelphia. www.benjamins.com; Chapter 6 from Victorian and Georgian Poetry, DQR (Dutch Quarterly Review of Anglo-American Letters), 14.3 (1984), pp. 200–213. Reprinted with additions, in Theo D'Haen (ed), *Linguistics and the Study of Literature*, 1986, pp. 111–127 by permission of Editions Rodopi BV; Chapter 8 from Nigel Fabb, Derek Attridge, Alan

CHAPTER 1

Introduction: about this book, its content and its viewpoint

My contributions to this book were written over a 43-year period 1964–2007, during which **stylistics** – the linguistic study of literary texts – has developed from being a fledgling offshoot of linguistics and literary studies to being quite an established discipline – or perhaps we should call it an 'interdiscipline' – in its own right. Stylistics, as it is understood today, began as a cautious application of linguistic techniques to literary texts in the late 1950s. Nowadays the interdisciplinary breadth of the field, as revealed tellingly in Wales's *A Dictionary of Stylistics* (2nd edn, 2001), for example, is impressive.

1.1 Stylistics as an 'interdiscipline'

However, the value of stylistics to its parent disciplines of linguistic and literary studies remains controversial, and this shows in the fact that the name of the field – 'stylistics' – is less firmly established than the subject itself. On the one hand, a sign that the field has come of age is the number of journals that support it: for example, *Style, Journal of Literary Semantics*, and *Language and Literature* are three journals of high quality in which linguistic and literary studies come together. On the other hand, none of these journals mentions the word 'stylistics' in its title. Moreover, the academic society which represents the discipline both in the United Kingdom and internationally also avoids the term: it is called the Poetics and Linguistics Association (PALA). There have been some uneasy attempts to confront the terminological problem – for example, a book edited by Carter and Simpson (1989), *Language, Discourse and Literature*, describes its subject as 'discourse stylistics', perhaps to emphasize how much stylistics has been advancing towards the same goals as discourse analysis. Other terminological proposals – such as literary pragmatics (Sell 1991) and critical discourse stylistics (Weber 1992) – go further in carving out a new conception of the field. But these terms, like 'poetics', have a habit of suggesting limitations of the field in one direction or another, and no term has been adopted generally as a substitute for 'stylistics'.

Strangely, then, the activity of studying literature using linguistic techniques appears to be more firmly rooted than the label or labels under which it is known. Why? On the one hand, this is partly because linguistics has been busy catching up with stylistics – some would say, overtaking it – by developing new techniques of interpreting language in use: overlapping fields such as pragmatics, discourse analysis and text linguistics have burgeoned since the 1960s. To that extent, stylistics may seem to have become simply a sub-field of other sub-fields in linguistics. On the other hand, in recent decades, the philosophy of literary studies has undergone such upheavals that it has been difficult to pin labels on definable areas of expertise relating to the study of literature. Questions such as 'What is literature?', 'What are the goals of literary studies?', which used to seem orderly, controllable issues in the reassuring world of Wellek and Warren's *Theory of Literature* (1949), have become ever more elusive and problematic. So how can a sub-field such as stylistics be defined, and how can its purposes be clarified? This has seemed problematic as well.[1]

Furthermore, in both literary theory and linguistic stylistics, the idea that there is something special about literature, and that there is a literary canon which deserves more respectful treatment than mundane texts, has been strenuously challenged. The classics have been toppled off their pedestals, so that nowadays one can scarcely appeal to the term 'literature' as something which self-evidently means something. This is a salutary change from some points of view, rejecting an earlier 'sacred cow' veneration of the classics and opening up to serious study bodies of texts which had previously been overlooked. But it is also a disorienting one.

Despite these uncertainties, this book will continue to rely on the term *stylistics* as the one which most neutrally represents the field acting as a bridge between linguistic and literary studies. There have been revolutionary developments in linguistics and literary theory since 1965, and yet the essential role and formulation of stylistics, as a discipline bridging the gap between the two, remains valid.

My contention, indeed, is that this notion of a 'bridge discipline' has actually acquired more secure linguistic underpinnings in the last 35 years, in the light of developments in pragmatics and discourse analysis. The earliest-published paper in this book (Chapter 3, published in 1965) aimed to demonstrate the interrelation between LINGUISTIC DESCRIPTION and LITERARY INTERPRETATION (see also Chapter 4, pp. 41–3). Such a distinction, in the light of the formalist and structuralist tenets which dominated linguistics 45 years ago, seemed scarcely tenable: in those days describing the formal or structural properties of a literary work was typically considered a sufficient exposition of its significance. But this distinction between a text – defined by the language code – and its interpretation, which has since been variously elaborated in other chapters of this book (especially Chapters 2, 4, 5, 7, 9 and 10),[2] fits well with dichotomies which have become commonplaces of linguistic thought since the later twentieth century. For example, linguists nowadays are very familiar with distinctions such as those between *form* and *function* (see Chapter 8), between *semantics* and *pragmatics* (Leech 1980, 1983), between what is '*said*' and what is '*meant*' (Grice 1975), between *decoding* and *inference* (Sperber and Wilson 1995), between *text* and *discourse* (see Chapter 7), and between *cohesion* and *coherence* (Widdowson 1978). Placing linguistics in a broad humanistic and social science perspective, it no longer seems controversial that when we describe the characteristics of a piece of language, we can (and should) also study its interrelations with those things which lie beyond it but nevertheless give it meaning in the broadest sense. These include the shared knowledge of writer and reader, the social background, and the placing of the text in its cultural and historical context.

This interface between linguistic description and interpretation is precisely the sphere of stylistics as I see it: by undertaking a linguistic *analysis* as part of the interrelation between the two fields of study, we facilitate and anticipate an interpretative *synthesis*. Within stylistics, that is, linguistic and literary concerns are as inseparably associated as are the two sides of a coin, or (in the context of linguistics) the *formal* and *functional* aspects of textual study. In fact, the distinction between form and function is as fruitful in linguistics and stylistics as it has ever been: the interplay of formal and functional approaches to a literary work is a recurrent theme in this book, and the principal focus of Chapter 8. In this connection, a key concept of stylistics, as I have perceived it, is FOREGROUNDING (see especially Chapter 2, pp. 15–19), and a cardinal value of this principle is that it is the meeting point of formal and functional points of view. Formally, foregrounding is a deviation, or departure, from what is expected in the linguistic code or the social code expressed through language; functionally, it is a special effect or significance conveyed by that departure.

The concept of foregrounding has been given overdue book-length investigations by van Peer (1986) and Douthwaite (2000).[3] More recently, an issue of *Language and Literature* (2007, **16** (2)) under the guest editorship of Willie van Peer focuses on the state of the art in the theory of foregrounding and its empirical bases. I can do no better, here, than to help define the concept in Douthwaite's words:

[C]ognitive psychology has demonstrated that habituation in perception and comprehension is a normal phenomenon in human life. Habituation routinises life, it dulls the senses and the critical faculties. One way of combating habituation is to experience an entity in a novel fashion so that our attention is arrested, and our automatic mode of processing together with the standard response we produce to the familiar stimulus are **impeded**, slowed down, surprised even. This obliges us to examine the entity more closely and from a new perspective. As a result we are challenged to place a new interpretation on reality.

Impeding normal processing by showing the world in an unusual, unexpected or abnormal manner is termed **defamiliarization**. Thus defamiliarization may be achieved by subverting the rules governing perception and behaviour. The **linguistic technique** employed in subverting the world in this manner is termed **foregrounding**.

(Douthwaite 2000: 178)[4]

The value and varied applications of the concept of foregrounding, in explicating the language of literature, can only be shown by illustration in depth, referring to particular literary works. It will be elaborated in later chapters, forming an evolving theme, a common thread, connecting the chapters of this book. Another recurrent theme, which links many of the contributions, is the importance of combining theory with practical application. It can be argued that, in an 'interdiscipline' such as stylistics more than in most subjects, *the proof of the pudding* must be in *the eating*. That is, since the justification for stylistics is in the application of *linguistic* methods and tools to *literature*, it is in its very nature an applied and practical discipline – which we put into practice by addressing the particular artistries of particular piece(s) of poetry or prose. 'Putting into practice' here means applying the methods and insights of stylistics to literary examples, and especially to substantial texts and extracts representing various genres and types of literature. At the same time, a practical hands-on engagement with literature, if successful and rewarding, goes a long way towards justifying any theory that underlies it. Hence most of the chapters which follow (particularly Chapters 3, 4, 5, 6, 7, 9, 10 and 11) begin by discussing theoretical ideas, arguments and frameworks, and then move on to apply these elements of general theory by using them to look closely at the detailed features of given texts.

1.2 The chapter-by-chapter progression of this book

I have emphasized a common thread connecting the book's various chapters. It would be reasonable to ask, now, what sort of stage-by-stage progression they represent, coming as they do from a period of forty-five years in which ideas have by no means stood still.

First and most obviously, the sequence of chapters represents movement in time: there is a general chronological progression from the two chapters following this, published in 1965 and 1966,[5] to the last three chapters, finished in 2007. The advantage of this is that the reader meets initial, and in some way more basic, ideas before their developments and extensions in later work.[6]

Secondly, there is roughly a progression from small-scale to larger-scale works. There was a common complaint, back in the 1960s and 1970s, that stylistic techniques lent themselves mainly to works in miniature, and particularly to lyrical poems, where the effects of foregrounding were most striking. Nowadays, this is no longer a reasonable complaint: developments in pragmatics and discourse analysis have enabled stylistics to evolve techniques for examining larger units than the sentence, and indeed quite lengthy texts. (Medd and Biermann 1998 catalogue the extensive range of literary works, long as well as short, studied in recent stylistics publications.) Most recently of all, the advent of corpus stylistics (see Chapter 11) has enabled us, in certain ways, to obtain a profile or overview of the language of a whole text, or even a whole series of texts such as the novels of Henry James. In the early days of stylistics, when the 'isms' in vogue were formalism, structuralism, practical criticism and new criticism,[7] it was natural to focus attention on the more formally striking features of literary language, such as abound in certain (especially modern) types of lyrical poetry, as those most inviting linguistic study. Later, the trend moved towards lengthier works of literature, as well as towards wider horizons outside literature, such as media discourse. The custom, in academic life, of justifying latest trends in thinking by wholesale rejection of the preceding ones, had brought the formalists, structuralists, and new critics to prominence in their own time. Not surprisingly, in their turn, these text-oriented approaches came in for some severe disapproval in the literary and linguistic world that followed theirs.

But here I prefer to emphasize, instead, the continuity of thinking and of techniques which we can share with these 'isms' of the previous generation. One dominant merit of these earlier schools of thought was that they lay great store by the careful, even rigorous, scrutiny of what texts were like, and how they hung together. To a considerable extent, this observational habit has been devalued in this age. It is true that we have since learnt to extend our horizons to the functional meanings of a text in their broadest sense, but this does not require us to neglect the importance of the evidence of the text itself, seen as a linguistic phenomenon. Thus I hope that it will be seen as a strength of this book that a sense of continuity is asserted, whereby formal and functional concerns are seen to develop side by side through the decades. It may be that formalism was much the more powerful influence in 1965, and that functionalism has taken the upper hand in more recent decades. But the important point is that both are necessary to a balanced approach, and the evolution of ideas and techniques over the past forty years has not changed that basic truth. Hence, a movement from small exemplars of literary language to more extensive ones is a natural way to expound not only the progress and enlargement of the subject, but also its continuity.

With this progression from *small* to *large* goes a third progression to be observed in the book: from poetry (Chapters 2–6) to prose and drama (Chapters 7–11). This genre-based ordering illustrates the way in which stylistics has developed, from a discipline most at home with lyrical poetry, to one exploring larger-scale and less tightly wrought works. And perhaps yet a further progression – a fourth one – may be noted here. Poetry, as the subject of earlier chapters, is literature in its most concentrated and (arguably) quintessential form. As we move from poetry to other genres in this book, we also move towards the periphery of 'the literary'. Specifically, few would deny that Johnson's 'Celebrated Letter' to Lord Chesterfield in Chapter 7 is a 'work of art' in the ordinary everyday sense; but is it a piece of literature? It is a letter Johnson wrote to fulfil a practical social function – to reject his lordship's claim to be his patron. Although it does not fit into the canonical core of literature, it is nevertheless rewarding to examine from the stylistic point of view. A similar point, perhaps, could be made about Woolf's 'The Mark on the Wall' in Chapter 10. Is it fact or fiction? Is it a short story or a fugitive essay? It appears not to fit into the regular genres of English literature, but nevertheless the techniques of stylistics can be as revealingly at home with it as they are with something in the mainstream of literary traditions. It has been widely accepted, in the last twenty years, that the techniques of stylistics are a practical implementation of linguistic methods which can be applied to literary or non-literary texts. They are not to be penned in by the fences that have traditionally been placed between literary genres, or around the literary 'canon' itself. Instead, stylistics helps to *reveal* the literary qualities of texts – not by applying criteria from some rigorous formal definition, but by applying techniques helping to bring out the (often latent) characteristics which people associate with literary texts and which they value. However, none of the tools of the stylistician's stock-in-trade are restricted in their application to literary phenomena. A moment's thought will remind us that the most typically 'poetic' characteristics of language, such as sound patterning, verse form, metaphor, irony and paradox, are found in 'non-literary' discourse as well: in political speeches, in advertising, in pop lyrics and indeed in the creativity of ordinary conversation (see Carter 2004).

1.3 A digression on 'literariness'

At this point, a digression on the theme of 'literariness' is relevant. Forty years ago, a common way for academics to keep themselves in employment was to define the notion of 'literature' in terms of some elusive quality of 'literariness'. Formalists or structuralists defined 'literariness' in terms of formal criteria – for example, Jakobson's (1960, 1966) criterion was parallelism. Functionalists defined it in terms of function – Jakobson (1960), being a functionalist as well as a formalist, elaborated a conception of the specific *poetic function* (see Chapter 8 below). While literary theorists often defined it in terms of criteria such as mimesis, linguists defined the literary by modelling the literary or poetic competence of the reader on the linguistic competence of Chomsky, or in terms of the latest linguistic theory, such as the performative hypothesis or speech act theory.[8] It seems to me, however, that all this ingenious effort was misguided, because 'literature' is pre-eminently a PROTOTYPE concept, in Eleanor Rosch's sense of prototype (1975), which has since become a commonplace of cognitive linguistics. What she demonstrated is that, unlike Aristotle's classic conception of categories, most conceptual categories in the human mind and in language are characterized by a core of clear cases, with a blurry periphery of unclear, borderline cases. (Examples often cited are natural kinds such as *bird* or *fruit* and categories of artefact such as *furniture*: we can name 'chair', 'table', 'bookcase' and so on as pre-eminently clear examples of *furniture*, whereas 'table lamp', 'computer', 'deckchair' and 'cooker' are more peripheral.)

The concepts of 'literature' and 'literariness' are prototypical in this respect. Few people who know anything about English literature would doubt the literary status of, for example, *The Mill on the Floss* or Shakespeare's sonnets; but many might have doubts about (say) *Murder on the Orient Express* or Chesterfield's letters to his son. There is no litmus test for literature, but rather a range of overlapping indicators of different kinds, such as sociocultural, aesthetic and linguistic criteria. The core of the concept of literature is identified by a convergence of these criteria, just as Rosch and others have shown it to be for categories like 'bird' and 'furniture'. In a number of chapters in this book, I stress the importance of FOREGROUNDING, as a stylistic trait we above all find in literature, and in Chapter 8 I mention another criterion, that of the AUTOTELIC nature of literature – the fact that goals of communication are fulfilled in the creative work itself. A third criterion, prominent in Chapter 2, is rich MULTIPLICITY OF SIGNIFICANCE. And I would argue that these three literary traits are interconnected. However, I would not want to give the impression that these stylistically oriented criteria are the only ones which matter in the identification of a text as a work of literature, or that they are always found in works which 'count as' literature. On the contrary, I would argue that an advantage of the stylistic approach I would advocate is its *negative capability* in this respect – its ability to be free from rigid preconceptions about what literature is. It can be said that by choosing to analyse a text stylistically, using techniques well adapted for the study of literature, we thereby treat the text *as* literature. If it had not seemed worthwhile giving the text this kind of attention, one would not have chosen it for that purpose.

The same quality of negative capability can be claimed for stylistics in confronting the positive evaluation often inherent in the use of terms such as *poem* and *literature*. This 'honorific' usage is evident, for example, when someone says 'That's not a poem – it's just a piece of doggerel', or 'That's not literature – it's just propaganda'. By choosing to take a text as a subject for stylistic analysis, we open ourselves to every possibility of establishing the nexus between form and interpretation in the text, and in this sense, of seeking its full communicative potential *as a literary text*. (This does not mean we are free to 'read into' the text whatever subjective interpretations we like – the notion of textual 'warranty', returned to in Chapters 2 and 3, pp. 24, 33, is a prerequisite to literary interpretation.) In this way, we give the writer the full credit for what is in the text; that is, we engage in *elucidation* and *appreciation* of the text, without needing to engage in *evaluation* of a text as being 'good', 'bad', 'better' or 'worse' than others. The same applies to features or aspects or parts of texts – a line of poetry, for example. It is not part of the brief of the stylistic analyst to make a negative judgement about a piece of literature. This is not to say that in stylistics we cannot make judgements in favour of or against a literary text, but merely to say that they are not an inherent part of the job. I will return to this theme in Chapter 12, in discussing the educational role of stylistics.

So, to revert to my main thread: the general picture presented in this book is one of evolutionary change in stylistics – particularly in the direction of expanding our horizons beyond the confines of any restrictive view of stylistics or of literature. Revolutionary poses will not be found in this book: instead, there is an emphasis on underlying continuity of model and method.

1.4 A list of texts examined

Chapter 2 – Various short extracts
Chapter 3 – 'This Bread I Break' by Dylan Thomas
Chapter 4 – 'Ode to a Nightingale' by John Keats
Chapter 5 – 'Ode to the West Wind' by Percy Bysshe Shelley
Chapter 6 – Various passages from Victorian poetry
Chapter 7 – The 'Celebrated Letter' from Samuel Johnson to Lord
                     Chesterfield
Chapter 8 – Various short extracts
Chapter 9 – 'You Never Can Tell' by George Bernard Shaw
Chapter 10 – 'The Mark on the Wall' by Virginia Woolf
Chapter 11 – 'The Mark on the Wall' by Virginia Woolf again.

Notes

1. The field of stylistics lost credibility for thirty years in the eyes of literary critics in the USA through the demolition job performed by Stanley Fish in 'What is stylistics and why are they saying such terrible things about it?' (1980). In the words of Sylvia Adamson (2003):

   > it crystallised the alarmed reaction of many in the literary establishment to the impact of stylistics in the 1960s and to the growing hegemony of linguistics across the humanities more generally. But the sheer virtuosity of Fish's rhetoric turned defence into attack and by the 1980s the essay had the status of a classic text of the anti-formalist movement, surviving recurrent rebuttals . . . to exercise a potent influence both on the internal development of stylistics and on its reputation abroad. By the millennium, stylistics had become, almost, a subject that dare not speak its name.

   Perhaps the time is ripe for rehabilitation.
2. The distinction between a *text*, as a linguistic phenomenon, and its interpretation is elaborated in Chapter 12. It is my contention that this cardinal distinction has been unhelpfully blurred or problematized in some recent thinking in linguistics and literary theory.
3. A related approach, perhaps describable as an updated, cognitive version of foregrounding theory, is that of Cook (1994), who defines literature as text in terms of *schema refreshment*. In the world of literary scholarship, the work of Derek Attridge should also be mentioned here. In two of his books (2004a [1988] and 2004b) he advances the theory of the essential *singularity, peculiarity* and creative *'otherness'* of literature – a view that seems to come close to the notion of 'defamiliarization' inherited by foregrounding theory from the Russian formalist school. However, he draws his inspiration from the French poststructuralists, rather than from linguistics and formalism.
4. Regarding the history of foregrounding theory, the following quotation from Willie van Peer (2007: 99) will be useful:

   > The study of foregrounding has been around for a while now. Its roots reach into Greek Antiquity, but it is in the last century that it received its full-fledged status as a theory, first in the years 1916–17 with the Russian Formalists, then a second time in the 1960s and 1970s, mainly through the reception of the formalists' principles and their further development in the West. We are now, some 40 years later, at a good moment to take stock.

5. Actually, Chapters 2 and 3 were written in their numerical order (in 1964–65), but were published in the opposite order (1966 and 1965 respectively). This is the one exception to the chronological ordering by publication of Chapters 2–9. In their original form, these two chapters had no section headings: these have now been added.
6. I have resisted the temptation to update the content of earlier chapters, as their interest lies partly in their reflection of the thinking of the time when they were written. However, there are some present-day additions to the footnotes (signalled in boldface), so that the present-day reader can benefit from more recent references.

7. See, for example Erlich (1965), Jakobson and Jones (1970), Lévi-Strauss (1963: 31–97, 206–31), Richards (1929) and Wimsatt (1954) for *loci classici* of these schools of thought, which can also be usefully followed up in their entries in Wales's *Dictionary* (2001).
8. On the definition of literature and the related question of literary or poetic competence, see Bierwisch (1970), Ohmann (1971), Culler (1975: 113–30); also Pratt's (1977: 3–37) attack on the 'Poetic Language Fallacy'.

CHAPTER 2

Linguistics and the figures of rhetoric

2.1 Introduction

If rhetoric is an outmoded discipline, its influence lives on in the present-day study of literature, at least in the 'figures of speech' (above all, metaphor), which form an important part of critical vocabulary. Neither the traditional 'definitions' of the rhetorical manuals, nor those of the more recent manuals of usage, provide a satisfactory account of these terms; and attempts to elucidate them by reference to the psychology or philosophy of language have met with only limited success, largely, it seems to me, because of the inadequacy of the linguistic part of the writers' explanatory equipment. In consequence, the subject of rhetorical figures has become an unjustifiably neglected department of literary education.[1]

This chapter is not an attempt to provide a practical remedy for this state of affairs, in the form of detailed descriptions of figures of speech. (This last term is used in a loose modern sense, roughly incorporating all that was meant by 'figures of speech', 'tropes' and 'figures of thought' in classical rhetoric.)[2] Many of these figures (particularly those which traditionally belong under the heading 'figures of thought') appear to lie altogether outside the linguist's sphere of competency; others do not entirely fall within it. Moreover, a consistent and accurate linguistic account of figures of speech can only be undertaken within the framework of a more general account of the characteristic linguistic features of literary texts. My primary aim, therefore, will be to suggest how linguistic theory can be accommodated to the task of describing such recurrent phenomena in literature as metaphor, parallelism, alliteration and antithesis.

Rhetoric only enters into the discussion in so far as it has provided us with most of our terminology for talking about these features. In a historical perspective, the *Ars Rhetorica* and *Ars Poetica* of classical tradition 'institutionalized' many of them, and combined with literary fashion to give special prominence to certain figures at certain historical periods. But my general concern is with characteristics of creative writing irrespective of author, period and language. It follows from this approach that such a question as 'How can we define a metaphor?' is, in a sense, misconceived: an unprejudiced examination of the recurrent linguistic features of literary texts may, or may not, yield a category which fits the traditional term 'metaphor' sufficiently well not to do violence to accepted usage. The terminology is logically subsequent to, not prior to, the system of classification.

2.2 A linguistic perspective on literary language

By popular definition, literature is the creative use of language; and this, in the context of general linguistic description, can be equated with the use of unorthodox or deviant forms of language. It is not surprising that until recent years, linguistics contributed little to stylistic analysis; a discipline has to attain a degree of maturity and confidence before it can profitably take into its ken a type of material guaranteed to produce exceptions to rules of general application.

The essential prerequisite of the linguist's approach to literature is that he should have means to assign different degrees of generality to his statements about language. There are two particularly important ways in which the description of language entails generalization. In the first place, language operates by what may be called *descriptive* generalization, in the sense that a number of heterogeneous terms $A_1, A_2, A_3, A_4, \ldots$ may be recognized as being in some sense 'the same thing', i.e. belonging to the same general category A. If the items *I, they, it*, etc., are given the general grammatical name 'pronoun', this is because it is necessary to discern their likeness, despite grammatical differences such as the selection of a singular verb after *I* and a plural verb after *they*. A scale of *descriptive delicacy*[3] permits the grammarian to take account of the likeness or equivalence of linguistic terms, whether in shape or function, whilst not neglecting, unless he so wishes, the differentiation to various degrees of refinement of items within general categories. Steps on this scale can be illustrated by the increasing delicacy of the grammatical classes 'pronoun': 'objective personal pronoun'; 'objective third-person pronoun'; 'objective third-person singular masculine non-reflexive pronoun' – the last class is of maximum delicacy, consisting of only one item (*him*). Any description of a language is relatively general and incomplete, or relatively detailed and complete, according to the depth of descriptive delicacy to which it penetrates.

The other type of generalization is implicit in the use of terms such as 'dialect' and 'language' (in the sense in which we talk of a particular language, such as English). The raw material for linguistic study is composed of numerous individual events of speaking, hearing, writing and reading; but it is assumed that from these events, generalizations can be made covering the linguistic behaviour of whole populations of large geographical areas. It is unfortunate that the word *language* commonly has to do service for at least three degrees of generalization, between which the linguist is bound to make a clear distinction. 'Language' (without the article) refers to the whole field of human behaviour which it is the linguist's task to study. 'A language' generally denotes a less general concept, convenient but in some cases arbitrarily defined, within which a particular linguistic enterprise or study is usually confined (e.g. English, Russian, Swahili). Further, 'language' is often used for a still less general aspect of linguistic behaviour, for example when it is said that 'Mr X speaks a different language from Mr Y' (although both are Englishmen born and bred); 'Mr X uses one language to his wife, another to his employer'; or 'the inhabitants of St Ives, Cornwall, speak a different language from the inhabitants of Barnstaple, Devon'. If it is decided to make a 'language', such as English, the upper limit of generality for a particular description (as is generally the case), then the degrees of generality applying to different varieties of English can be plotted on a scale of increasing delicacy or differentiation, until such relative minutiae as 'the language Mr X uses in addressing his young daughter, aged 2' are taken into account. This type of delicacy, which may be entitled *institutional delicacy*,[4] operates on a scale which relates linguistic behaviour to other forms of social behaviour, and to the structure of society as composed of successively larger groupings of individuals and communities.

In fact it is more accurate to distinguish two scales of institutional delicacy. The first, the *register scale*,[5] handles various registers or roles of linguistic activity within society, distinguishing, for example, spoken language from written language; the language of respect from the language of condescension; the language of advertising from the language of science. The second distinguishes the linguistic habits of various sections of society, differentiated by age, social class, sex and geographical area. The end point of this *dialect scale* is reached with the *idiolect*, or the aggregate of the characteristic linguistic habits of a particular individual within the linguistic community. The two scales can be visualized as intersecting axes; the literary works of a particular author, for instance, would have to be plotted, as a subject for linguistic study, with reference to both the register scale and the dialect scale.

These scales are not merely conveniences for the linguist's description, but reflect the nature of language itself. If we started from the assumption that all differences in linguistic events are equally important, we would not only conclude that language is amorphous and incapable of systematic study, but would also be at a loss to explain how it acts as a vehicle of communication. Likenesses are more important than dissimilarities. Thus with reference to the dialect and register scales, it may be appropriate to study different varieties of English as if they were self-contained languages, before relating them in a total description of the language; but the fragmentation presupposes a synthesis.

It has been necessary to go at some length into the question of generality in language, in order to clarify the notion of *linguistic deviation* which is essential to a linguistic account of literary language. It is a commonplace that poets and other creative writers use language in unorthodox ways: that they are by convention allowed 'poetic licence'. But we also need to recognize *degrees* of unorthodoxy, and it is here that the scales of descriptive and institutional delicacy become relevant.

Degrees of deviation can initially be defined by reference to the scales of institutional delicacy. A linguistic feature will be highly deviant if it is unique to a low-generality variety of English; if it is common to a number of low-generality varieties, or unique to a variety of higher generality, it is to that extent less deviant. The least deviant, or 'most normal' feature of all, will be that which is common to all varieties of English.

The scale of descriptive delicacy is brought in to assess the degree of structural importance of a feature which is institutionally deviant, or, in subjective terms, the degree of surprise it is capable of eliciting in the uninitiated reader (or listener). If, in most varieties of English, adverbial clauses beginning with *if* are distributed so that more *if* clauses precede than follow the main clauses on which they depend, whereas in one particular variety of English this tendency is reversed, this will constitute a relatively trivial deviation, identifiable only at a considerable depth of descriptive delicacy. A contrast to this is the frequently instanced case of the pronoun *thou/thee/thine/thy*, which is restricted to only a few varieties of English (e.g. religious English), and moreover represents a deviation of descriptive importance, involving a restatement of the systems of number and person, and the introduction of a new relation of concord (*thou canst*, etc.). In terms of social meaning, *thou* has a high 'strangeness value' or 'connotative value', being fraught with overtones of piety, historical period, 'poeticalness', and so forth.

A final word is necessary concerning the use of the word 'deviation'. This term has acquired a specific meaning with reference to a statistical norm, and it seems that this statistical use may well coincide, in practice, with the use adopted here.[6] If it is imagined that a corpus of material has been selected to represent a variety of English at a given degree of institutional delicacy, and that this analysis has revealed two occurrences of the pronoun *thou* against 10,000 occurrences of the pronoun *you* in comparable conditions, the item *thou* will be statistically deviant. On increasing the depth of delicacy, the occurrences of *thou* would no doubt be found to coincide with a less general variety of the language: for example, if the original corpus was of educated spoken British English, the *thou*'s in question might well be found to occur in the language of strict Quakers, of Shakespeare quotation, or of the jocular simulation of a North Country dialect.

Now that a theoretical value has been assigned to the word 'deviation', we may proceed to a closer examination of its function in literary language. Literature is distinguished from other varieties of linguistic activity above all by the number and the importance of the deviant features it contains. The highly deviant character of these features is to be measured not only by the important degree of descriptive delicacy at which they operate, but also in most cases, by an extreme lack of institutional generality. To all intents and purposes, the typical deviation in literary language can be considered unique to the text in which it occurs, and to this extent it resembles linguistic 'errors' and slips of the tongue, rather than such cases as the pronoun *thou*, which is associated with certain registers, and therefore has an accepted social meaning. This raises a descriptive problem. If literary English is viewed as a variety of English identified with reference to the register scale, how will its description fit into the total description of the language? A self-contained description of a 'literary language' would prove an impossible or at best an uninforming task. Since it would abound in unique deviations, it would be found to contain few of the restrictions on usage observed in other varieties of English, or at least whatever restrictions were perceived to exist through analysis of a working sample would be likely to evaporate on inspection of a further sample. In fact any corpus of material, however large, would be inadequate for a complete description of literary language: every new metaphor, for instance, would require an alteration of the existing description.

The difficulty of conceiving of a literary language as a describable language in its own right confirms the need to study it in the light of comparison with other varieties of the language, that is, chiefly in terms of linguistic deviation. This is not to suggest that literary language tends to amorphism: an individual text will be linguistically highly organized, but the features of organization (e.g. a recurrent lexical pattern carrying the symbolic theme of the work) will tend to be peculiar to that text, not general to literature as a whole. A linguistic analysis of a limited text, such as a poem, is indeed a practicable exercise; but this again presupposes comparison with other varieties of English.[7]

2.3 Figures of speech as deviant or foregrounded phenomena in language

The adoption of an approach *via* general linguistic description has governed my choice of the adjective 'deviant' to characterize an essential (perhaps *the* essential) feature of literary language. This is unflattering to creative writers, classing them with eccentrics, Mrs Malaprops, and anyone else who makes unorthodox or idiosyncratic use of language. Later we shall face the problem (crucial from the aesthetic point of view) of how to distinguish between a unique deviation which is meaningful and one which is merely an unmotivated aberration. But our immediate task is to exemplify and classify such deviations without respect to their artistic or other significance.

An exceptionally bold linguistic device employed by Dylan Thomas has caught the attention of more than one linguist,[8] and will provide an illustrative starting point. In phrases such as *all the sun long, a grief ago,* and *farmyards away* the deviation consists in an unrestricted choice of nouns (*farmyards, sun, grief*) in a position where normally only members of a limited list of nouns appear (in the last case, nouns of linear measurement such as *inches, feet, miles*). The effect of this is to upset the normal system of contrasts at this place in structure, and to substitute a new dual opposition between the deviant occurrence and the expected set.[9]

The difference between the normal paradigm and the new ad hoc paradigm can be represented as follows:

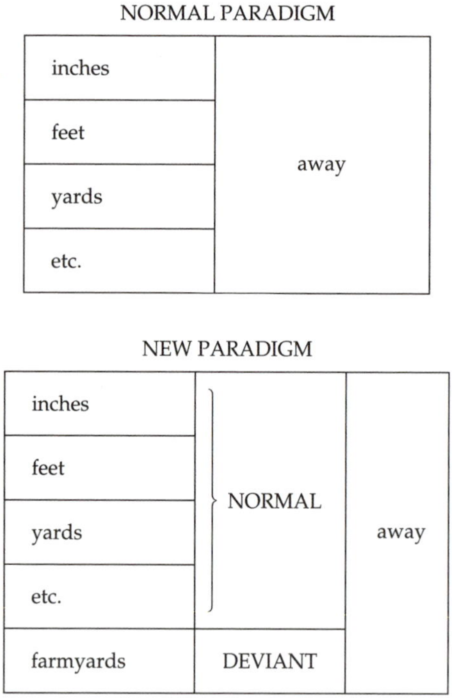

NORMAL PARADIGM

inches	
feet	away
yards	
etc.	

NEW PARADIGM

inches		
feet	NORMAL	
yards		away
etc.		
farmyards	DEVIANT	

Figure 2.1 Deviant and normal paradigm

Here there is a clear division between 'deviant' and 'normal'. But for those aspects of linguistic organization where there are no closed lists of equivalent terms, the distinction is relative: that is, between 'more deviant' and 'less deviant'. The deviation constitutes an unaccustomed extension to the range of choices, but not a disruption of established oppositions. Grammatical deviation is of this kind in the case of iterative structures. For example, the last verse of *This is the House that Jack Built* is a linguistic oddity in that it contains a long series of embedded relative clauses. Each verse after the first adds an extra clause, and represents a step in the direction of greater deviation; but it would be impossible to say at what point in this language game deviation 'sets in'.

Lexical deviation, studied with reference to the frequency of collocations, or groups of lexical terms in proximity,[10] is again a matter of gradience. One would have no hesitation in dubbing the collocation *damp smile* as deviant, but it would have to be placed on a scale of lesser-to-greater deviation on the lines of:

(1) broad smile (most normal)
(2) free smile
(3) damp smile
(4) high smile (most deviant)

Nevertheless, it appears that something akin to the direct contrast between deviation and normality postulated in the case of *farmyards away* is needed to account for the phenomenon of literary metaphor. In Edith Sitwell's phrase *fruitbuds that whimper, fruitbuds* occupies a position relative to *whimper* normally filled by a relatively homogeneous set of animate nouns *dog, cub, animal, child*, etc. This group of customary collocates might be said to constitute a 'collocational core' of items, such that an opposition is set up between the deviant collocation with *fruitbuds* and the total 'collocational core'. Hence from the viewpoint of literary appreciation, it is within the capability of metaphor (as opposed to simile) to suggest a connection between the explicit *vehicle* (represented by the deviant item) and a less tangible cluster of associations constituting the *tenor* (and represented by the 'core' of customary collocations).[11] Other figurative uses of language can be better explained in terms of discrete grammatical oppositions. Contrasts such as personal/impersonal, animate/inanimate and concrete/abstract distinguish grammatical classes of nouns, and the use of an inanimate noun in a context appropriate to a personal noun, as in Milton's

And caused the golden-tressed sun
All the day long his course to run

is a type of deviation we recognize as *personification.* Other common metaphoric effects are produced by the substitution of a concrete for an abstract noun, or an animate for an inanimate noun.

The Czech term *aktualisace*, translated by Garvin as 'foregrounding', was used by the pre-war Prague School of linguistics in a sense roughly corresponding to my 'unique deviation'.[12] Deliberate linguistic 'foregrounding', according to the Prague linguists, is not confined to creative writing, but is also found, for example, in joking speech and children's language games. Literature, however, is characterized by the 'consistency and systematic character of foregrounding'.[13] The metaphorical term 'foreground' suggests the figure/ground opposition of gestalt psychology: the patterns of normal language are relevant to literary art only in providing a 'background' for the structured deployment of deviations from the norm. If the gestalt metaphor is retained, the word 'figures' of 'figures of speech' is reanimated by a technical pun. There is no need, however, to explore the psychological implications of the analogy. 'Figures', in the sense of deviant or foregrounded features of literary language, are observable and classifiable features of texts; how they register on the mind is beyond the scope of linguistic study, and irrelevant to the present stage of the discussion.

Figures can be initially classified as either *syntagmatic* or *paradigmatic*. An elementary distinction is often made between these two complementary aspects of linguistic patterning: items are associated syntagmatically when they combine sequentially in the chain of linguistic events, and paradigmatically when they enter into a system or set of possible selections at one point in the chain. The distinction is conventionally indicated in grammars by horizontal and vertical presentation on the printed page; for example, clause elements in chain relation are represented *Subject–Verb–Complement*, etc., whereas case endings in choice relation are shown in vertical display in the declension of a Latin noun. Types of figure illustrated so far have been paradigmatic: they have consisted in the selection of an item which is not a member of the normal range of choices available at its place in the linguistic chain. In other words, where there is a choice between equivalent items, the writer chooses one which is not equivalent to (i.e. in contrast to) the normal range of choices. Syntagmatic foregrounding results from the opposite process: where there is choice to be made at different points in the chain, the writer repeatedly makes the same selection. This, in Jakobson's words, is the projection of 'the principle of equivalence from the axis of selection into the axis of combination.'[14] A syntagmatic figure introduces a layer of patterning additional to those normally operating within the language; for example, in an alliterative figure such as *the furrow followed free* (S.T. Coleridge), the selection of the same initial phoneme /f/ on successive accented syllables imposes a repetitive pattern ($\times$ f $\times$ f $\times$ f) which in other types of discourse would be fortuitous and of no communicative value. The notion of figure and ground may again be useful in furnishing a visual analogue of the two types of foregrounding:

   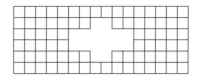

Syntagmatic Figure   Paradigmatic Figure

Figure 2.2 Figure and ground

The syntagmatic figure can be imagined as a pattern superimposed on the background of ordinary linguistic patterning, the paradigmatic figure as a gap in the established code – a violation of the predictable pattern.

Our understanding of the term 'foregrounding' should, of course, accommodate both the discrete and the relative types of deviation. The latter category is applicable to syntagmatic as well as paradigmatic figures. A syntagmatic figure may be thought of as a realization, to a greater or lesser degree, of the potential syntagmatic regularity of a language. A trivial degree of regularity is present in the repetition of the verb + object construction (a weak form of parallelism) in

He found his key and opened the door.

However, as the clause with a direct object is very common in English, the general probability of such a pattern is in any case fairly high. In contrast, the two clauses in Othello's

I kissed thee ere I killed thee

exhibit a high order of syntagmatic correspondence. Apart from identity of structure (subject + verb + object), the second clause echoes the first in containing identical pronouns (*I, thee*) and an identical morpheme (*-ed*) in equivalent syntactic positions. This formal pattern is further reinforced at the phonological level in the initial phonemic correspondence of *kissed* and *killed*.

With the syntagmatic category, a further important division is to be made between *schematic* and *prosodic* foregrounding. The preceding examples of syntagmatic figures have illustrated the former; the latter is the type of syntagmatic regularity that distinguishes verse from prose literature. The most satisfactory criterion by which they may be distinguished is this: prosodic foregrounding, although deviant in respect of general linguistic norms, is itself a norm for the type of text (a poem) in which it functions.[15] Hence the phenomenon of defeated expectancy in verse, a failure of the predicted prosodic foregrounding to materialize, constitutes a deviation from the secondary, or textual norm (see further pp. 62–4).

19

2.4 Classifying figures of speech

Further consideration need not be given to prosodic foregrounding, which is outside our subject, nor to the subtleties of its delimitation in different languages, cultures and literary modes.[16] The next step is a further linguistic classification of paradigmatic and schematic figures.

We distinguish, in the first place, between the different levels of linguistic function at which a figure is to be identified and described. On this basis, a figure is classified as formal (grammatical or lexical), phonological, orthographic, or semantic (referential or contextual),[17] or perhaps assigned to a combination of these categories. For example, alliteration, rhyme, vowel harmony, and assonance (where these are not prosodic phenomena) are *phonological* schematic figures, all consisting in an adscititious regularity of phonematic sequences. Parallelism, anaphora and many of the schemes distinguished in Renaissance rhetoric (such as antistrophe and epanalepsis)[18] are *formal* schematic figures, consisting in an adscititious regularity of various types of formal patterning. In distinguishing between these various types, it is important to stipulate the degree of abstraction at which the pattern is recognized. Highly abstract grammatical patterns, such as clause structures expressed in terms of subject, verb, complement, etc., often form the basis of a schematic figure which is manifested in a more specific regularity. Thus the parallelism of Goldsmith's

Where wealth accumulates, and men decay

does not consist only in the repetition of like clause structures (subject + verb), but in the fact that in each case the clause elements have single words as their exponents (*wealth, accumulates, men, decay*). A more highly organized schematic pattern will extend to a regularity at the most specific level of formal patterning: a repetition of individual formal items such as *my, for* and *a* in the following passage from *Richard II*:

I'll give my jewels for a set of beads,
My gorgeous palace for a hermitage,
My gay apparel for an almsman's gown,
My figured goblets for a dish of wood,
My sceptre for a palmer's walking staff,
My subjects for a pair of carved saints,
And my large kingdom for a little grave,
A little, little grave, an obscure grave.

Anaphora, at least in H.W. Fowler's sense (marked repetition of a word or phrase in successive clauses or sentences),[19] operates predominantly on

the plane of individual formal (lexical or grammatical) items. In David's
lament for his son,

> O my son Absalom, my son, my son Absalom! Would God I had died for
> thee, O Absalom, my son, my son!
>
> (II Samuel)

the repetition of individual sequences of words is more significant than the
grammatical parallelism which accompanies it.

A comparison of formal and phonological schematic figures reveals that
we cannot always handle the different linguistic levels in isolation from one
another. The presence of formal schematic patterning to some extent implies
the presence of phonological schematic patterning (i.e. to repeat a word is
to repeat the sounds of which it is composed). Hopkins's extensive use of
anaphora appears to be one with his deployment of phonological schemes.
The lexical repetitions in his lines

> My aspens dear, whose airy cages quelled,
> Quelled or quenched in leaves the leaping sun,
> All felled, felled, are all felled
>
> (*Binsey Poplars*)

contribute to the effects produced by alliteration, rhyme and vowel harmony. But the dependence is not reciprocal: phonological repetitions (e.g.
the repetition of /li:/ in *leaves* and *leaping*) may be independent of formal
correspondences.

Another type of dependency exists between formal paradigmatic and
semantic foregrounding. We have already noted that figurative meaning is
expressed by some kind of formal deviation, whether in the selection of
an inappropriate grammatical class or in the collocational foregrounding of
a lexical term. Nevertheless, the figurative/literal dichotomy is primarily a
matter of referential semantics. The term 'figurative' implies that an item
has been given a referential meaning outside its normal range of meanings
(as listed, for example, in a dictionary entry). A sober rereading of a well-
known passage from Bacon

> Some books are to be tasted, others to be swallowed, and some few to be
> chewed and digested
>
> (*Of Studies*)

will show that by the standards of the accepted code (i.e. 'literal meaning')
a literary metaphor is a semantic absurdity. Our dictionaries are full, however, of metaphorical meanings which in the course of linguistic history
have lost their deviant character ('dead metaphors').

At least three kinds of semantic foregrounding can be signalled by deviant collocation. In Hopkins's

> Then let the march tread our ears
>
> (*At the Wedding March*)

the collocation of *tread* and *ears*, like that of *books* and *tasted*, etc., in Bacon's apophthegm, is a juxtaposition of semantic incompatibles – the linguistic basis of metaphor. Antonymy is a special case of semantic incompatibility; when Milton's Samson collocates *living* and *death*,

> To live a life half-dead, a living death

he produces a particular type of semantic absurdity we recognize as paradox or oxymoron. This line also illustrates, in the collocation of *live* and *life*, a third kind of oddity: a pleonasm, or semantic redundancy consisting in the combination of synonymous items. The verse from Ecclesiastes

> I praise the dead which are already dead more than the living which are yet alive

contains two more obvious examples of this type of foregrounding.

After the description of figures by the linguistic levels at which they function, an obvious next stage in the analysis is to classify them according to relevant features of organization within each level. For instance, to the preceding examples of parallelism of clause structure we may add an example of parallelism of nominal phrase structure, Pope's

> A tim'rous friend and a suspicious foe
>
> (*Epistle to Dr Arbuthnot*)

(a + Adjective + Noun, a + Adjective + Noun). In calling this 'a different kind' of parallelism from the others, we call into play the ordinary descriptive categories of English grammar. But in fully accounting for possible varieties of formal parallelism on these lines, we would need to specify (a) the largest grammatical unit entering into the structural equivalence (e.g. sentence, clause, phrase, etc.); (b) the degree of identity of the class exponents of the element of structure (e.g. whether they are both nouns, animate nouns, personal nouns, etc.); and (c) the extent to which the structural elements have identical exponents at lower ranks (the maximum similarity here would be complete identity of formal items, which would also imply complete identity under (b)). A similar type of classification might be made of paradigmatic figures. As the number of distinctions that can be made on the basis of linguistic categories is virtually boundless, we have to decide on the amount of detail we wish our classification to include.

Schematic figures can be further analysed abstractly as configurations of foregrounded regularities: that is, as patterns in their own right, without reference to the 'background' of normal linguistic patterning. In its simplest manifestation, a schematic figure is a pattern consisting of two equivalent phases or segments, representable as *aa* (*a-a-* if they are separated by a sequence of unforegrounded material). Although there is no clear limitation on the number of phases in a schematic pattern, in literature the pattern which is simplest in this respect seems also to be the most important: a symptom of this is our preference for a separate critical term (balance) for a parallelism consisting of two phases only. All the parallelisms so far quoted have been binary, even the passage from *Richard II*, which has the structure *ababab*. Elizabethan stage rhetoric, in fact, provides many examples of this more complex type of configuration, in which there is an alternation of two or more sets of equivalent phases:

> He spake me fair, this other gave me strokes:
> He promised life, this other threatened death:
> He won my life, this other conquered me . . .

This schematic pattern from Kyd's *The Spanish Tragedy* has the structure *ababab*. There is yet the further possibility that two phases may be in a symmetrical relation, such that the second is in some sense the mirror image of the first. The placing of equivalent formal items in Hamlet's line

> What's Hecuba to him, or he to Hecuba

yields the formal pattern *abccba*, and an analogous configuration of grammatical elements defines the rhetorical figure *chiasmus*. Such dimensions of description need to be recognized, although their relevance to literary appreciation is perhaps marginal, and their potential complexities are more fully realized in prosodic than in schematic foregrounding.

A linguistic classification of literary figures such as that outlined above can proceed from the most general distinctions towards the most specific; but the only complete classification would be that which has a separate characterization of each unique deviation. Quintilian was justified in complaining that the practice of enumerating figures of speech was an overestimated pastime among rhetoricians:[20] the inventory of such figures is potentially infinite. Whereas linguistics provides the technique for pursuing this classification to the point of boredom, it also provides a criterion (in the scale of descriptive delicacy) for deciding which are the most significant (least trivial) distinctions.

2.5 Linguistic analysis and critical appreciation

I return finally to the question which looms over the gap between linguistic analysis and critical appreciation. When is a unique deviation meaningful, and when is it merely a piece of nonsense? In one sense, the first part of this question is a contradiction in terms: a broad definition of meaningfulness equates it with the appropriate use of linguistic conventions. Similarly, if we want to find a technical definition of nonsense, none will suit it better than 'that which contravenes the established rules of the language'. From this point of view, therefore, poetry is a variety of nonsense (as, indeed, it is to some people). But another interpretation of 'nonsense' might be 'language that communicates nothing'; and it must be admitted that this 'nonsense' is virtually a fiction. Even a linguistic error or aberration communicates something: to write *authoritis* for *arthritis*, for example, might be to convey to your reader that you are unfamiliar with the language, a bad speller, or the kind of semi-educated person who commits malapropisms. It is in this wider sense of meaningfulness that literary foregrounding communicates. Nevertheless, we must hasten to distinguish between the 'significant deviations' of literary language, and unmotivated deviations which have a trivial and unintended meaning.

The approach to this problem of 'significance' depends very much on whether paradigmatic or schematic foregrounding is under consideration. The former, it has been suggested, constitutes a disruption, at one particular level, of the normal pattern of linguistic organization. The gap can be filled, and the deviation rendered meaningful, only if some latent relation (linguistic or non-linguistic) implied in the nature of the deviation compensates for the overt linguistic relation. We may speak of the latent connection by which we interpret a paradigmatic deviation as its *warranty*, implying that the connection is a positive requirement if sense is to be made of the linguistic event as a whole. But in the case of schematic foregrounding, the normal functions of the language are undisturbed, and the total linguistic event is meaningful even if the deviation is unmotivated (as it might be in an adventitious alliteration such as *Tell Tom it's teatime*). It is more fitting to refer to the interpretative connection of a schematic figure as its *reinforcement*: we do not have to make good a deficiency, but to explain a superfluity of patterning. The medieval labels for schemes and tropes, *ornatus facilis* and *ornatus difficilis*, are perhaps a reflection of the nature of the difference between these processes.

One kind of warranty for a paradigmatic figure is a connection established at some other level of linguistic function. The morphological extravagances of *Finnegan's Wake* (e.g. *wholeborrow*, *Gracehoper*) are interpreted in the light of their phonological resemblance to established words in the language (*wheelbarrow*, *grasshopper*). Most examples of wordplay are to be explained in terms of a phonological compensation (homonymy or partial homonymy) for formal deviation. Another kind of warranty consists in the preservation of a prosodic pattern: the need for a rhyme or for metrical regularity supplies a motive (aesthetically dubious) for a foregrounded arrangement of grammatical elements. This type of grammatical foregrounding, for which the rhetorical term 'hyperbaton' is available, may also contribute to a schematic figure. In Francis Thompson's *The Hound of Heaven*,

> Yea, faileth now even dream
> The dreamer, and the lute the lutanist

the transposition of the clause elements out of their normal affirmative order into verb + adjunct + subject + object upholds the parallelism of *dream the dreamer* and *lute the lutanist*.

No linguistic warranty can be found for metaphor: instead, the compensatory connection is to be sought outside language, in some kind of psychological, emotional or perceptual relation between the literal and figurative meanings of the item(s) concerned. In the line from Donne's *The Apparition*,

> Then thy sick taper will begin to wink

the deviant terms *sick* and *wink* become meaningful on the recognition of appropriate analogies – between someone who is ill and a candle which is burning out, and between the intermittent light of a candle and the winking of an eye. In probing more deeply into the meaning of these metaphors, we attach further significance to them in the light of the total symbolic context of the poem. A similar type of semantic deviation in *Humphry Clinker* has a very different kind of extra-linguistic warranty:

> Hark ye, Clinker, you are a most notorious offender. You stand convicted of sickness, hunger, wretchedness and want.

The juxtaposition of semantic incompatibles here leads to the equation 'crime = misfortune', an absurdity which gains its point through ironic interpretation.

The linguistic/non-linguistic distinction also applies to the reinforcement of schematic figures. The Biblical

> Absent in body, but present in spirit
>
> (I Corinthians)

exemplifies a marked form of antithesis in which parallelism is reinforced by antonymy, i.e. by a linguistic connection at the level of referential semantics. The phases of the schematic figure establish an equivalence between *absent* and *present, body* and *spirit,* and this relationship in each case corresponds to a systemic semantic contrast.[21] The parallelism of *I kissed thee ere I killed thee,* on the other hand, has no linguistic reinforcement. The two words equivalent in respect of the pattern, *kissed* and *killed,* are in no easily definable semantic relationship; their antithetic reinforcement comes rather from emotive contrast and from the dramatic context. The reinforcement of phonological schemes may be found in their contribution to figures at other levels. Alliteration, for example, underlines the grammatical parallelism of Marlowe's

Of conquer'd kingdoms and of cities sack'd

(I *Tamberlaine*)

and the paradox of Shakespeare's

So foul and fair a day I have not seen.

(*Macbeth*)

In other cases, we look for a non-linguistic connection: some kind of imitative connection between the sound pattern and other extralinguistic implications of the text, such as is suggested by the final sibilants of Keats's:

Thou watchest the last oozings hours by hours.

(*To Autumn*)

Of all reinforcements, such onomatopoeic effects are perhaps the least accessible to study.

The discussion of non-linguistic warranty and reinforcement has brought us beyond the bounds of linguistic study, although for the critic it is perhaps the most important aspect of the study of figures of speech. Linguistic warranty and reinforcement account for only the most obvious effects of literary language: the kind of effects which explain the point of a linguistic game or joke, but in literary explication only serve to point the way to further relevant non-linguistic connections. The conclusion is not surprising: that the most interesting and illuminating aspect of communication in literature is beyond the scope of linguistics. The literary writer's object, after all, is to transcend the limitations of ordinary language, and this is the real sense in which he can be said to use language creatively. But meaning in literature cannot be studied without constant reference to the observable patterns of language, and I have attempted to show to what extent linguistics can contribute to this study, by describing and classifying the mechanisms of deviation which are basic to the creative use of language.

Notes

1. **Particularly with regard to metaphor (and metonymy), this is now a very dated assessment. For more recent treatments of metaphor, see Kövecses (2002), Lakoff and Turner (1989) and Barcelona (2000).**
2. See Atkins (1934: 18, 272). This and other volumes by Atkins document the history of rhetorical figures from their classical origins to the eighteenth century. More recent descriptions and exemplifications are to be found in Bain (1887) and Fowler (1965 [1926]).
3. Halliday (1961: 258–9, 272–3).
4. The use of 'institutional' in this sense derives from Hill (1958: 441–55).
5. Following the use of 'register' by Reid (1956: 32 ff.) and others.
6. **See Chapter 11, especially pp. 164–7, for a more technical discussion – and tentative implementation – of the notions of statistical norm and deviation with respect to literary style.**
7. Cf. Halliday (1964: 303): 'Linguistic stylistics is . . . essentially a comparative study.'
8. E.g. Samuel R. Levin discusses *a grief ago* in Levin (1964).
9. Levin (1964) suggests two other ways of accounting for a deviation such as this: (a) the deviant item is added on to the list of items ordinarily in contrast; and (b) a sub-class of nouns *containing* the deviant term (e.g. nouns of emotional state) is added to the list of items ordinarily in contrast. The explanation I offer is based on the principle that having diagnosed a violation of linguistic restraints, we have no grounds for supposing that the deviation implies further restraints (e.g. that it is a member of a 'class' of possible deviations including a *disappointment ago, a happiness ago*, etc., but not *a meal ago, a frost ago*, etc.).
10. For the place of collocation in linguistic study, see Firth (1957: 194–5); and Halliday (1961: 276). **More recent treatments of collocation include Sinclair (1991).**
11. The terms *tenor* and *vehicle* are taken from Richards (1936: 96 ff). **More commonly nowadays the terms 'target (domain)' and 'source (domain)' are used (see Lakoff and Johnson 1980; Lakoff and Turner 1989).**
12. See Garvin (1958), esp. B. Havránek's contribution, 'The functional differentiation of the standard language', pp. 1–18.
13. J. Mukařovský, 'Standard language and poetic language', in Garvin (1958: 23).
14. Roman Jakobson (1960: 358).
15. This amounts to the same as saying, with Levin (1962: 59), that 'many features distinguishing poetry from ordinary discourse result from the mere fact that a writer addresses himself to writing a poem'.
16. See J. Lotz, 'Metric typology' in Sebeok (1960: 135–48).
17. On linguistic levels see J.R. Firth (1957: 190–215) in his paper 'Modes of meaning'; also Halliday (1961: 243–4).
18. See, for example, George Puttenham's seven figures of 'repetition' (Puttenham 1936[1589]: 198–202).
19. Entry in H.W. Fowler, *A Dictionary of Modern English Usage* (Fowler 1965[1926]).
20. See Atkins, vol. ii (1934: 273).
21. The importance in poetry of such phenomena as this is discussed by Levin (1962: 30 ff.) under the heading of 'coupling'. The distinction I make between *Absent in body, but present in spirit* and *I kissed thee ere I killed thee* presupposes a structural approach to referential semantics which Levin, in common with many other linguists **(of the 1960s)**, does not entertain.

CHAPTER 3

'This bread I break' – language and interpretation

This bread I break

This bread I break was once the oat,	1
This wine upon a foreign tree	2
Plunged in its fruit;	3
Man in the day or wind at night	4
Laid the crops low, broke the grape's joy.	5
Once in this wine the summer blood	6
Knocked in the flesh that decked the vine,	7
Once in this bread	8
The oat was merry in the wind;	9
Man broke the sun, pulled the wind down.	10
This flesh you break, this blood you let	11
Make desolation in the vein,	12
Were oat and grape	13
Born of the sensual root and sap;	14
My wine you drink, my bread you snap.	15

Dylan Thomas

Linguistic description and critical interpretation are, to my mind, distinct and complementary ways of 'explaining' a literary text. By reference to Dylan Thomas's poem quoted above, I shall attempt to show how they are related, and indirectly, what the former can contribute to the latter.

According to a widely held view, the linguist's aim is to make 'statements of meaning'.[1] 'Meaning' here is interpreted in a broader sense than usual, sometimes including every aspect of linguistic choice, whether in the field of semantics, vocabulary, grammar or phonology. One advantage of this extended use of the word 'meaning' is that it liberates us from the habit of thinking that the only type of meaning that matters is 'cognitive' or 'referential' meaning: a view that literary critics have long found unsatisfactory.[2] On the other hand, a work of literature contains dimensions of meaning additional to those operating in other types of discourse. The apparatus of linguistic description is an insensitive tool for literary analysis unless it is adapted to handle these extra complexities.

3.1 Cohesion in a text

Cohesion is a dimension of linguistic description which is particularly important in the study of literary texts.[3] By this is meant the way in which independent choices at different points of a text correspond with or presuppose one another, forming a network of sequential relations. In Dylan Thomas's poem, the selection of present tense in lines 1, 11 and 15, and of the past tense in lines 1, 3, 5, 7, 9, 10 and 13 are of little interest as isolated facts. What is of interest is the way these choices pattern together: from a starting point in the present, the poet makes an excursion into the past, returning to the present at the beginning and end of the final stanza. Notice, too, how the present tense patterns with the first and second person pronouns 'I' (1), 'my' (15 twice), and 'you' (11 twice, 15 twice), whereas the past tense patterns with 'man' (4, 10), the only personal noun in the text (third person), and the adverb 'once' (1, 6, 8). The distributions accord with the semantic opposition between immediacy ('thisness') and non-immediacy ('thatness') of temporal and spatial reference. The word 'this' (1, 2, 6, 8, 11 twice) is, in fact, a bridge between the two distributional patterns: it occurs with both present and past tenses.

Lexical cohesion in this poem is even more marked than grammatical cohesion. The most obvious kind of lexical cohesion consists in the repetition of the same item of vocabulary: 'bread' (1, 8, 15), 'break' (1, 5, 10, 11), 'oat' (1, 9, 13), and many other items occur more than once. But apart from this, choice of vocabulary is largely restricted to items which have a clear semantic connection with other items in the text. One path of semantic connections links 'bread', 'oats', 'crops'; others can be traced through 'wine', 'tree', 'fruit', 'grape', 'vine', 'drink'; 'day', 'night', 'summer', 'sun'; 'blood', 'flesh', 'vein'; 'joy', 'merry', 'desolation'; 'break', 'snap'.

In studying cohesion, we pick out the patterns of meaning running through the text, and arrive at some sort of linguistic account of what the poem is 'about'. In this case, we also notice how tightly organized the relationships are: it might almost be said that the poet makes it too easy to follow his meaning. But this is a very superficial kind of 'meaning', yielded by an analysis which could be equally well applied to any text in English – say, a Home Office memorandum or a recipe for apricot soufflé. It is superficial, because we have only considered how selections are made from the range of possibilities generally available to users of the language. But poetry is above all the variety of discourse which exploits linguistic unorthodoxy. To bring to light what is of most significance in the language of a poem, we have to deal with choices which would not be expected or tolerated in a normal language situation.[4] This is another dimension of analysis.

3.2 Foregrounding

Foregrounding or motivated deviation from linguistic, or other socially accepted norms, has been claimed to be a basic principle of aesthetic communication.[5] Whether or not the concept is applicable to any great extent to other art forms, it is certainly valuable, if not essential, for the study of poetic language. The norms of the language are in this dimension of analysis regarded as a 'background', against which features which are prominent because of their abnormality are placed in focus. In making choices which are not permissible in terms of the accepted code, the poet extends, or transcends, the normal communicative resources of the tongue. The obvious illustration of foregrounding comes from the semantic opposition of literal and figurative meaning; a literary metaphor is a semantic oddity which demands that a linguistic form should be given something other than its normal (literal) interpretation.

A metaphor frequently manifests itself in a highly unpredictable collocation, or sequence of lexical items. In 'Broke the grape's joy' (5) there is a collocative clash between 'broke' and 'joy', and between 'grape's' and 'joy': to make the sequence 'sensible' we would have to substitute a concrete noun like 'skin' for 'joy', or else replace 'grape' by an animate noun and 'broke' by a verb such as 'spoiled'. Of the many foregrounded groupings of lexical items in the poem, two kinds are prominent: those which yoke together inanimate nouns and items denoting psychological states ('grape's joy' (5), 'the oat was merry' (9), 'desolation in the vein' (12), 'sensual root' (14)); and those which consist in the use of verbs of violent action in an 'inappropriate' context ('plunged in its fruit' (3), 'broke the . . . joy' (5), 'knocked in the flesh' (7), 'broke the sun' (10), 'pulled the wind down' (10), 'this flesh you break' (11), 'my bread you snap' (15)). The deviation consists in the selection of an item which lies outside the normal range of choices at a particular place in structure. If we set up the frame 'pulled the . . . down', it is easy to make a list of nouns (mostly concrete and inanimate) which could predictably fill the empty space. But the noun 'wind' is not available for selection in this position: the poet has disregarded the normal conditions of choice.

Less obviously, 'foregrounding' can apply to the opposite circumstance, in which a writer temporarily renounces the permitted freedom of choice, introducing uniformity where there would normally be diversity.[6] An example is the grammatical parallelism in line 4: one noun phrase of the structure noun + prepositional phrase ('Man in the day') is followed by another noun phrase of like structure ('wind at night'). Although the language tolerates a great variety of noun-phrase structures (deictic + noun, adjective + noun + prepositional phrase, noun + relative clause, etc.) the poet successively restricts himself to the same pattern, thereby setting up a special relationship of equivalence between the two grammatical units. A more striking parallelism is found in the last line of the poem, which divides grammatically into two sections, each having the structure 'my' + noun + 'you' + verb. I shall refer to such foregrounded patterns, whether in grammar or phonology, as 'schemes'.

3.3 Cohesion of foregrounding

Cohesion of foregrounding constitutes a separate dimension of descriptive statement, whereby the foregrounded features identified in isolation are related to one another, and to the text in its entirety. A certain pattern of similarities has already been observed in the poet's deviant lexical collocations. There is also cohesion of schemes: for example, other parallelisms in the poem reinforce the initial correspondence of 'This bread . . . This wine . . .', by setting up semantically analogous equivalences: 'Laid the crops low', 'broke the grape's joy' (5); 'My wine you drink, my bread you snap' (15); etc. If a single scheme extends over the whole text, it can itself be regarded as a form of cohesion. Since it is unlikely that absolute uniformity will be preserved in any sequential aspect of a poem, this type of scheme is to be distinguished from cohesion as discussed earlier only by the *degree* of regularity of a certain pattern running through the text. It is ultimately a matter of subjective judgement whether we choose to regard such a pattern as an example of schematic foregrounding – that is, whether the regularity seems remarkable enough to constitute a definite departure from the normal functions of language. The verse structure of a poem is a special case of an extended scheme. Space forbids an analysis of this interesting and complex aspect of the poem.[7] I will only observe that the half-line is an important prosodic unit, and that the final line of each stanza is distinguished from the others by a special metrical pattern.

Further extended foregrounding is observed in the phonology of words: the phonemic congruity of 'wind', 'wine', 'vine', 'veins', and the striking predominance of monosyllabic words in the text as a whole. Of the hundred words in the poem, only five have more than one syllable. This is largely owing to the poet's almost exclusive choice of monosyllabic nouns and verbs. In such words the 'closed syllable' structure (consonant cluster + vowel + consonant cluster) is prevalent, whereas in polysyllables the 'open syllable' structure (with only one consonant or consonant cluster) is the more usual. A high frequency of monosyllables therefore tends to go with a high density of consonants – another noted characteristic of this text. We can compare in this respect the syllabic structure of line 3 (/plʌnʤd . . . fruːt/: CCVCCC VC VCC CCVC) with that of the word /desəleɪʃ(ə)n/ (13) (CVCVCVC[V]C). Both have four syllables; the one has 11 consonants, the other only 5. The difference between them, in terms of ease and speed of articulation, is considerable; and it is intuitively noted in the quickening of rhythm at the point where the polysyllable occurs. After the vowel, in most monosyllabic nouns and verbs in the poem, there is a voiceless plosive consonant (/p/, /t/ or /k/) or a voiced plosive /d/ ('bread', 'wind', 'pulled'). This foregrounding of particular consonants, together with the overall consonantal foregrounding, builds a characteristic phonological 'texture' which strikes the ear as austere and unresonant.

The different types of schematic pattern in the poem are frequently coincident. Formal parallelisms in every case coincide in extent with prosodic units. In several instances, the operative prosodic unit is the half-line (hemistich): the second half-line repeats both the phonological and the grammatical pattern contained in the first. Further, none of the parallelisms have more than two phases or elements. This is by no means a necessary restriction, but it matches other paired features in the poem: the division of the verse line into half-lines, and the coupling by coordination of *oat* and *grape* (13) and *root* and *sap* (14): structures which whilst scarcely meriting the name 'parallelism' contribute to the general foregrounding of duality. In fact both phonologically and grammatically, the poem is almost entirely divisible into binary segments.

I have dealt with what I consider to be the principal dimensions on which a linguistic analysis of this poem (or any poem) might proceed, and have exemplified some of the features of each dimension. Such features are, in the linguistic sense, part of the 'meaning' of the poem: they are matters of linguistic choice, and can be described in terms of the categories of the language. But in a broader sense, 'meaning' is 'whatever is communicated to this or that reader': it includes the factor of interpretation. If the task of linguistic exegesis is to describe the text, that of critical exegesis is, from one point of view, to explore and evaluate possible interpretations of the text.

The distinction I make between the text and its interpretation certainly has nothing to do with the familiar dichotomy between 'form' and 'meaning'; indeed, it has already been made clear that the former includes all that would be traditionally accounted 'meaning' in a non-literary text. Instead, the line is drawn between that which the reader is given, and that which the reader supplies in order to make what is given by the language fully meaningful. For the purpose of ordinary linguistic communication, it is justifiable to define 'intelligibility' as conformity to the linguistic code. A foregrounded feature, as an infringement of the code, is by this standard 'unintelligible' – indeed, it can be a positive disruption of the normal communicative process. From the linguistic point of view, literary interpretation can be seen as a negative process: a coming to terms with what would otherwise have to be dismissed as an unmotivated aberration – a linguistic 'mistake'. Again the simplest illustration is metaphor. An invented metaphor (as distinct from a 'dead' metaphor which has become accepted in the language) is unintelligible in the above sense, and communicates only to those who perceive some kind of compensatory connection outside language. To say that the connection is outside language is not to exclude the importance of linguistic context – that is, relations of cohesion – in providing interpretative clues. For example, 'the summer blood Knocked in the flesh that decked the vine' (6–7) scarcely admits of any interpretation in isolation. But the words 'flesh' and 'vine' here look back to 'wine', 'tree' and 'fruit' in stanza 1, and forward to 'flesh' and 'blood' in stanza 3. What of the interpretation of schematic figures? The parallelism 'Man in the day or wind at night' (4) sets up implications of equivalence between 'man' and 'wind' on the one hand, and 'day' and 'night' on the other. The latter two words have an obvious referential connection; the former apparently have none. Interpretation here consists in finding some plausible sense in which 'man' and 'wind' are equivalent. We are thus invited to think of the foregrounded aspects of a poem as so many question marks, to which the reader, as interpreter, consciously or unconsciously attempts to find answers. The interpretation of the whole poem is built up from a consistency in the interpretation of individual features.

3.4 Implications of context

But there is another aspect of a poem which requires interpretation: its implications of context. Normal discourse operates within a describable communicative situation, from which an important part of its linguistic meaning derives. In literature, it is usually true to say that such contextual information is largely irrelevant. Instead, we have to construct a context by inference from the text itself, by asking such questions as 'Who are the "I" and the "you" of the poem, and in what circumstances are they communicating?' Obviously these questions relate to the distinction between fiction and actuality. But it is not suggested that the reader is obliged to supply a fictional context: the option of fiction and non-fiction is left open. The reader may decide to interpret 'I' and 'you' as author and reader respectively, as other 'real' people, or as fictional creations.

This choice is indeed open in the present poem: according to one interpretation, it is an allegory of poetic creation, and 'I' and 'you' are actually 'I

who am writing this poem' (Dylan Thomas himself) and 'you who are reading it'. But this in turn presupposes another interpretation, in which 'I'
stands for Christ and 'you' for those who partake in the Lord's Supper. This
transferred situation is suggested at the very beginning, in the collocation of
'bread' and 'wine'. Taking it as a starting point, I shall follow its implications through the text, pointing out how it may be used to explain some of
the foregrounded features. The Last Supper carries with it a mystical or
symbolic identification of 'bread' with 'flesh' and 'wine' with 'blood'. This
association, which is upheld by grammatical parallelism throughout, has a
two-fold implication: (a) that vegetable growth is invested with the characteristic of animal life (and, in the context of Christ's sacrifice of his own
flesh and blood, of humanity): thus the 'vine' is 'decked' with 'flesh' (7);
the 'grape' is capable of 'joy' (5); the 'oat' is 'merry' (9); (b) that the human
animal takes on inanimate characteristics: 'man' is represented as an impersonal, destructive force on a par with 'wind' (4). The basic argument seems
to run as follows: 'Christ (the speaker) offers bread and wine, which are the
result of the destruction of life in nature (1–5). In this destruction, man col-
laborates with natural forces (the wind, 4); but whereas natural forces (sun
and wind) both destroy (4, 5) and sustain life (5–9), man alone is wholly
destructive; he even, in a manner of speaking, destroys the sun and wind
(10), by interfering with the normal course of nature.' The last stanza draws
on a further element of symbolism. Christ, in the Last Supper, makes a
sacrifice of himself; it is his flesh and blood that provides the meal. The 'you'
of line 11 might initially be taken merely as table companions: those sharing
in the meal. But in line 15, it is clear that they are not so much feeding *with*
the Speaker, as feeding *on* him.

This account illustrates the cumulative nature of the interpretative
process. One enigmatic feature provides the clue to a succeeding one, which
in turn strengthens the preceding interpretation. In the final line, this total
interpretation is resolved on what could without apology be termed its
'logical conclusion': 'Man destroys life; so man destroys life in man.' The
compression of signification in this last line is achieved partly by intensity
of foregrounding: by the rhyme of 'snap' with 'sap'; by the collocation of
'bread' with 'snap' (in contrast with 'break' in line 1); and by the deviant
order of clause elements, object + subject + verb. By such detailed observations as these it is possible to see a basis in linguistic observables for those
most elusive of critical concepts: climax, resolution, artistic unity.

3.5 Conclusion: interpretation

I have presented only one possible level of interpretation, and a very
partial one at that. The whole notion of 'interpretation' is bound to that of

ambiguity and indeterminacy of meaning. When ambiguity arises in poetry, in contrast to other kinds of discourse, we generally give the writer the benefit of the doubt, and take it to be intentional. Intentional ambiguity can only be understood in one way: by supposing that the poet intends a peaceful coexistence of alternative meanings. There are at least two examples in this text of the type of grammatical ambiguity that is liable to occur in non-literary language: 'plunged' (3; finite verb or past participle?) and 'you let' (11; a complete clause, or part of a clause running into the next line?). But in this discussion I have touched on much more important sources of indeterminacy of meaning: foregrounding, and implication of context – both of which can only be rendered 'intelligible' by an act of the imagination. Further, foregrounding is a relative concept: there are degrees of deviation, and in most cases there are no absolute grounds for regarding feature A as normal and feature B as foregrounded. So there is room for disagreement on what aspects of a poem *require* interpretation.

Finally, some foregrounded features may not be readily interpretable. For example, why 'plunged' in line 3; why 'knocked' in line 7? We have the option of being content to regard them as unintelligible; of explaining them in a non-constructive way (e.g. by saying that this sort of collocative clash is a stylistic trick of Thomas's earlier poetry); or of attempting to 'stretch' our interpretation of the poem to give them communicative value. Only the last course satisfies Tindall,[8] who in his commentary explains 'plunged' and 'knocked' as sexual references. Whether or not this is regarded as taking interpretation too far, it illustrates another variable entering into critical explication: the choice of whether to entertain a dubious interpretation, or to let obscurities remain obscurities.

Notes

1. See Firth (1957, especially pp. 32–3 and 190–215).
2. Notably I.A. Richards and 'new critics' influenced by him. Cf. Ogden and Richards (1923: 149–50, 158–9).
3. See Halliday (1964: 303–5).
4. The stylistic importance of deviation is discussed by Voegelin (1960: 58). In 'Linguistics and the figures of rhetoric' **(Chapter 2 of this book)**, I suggest how 'deviant' and 'normal' can be given an exact linguistic significance.
5. This is the theory of aesthetics and language expounded in contributions to Garvin (1958). For the concept of 'foregrounding', see esp. J. Mukařovský, 'Standard language and poetic language', ibid., p. 23.
6. For varying treatments of this special aspect of poetic language, see Jakobson (1960: 350–77, especially 358–9); and S.R. Levin (1962: 30 ff).
7. **In submitting this article to Review of English Literature in 1964, I had to comply with a word limit. But it seems appropriate here to add a few remarks on the poem's metre. Each half-line consists of four syllables, and each full line (consisting of two half-lines) of eight syllables, except for the middle line of each**

stanza, which contains only one half-line. Each half-line has two stressed and two unstressed syllables. The last line of each stanza has a comma (representing a caesura) between its two half-lines. The poem has no end rhymes, apart from the rhyme of *sap* and *snap* at the end of the last stanza. In general, the poem is highly schematized in its form.

8. Tindall (1962: 97).

CHAPTER 4

Literary criticism and linguistic description

Ever since linguistics began to take an interest in the language of literature, the relation between critic and linguist, in the English-speaking world, has tended to be an uneasy one of mutual distrust rather than mutual respect. True, linguists have been increasingly active in this area, and there have been one or two successes, such as the conversion of I.A. Richards to the value of linguistic analysis through the study of Shakespeare's 'Sonnet 129' by Jakobson and Jones.[1] Yet the literary critic is still typically cast in the role of the coy bride-to-be, who rejects the advances of the linguistic bridegroom, and his promise of a fruitful union between the two disciplines. In the USA, the course of this unhappy liaison has been charted (from an anti-linguistic point of view) by W. Youngren, in his book *Semantics, Linguistics, and Criticism*,[2] and in the United Kingdom, it can be traced most openly in the dispute between F.W. Bateson (for the critics) and R. Fowler (for the linguists) in the pages of *Essays in Criticism*, 1967–8,[3] a dispute sparked off by a review in that journal of Fowler's volume *Essays on Style and Language*.

My aim here will be to argue that the linguist–critic disputes over the linguistic analysis of literary texts have resulted from false assumptions, by members of both parties, about the theoretical relation between the two disciplines. I shall try to dispel this confusion, and to clarify the way in which linguistics may be said to contribute to the study of literature, by addressing myself to the following questions:

(a) What is the nature of literary critical statements about a literary text?
(b) What is the nature of linguistic statements about a literary text?
(c) In what sense can linguistic statements be said to *explain* or *support* critical statements?

To illustrate the argument, I shall take as an example of literary critical discussion a well-known essay by F.R. Leavis on the poetry of Keats, concentrating on Leavis's treatment of the first stanza of the 'Ode to a Nightingale';[4] this discussion I shall relate to the sort of statements one can make about the stanza from a stylistic point of view.

I shall not attempt to rehearse here the various arguments about the merits or demerits of 'the New Stylistics'.[5] The formulation of the above questions, however, disposes of one unnecessary source of acrimony: the tendency to think of linguists and critics as two separate breeds of scholar, separated by their differences of temperament and methodology. As soon as we think of 'linguistic statements' and 'critical statements' rather than 'statements by linguists' and 'statements by critics', we realize that 'critic' and 'linguist' are two roles that may be assumed by the same person: any critic who turns their attention to linguistic detail can scarcely avoid acting as a linguist (however tentatively or imperfectly); likewise, any linguist who turns their attention to the interpretation and evaluation of a work of literature can scarcely avoid acting as their own critic (however tentatively or imperfectly). The question is: how do linguistic statements and critical statements interrelate, and what is the purpose of their interrelation?

4.1 The nature of critical statements

It will be generally agreed that the function of literary criticism is to *interpret* and *evaluate* literature or a literary work. In *interpreting*, the critic arrives, both from linguistic evidence and from knowledge of extralinguistic background, at an assessment of the meaning of a work, by showing the interrelations between the meanings of its parts and elements. In *evaluating*, the critic uses his interpretation in arriving at a verdict about the merit of the work. Interpretation and evaluation are often in practice difficult to separate; we might, indeed, subsume the two activities under the single heading of literary *appreciation*. The two activities seem, indeed, to fuse in the use of 'aesthetic terms' (such as *elegant, sad, delicate, stately, unity, atmosphere, enchantment, expressive, buoyant*) which make up an important part of the vocabulary of literary criticism.

The notion of 'aesthetic term' I understand in the sense that has been explained by the philosopher Frank Sibley.[6] Sibley regards aesthetic terms as terms which require, for their correct application, taste, discrimination and judgment. Thus to call a painting 'elegant', 'forceful', 'evocative', etc. is to exercise discriminatory judgment in a way that is not required for the description of a painting as 'pale in colour', 'executed with thick brush strokes', 'composed of straight lines', etc. The description of a painting's mere visual appearance can be carried out by the use of non-aesthetic terms. Sibley points out that a critic often feels the need to explain, or in some way justify, his use of aesthetic terms, by the use of non-aesthetic terms. Thus he may argue that a piece of music is 'lugubrious' *because* it is written in a minor key and moves at a slow tempo. But this use of the word *because* requires careful scrutiny: one cannot do more than partially define an aesthetic term by means of non-aesthetic terms, nor can one predict with certainty, from the observation of non-aesthetic qualities in a work, the applicability of an aesthetic term. Thus a slow piece of music written in a minor key may well strike one as 'grand', 'sublime', or 'stately', rather then 'lugubrious'. The most one can do is to establish a *typical* dependence of an aesthetic term on a particular non-aesthetic term or combination of non-aesthetic terms ('A sad piece of music is typically slow and in a minor key'). Another important point made by Sibley's account of aesthetic concepts is that 'the particular aesthetic character of something may be said to result from the *totality* of its relevant non-aesthetic characteristics'.[7] What this implies is that aesthetic appreciation and its 'explanation' in terms of non-aesthetic description must be taken anew for each work studied: one cannot mechanically generalize on the aesthetic value of non-aesthetic features from one work to another. This point of view finds an echo in the critic's instinct to regard each work as a particular unity, which must be explicated in its own terms.

The activity of criticism, of course, involves much more than the appreciation of the character of a work by means of aesthetic terms. A critic may use aesthetic terms to support a pure value judgment (e.g. because a drawing is 'balanced' and 'graceful', it may be argued that it is 'good'); a critic's endeavour to persuade the reader of a work's artistic character may involve paraphrases or metaphorical explanations of its meaning, etc. But whatever else may be involved in criticism, it can scarcely be denied that criticism typically involves an attempt to support an aesthetic judgment by *reasoned argument*, and that an important part of this argument is the appeal to non-aesthetic terms as a justification for the use of aesthetic terms. In certain schools of English literary criticism, notably the 'Cambridge critics' in England and the 'New Critics' in the USA, the type of argument which relates aesthetic appreciation to the observed properties of the text is particularly prominent. We may say that an explanation or justification of aesthetic statements in terms of non-aesthetic statements is a 'reasoned argument', even though the argument can go no further than pointing out non-aesthetic properties which are *typically* associated, rather than *invariably* associated, with a particular aesthetic effect.

4.2 The nature of linguistic statements

How does the distinction between aesthetic terms and non-aesthetic terms (or, correspondingly, between aesthetic statements and non-aesthetic statements) relate to the argument about the value of linguistics to literary criticism? I have discussed Sibley's account at some length, because it is used by Youngren as a means of refuting the claim that linguistics can somehow make the arguments and judgments of the critic more precise. Youngren's contention is that linguists (likewise the philosophical critic I.A. Richards) have wrongly claimed that their formulations can be used to define, in more precise logical, or objective terms, those things which the literary critic is attempting to elucidate or describe. But since, as Sibley shows, there can be no non-aesthetic definition of aesthetic terms, this endeavour (according to Youngren) is a wholly misguided one, based on a 'theoretical mistake'.

There is no point in resurrecting here the various claims that linguists have made about the value of linguistics as a precise or objective 'underpinning' of literary criticism. Such claims have sometimes been made with ill-advised confidence, implying that criticism suffers from excessive impressionism and subjectivity, from which it might be rescued if the objective formulations of the linguist could explicate, or even entirely displace, the subjective statements of the critic. I have no desire to defend such claims. Yet Sibley's account of aesthetic and non-aesthetic terms can, I believe, be used to defend the proper role of linguistics in critical theory.

My argument depends on first of all clarifying the role of linguistics as that of making non-aesthetic statements about a literary text. In other art forms (such as painting and music), non-aesthetic statements often take the form of statements about the sensory properties of the work (colour, lines, tones, harmonies, melodic progressions, etc.). Such statements can (leaving aside certain philosophical reservations) be directly verified by observation. For literature on the other hand, the medium of a work is linguistic rather than directly sensory. Therefore a non-aesthetic statement about a literary text is, at least in the first instance, a linguistic statement: a statement, for example, about the meaning of a word, about the grammatical structure of a sentence, about a phonological pattern of repetition. To make linguistic statements about a text, one has to have, of course, an adequate linguistic metalanguage; and such a metalanguage gains precision and clarity to the extent that it is based on an adequate linguistic theory. Linguistic statements, so conceived, are not 'objective' in the sense that applies to statements about sensory data; indeed, it is debatable whether they should be considered 'objective' in any sense; but they are well defined if the linguistic theory within which they have meaning is well defined, and justified by empirical criteria. (Linguists can be expected to agree in the main that a phoneme is a phoneme without the exercise of 'taste' and 'personal judgment'.) Therefore, there is a valid distinction to be made between the aesthetic statements of criticism and the descriptive statements of linguistics. Sibley's distinction between aesthetic and non-aesthetic concepts can be applied to the distinction between linguistic statements and literary critical statements about a text, and can replace the, in some ways misleading, subjective/objective distinction which has sometimes been applied in this connection.

4.3 The relation between critical and linguistic statements

Further, we can use this conclusion to justify (although in more guarded terms than has been common) the role of linguistics in critical theory. Criticism involves giving reasons in favour of a given aesthetic appreciation, and since such a reasoned argument can take the form of 'explaining' aesthetic terms by means of non-aesthetic terms (which are subject to independent validation), linguistic statements can be regarded as 'explanatory' (in the limited sense of 'explanatory' already discussed) of critical statements.

In putting this distinction into practice, however, we come across a number of difficulties. One difficulty is that critical discussion is of a 'mixed' genre, which involves aesthetic observations and linguistic observations intermingled with many other elements. We have to distil the aesthetic statements which have linguistic relevance from the other factors before we can embark on the task of explaining or supporting them linguistically. It must also be acknowledged that a complete explication of aesthetic terms by means of non-aesthetic terms is out of the question. If Sibley is right in holding that the aesthetic character of a work depends on a *unique* combination of the non-aesthetic features composing the work, all the linguistically inclined critic can do is to point to a number of the non-aesthetic features most prominently contributing to the aesthetic effect.

At the linguistic end, there is a parallel difficulty: a complete linguistic analysis, comprising all the linguistic statements that can be validly made about a text with a given theoretical framework, is a practical impossibility, and in any case most of the linguistic statements that can be made (such as the statement that the word *of* occurs nine times in the 'Ode to a Nightingale') have no conceivable aesthetic relevance. Therefore in practice, a critic's statements about a text are confined to the location of a few *prominent* features of language, and the linguistic analysis that might be used for a more detailed explanation of the critic's observations must in practice confine itself to a selection of the more aesthetically relevant features. We must also notice that linguistic statements can be of a lower or higher order of abstraction: a statement to the effect that there is a pattern of repeated fricatives in a given line is ultimately dependent on a statistical statement about a relative frequency of certain phonemes in this or that part of the poem, or in the language generally.

Without too much simplification, however, we can draw a distinction between three levels of exegesis: the *linguistic level* of non-aesthetic discussion (Level 0), the *literary critical level* of aesthetic discussion (Level 2) and an intermediate level (Level 1) which I shall call the *stylistic level*. The stylistic level is the level on which linguistic statements that can be made on Level 0 (often at a relatively high level of abstraction) are selected for their relevance to the aesthetic discussion on Level 2. The selection of features for attention on Level 1 need not be based solely on aesthetic considerations. A general theory of stylistics should provide purely formal criteria for identifying features which are likely to have aesthetic implications. For example, the theory of *foregrounding*[8] leads us to assume that a linguistic deviation, or a pattern of repetition, or an abnormal clustering of features, is worth special consideration. In this way, the linguistic analysis may bring to light features which might be overlooked in a critical assessment, but which might, on further investigation, prove to have an important aesthetic function. Thus the diagram below may be interpreted as analogous to Spitzer's 'philological circle',[9] in that it implies a 'to-and-fro' motion between linguistic analysis and critical appreciation, in which non-aesthetic discussion explains or supports aesthetic discussion, and aesthetic discussion is further elucidated and enriched in the process.

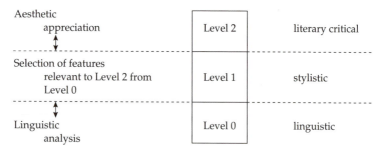

Figure 4.1 Three levels of studying a poem

   Having attempted to justify the role of linguistics within a general framework of stylistic exegesis, I am aware that scepticism about the value of linguistic analysis cannot be dispelled by theory alone: 'by their fruits you shall know them' is a slogan that might fittingly represent the most common objections of critics to linguistics. 'Show me an example where stylistics actually tells me something useful, and I shall believe.'[10] But often, I think, this sort of question has been posed in the wrong way. A critic, on his home territory of Level 2, finds himself at odds with a linguist who sticks relatively firmly to Level 0. He finds that the linguist does not give him any new insight into the aesthetic functions of language, and therefore rejects his painstaking analysis as useless. I feel that in such a situation, both the critic and the linguist may be at fault for not realizing that their true meeting ground is neither on Level 2, nor on Level 0, but on Level 1. The linguist should realize that 'objectivity' and 'precision' are not goals in their own right; the critic should realize that linguistic analysis should not be read as if it were criticism manqué.

4.4 Leavis on Keats's 'Ode to a Nightingale'

To elucidate the different but complementary roles of criticism and linguistics, I turn now to an account of Keats's 'Ode to a Nightingale' by F.R. Leavis. I shall try to use linguistic observations not to undermine Leavis's account of the poem, but to add to it, as it were, a further dimension of analysis. I suspect that Leavis himself would have seen little point in this procedure, but it may be of value to other critics, particularly those who are deeply concerned with understanding the linguistic means by which a writer achieves an aesthetic effect, and with the philosophical respectability of critical argument. Leavis's own position can be judged from the following:

> In criticism, of course (one would emphasize), nothing can be proved; there can, in the nature of the case, be no laboratory-demonstration or anything like it. Nevertheless, it is nearly always possible to go further than merely asserting a judgment or inviting agreement with a general account. Commonly one can call attention to this, that, or the other detail by way of making the nature and force of one's judgment plain.[11]

Whereas Leavis is content to 'call attention' to certain features of the text, I shall want to go further, and to analyse certain structural aspects of the text, confining myself in the main to the first stanza. I shall concentrate on two particular aesthetic judgments that Leavis makes about the poem:

(a) That it has a 'fine organization':

> The rich local concreteness is a local manifestation of an inclusive sureness of grasp in the whole. What the detail exhibits is not merely an extraordinary intensity of realisation, but also an extraordinary rightness and delicacy of touch; a sureness of touch that is the working of a fine organization. The Ode, that is, has the structure of a fine and complex organism . . .
>
> (p. 245)

(b) That this 'fine organization' manifests itself in an interplay or balancing of contrasting emotional movements:

> In the first stanza, there is a balance of the 'death-wish' enunciated in the first four lines against the 'life-wish' of the remaining part of the stanza. These are not static moods, but dynamic 'motions'.

43

> . . . the Ode is, in fact, an extremely subtle and varied interplay of
> motions, directed now positively, now negatively . . . It starts Lethe-
> wards, with a heavy drugged movement ('drowsy', 'numb', 'dull')
> down to 'sunk' . . . In the fifth and sixth lines, with the reiterated
> 'happy', the direction changes, and in the next line comes the key-
> word, 'light-wingéd'. The stanza now moves buoyantly to life, the
> fresh air, and the sunlight ('shadows numberless') – the thought
> of happy, self-sufficient vitality provides the impulse. The common
> medium, so to speak, in which the shift of direction takes place with
> such unobtrusive effectiveness, the pervasive sense of luxury, is given
> explicitly in the closing phrase of the stanza, 'full-throated ease'.
>
> (p. 246)

4.5 Linguistic support for Leavis's account

Leavis's reference to language confines itself mainly to a noting of words
whose symbolic and emotive connotations point to shifts and developments
in the unfolding theme. But if a poem is a 'fine and complex organism', one
would expect to find not just its vocabulary, but its organization on various
linguistic levels, working towards the same end. I shall therefore consider
aspects of the structure of the stanza mainly on three levels: on the level it
will be convenient to call *phonemic* (i.e. that of individual speech sounds);
on the *metrical* level, and on the *syntactic* level. I shall finally add a comment
or two about contextualization. On all these levels, I shall try to show that
the 'change of direction' noted by Leavis after line 4 is reflected in changes
of linguistic pattern.

> My heart aches, and a drowsy numbness pains
> My sense, as though of hemlock I had drunk,
> Or emptied some dull opiate to the drains
> One minute past, and Lethe-wards had sunk:
> 'Tis not through envy of thy happy lot,
> But being too happy in thine happiness, –
> That thou, light-wingéd Dryad of the trees,
> In some melodious plot
> Of beechen green, and shadows numberless,
> Singest of summer in full-throated ease.

4.5.1 The phonemic level

The transcription I shall use for this analysis assumes that a careful and
deliberate style of recitation is appropriate to the Ode:[12]

maɪ hɑːt eɪks ənd ə drɑuzɪ nʌmnəs peɪnz   1
maɪ sɛns, əz ðəu əv hemlɒk aɪ həd drʌŋk,   2
ɔː ɛmptɪd sʌm dʌl əupɪət tə ðə dreɪnz   3
wʌn mɪnɪt pɑːst, ənd liːθiːwədz həd sʌŋk;   4

tɪz nɒt θruː ɛnvɪ əv ðaɪ hæpɪ lɒt   5
bət biːɪŋ tuː hæpɪ ɪn ðaɪn hæpɪnɛs,   6
ðət ðɑu, laɪt-wɪŋɪd draɪæd əv ðə triːz   7

ɪn sʌm mələudjəs plɒt   8
əv biːtʃən griːn ənd ʃædəuz nʌmbələs,   9
sɪŋəst əv sʌmər ɪn ful-θrəutɪd iːz   10

I have marked here not only the major stanza division after line 4, but a minor division after line 7, since, as Leavis hints, and as further analysis will bear out, the end part of the stanza reasserts, to some extent, the mood of the opening lines: 'The common medium, . . . in which the shift of direction takes place with such unobtrusive . . . effectiveness, the pervasive sense of luxury, is given in the closing phrase . . . "full-throated ease".' These two divisions correspond to the most important divisions within the rhyme scheme: *abab cde cde*.

The 'drugged' movement towards Lethe in the first four lines is dramatized by a density of certain sounds and sound combinations:

(a) Frequency of nasals: there are as many as 18 nasal consonants in the first four lines, the greatest number (6) being in the first line: *m*y, a*n*d, *n*umb*n*ess pai*n*s.

(b) Frequency of sibilants (/s/, /z/): there are 12 such consonants in the first four lines, again the highest number (4) being in line 1: ache*s*, drow*s*y, numbne*s*s, pain*s*.

(c) Especially noteworthy are clusters of postvocalic consonants, where either the first consonant is a nasal (nu*mb*ness, pai*ns*, se*ns*e, dru*nk*, etc.) or where the second consonant is a sibilant (ache*s*, sen*se*, drain*s*, -war*ds*, etc.)

(d) More generally, stressed positions are frequently occupied by long syllables, containing long vowels, diphthongs, or consonant clusters. Notice, in particular, the first line's heavy syllables *heart*, *aches*, *drows-*, *pains*.

One does not have to be a blind believer in sound symbolism to accept that the density of these particular phonemic features in some degree reinforces the mood expressed in the lines. Nasals and sibilants are both continuant consonant-types, favouring prolonged articulation (their power to suggest seductive lassitude is recalled, for instance, in Tennyson's 'The moan of doves in immemorial elms, / And murmuring of innumerable bees' and Spenser's 'Sweet-breathing Zephyrus did softly play'). The consonant clusters and long vowels contribute, in addition, to a slow, lingering, consonant-clogged movement in the opening lines. There is a particular density of these features in line 1, which strongly establishes, from the start, the dominant pattern of sound.

In the next section of the stanza, these features are markedly less frequent, and instead we have the thrice-repeated word *happy* (noted by Leavis), a word containing two very brisk syllables with the simple structure CV, the consonant being plosive and the vowel being short in both cases. (Compare, for example, the length of this disyllable with that of the antonymous mono-syllable *pains* in line 1.) This contributes to a lightness of rhythm in lines 5–6, which may be seen as a phonetic correlate of Leavis's reference to the 'buoyant' movement towards 'life'.

Another indication of the change of mood is the contrast between the six-times repeated vowel /ʌ/ in the opening quatrain, and the thrice-repeated /æ/ in 5–6: the former belonging with the soporific associations of the words *dull* and *numb*, the latter with the opposed associations of the word *happy*. It is worth observing that /æ/ does not occur at all before line 5, and that it occurs only once later, in the final tercet (*shadows*).

The last three lines show a return to the predominance of nasals, sibilants and the /ʌ/ vowel of the opening lines, but now the consonant clusters of the opening lines are rare. However, the phrase *full-throated ease* not only recalls the opening mood by sounding a 'note of luxury', as Leavis suggests, but also, through the length of its constituent syllables, brings a final return to the initial slowness of rhythm.

The distribution of these features is shown by the following table, in which changes in relative frequency show the transition at line 5, and the partial resumption of the opening pattern in line 8:[13]

Table 4.1   FREQUENCY OF PHONEMES

	Lines 1–4	Lines 5–7	Lines 8–10	General %age frequency in English
Total number of phonemes	111	75	70	
No. of nasals /m/ /n/ /ŋ/	18	7	11	
(%age of all phonemes)	(16.2)	(9.3)	(15.7)	(11.95)
No. of sibilants /s/ /z/	12	3	8	
(%age of all phonemes)	(10.8)	(4.0)	(11.4)	(7.27)
No. of nasal + consonant occurrences	9	2	2	
(%age of all phonemes)	(8.1)	(2.6)	(2.9)	
No. of consonant + sibilant occurrences	5	0	0	
(%age of all phonemes)	(4.5)	(0.0)	(0.0)	
No. of occurrences of /ʌ/	6	0	3	
(%age of all phonemes)	(5.4)	(0.0)	(4.3)	(1.75)
No. of occurrences of /æ/	0	4	1	
(%age of all phonemes)	(0.0)	(5.3)	(1.4)	(1.45)

The rough indications of relative frequency provided by the percentages of this table give reasonably clear support to the claim that the tercet (lines 5–7) contrasts with the opening quatrain in terms of all the features considered, and that the second tercet (lines 8–10) returns to the pattern of the quatrain with respect to all features considered except that of consonant clustering.[14]

These observations are consistent with Leavis's interpretation of the stanza, if we accept that what he calls the 'pervasive sense of luxury' shows itself in the re-emergence, in the final tercet, of the mood established in lines 1–4, minus the dragging effect of the consonant clusters. The data suggest, however, a slight rethinking of Leavis, whereby lines 8–10 are seen to merge and reconcile the different 'motions' of lines 1–4 and lines 5–7. There are two reasons why this should make sense in terms of the thematic development of the poem. First, the end of the stanza does not present a mood opposed to the opening 'lethargy', but rather a reinterpretation of that 'lethargy', as the poet's ecstatic response to the nightingale's song. Secondly, both the languor of the opening lines and the related 'luxury' of the final lines can be seen, in the context of the whole poem, as offering an ultimately illusory promise of self-realization – hence it is appropriate, in retrospect, that the last lines, expressing a purely hedonistic delight in the nightingale's song, should be tinged with the negative associations of the first quatrain.

4.5.2 The metrical level

Of most interest on the metrical level is the interplay between the binary iambic rhythm X / X / X / . . . and the trisyllabic 'dactylic' rhythm / X X / X X . . . It is a commonplace of traditional metrics that a trisyllabic rhythm (anapaest, dactyl, etc.) is conducive to liveliness, light-heartedness, even levity; presumably because there is a tendency (if one assumes a version, however weak, of the isochronous stress theory) for tempo to increase in proportion to the number of unstressed syllables per stress. Apart from at the beginning of the first line, where the strong stresses on the adjacent long syllables *heart aches* set the stanza off with adagio emphasis, there is no disturbance of the iambic rhythm in the first quatrain. This, combined with the pervasive phonemic texture noted above, gives the quatrain a steady, languid movement in keeping with the mood it expresses, as shown pre-eminently in line 2:

X   /   X   /   X / X   / X   /
My sense, as though of hemlock I had drunk.

But this rhythm is progressively interrupted in the last six lines, by the intrusion of trisyllabic (dactylic) patterns:

/   X X   / X X
Light-wingéd Dryad of . . .

The trisyllabic rhythm takes over triumphantly in the last line, which may be recited as dactylic throughout:

/ X X /   X X /   X X   /
Singest of summer in full-throated ease.

The 'note of luxury' sounded in the last phrase is reinforced metrically, by the secondary stress on -*throat*-, which produces a rallentando effect comparable to that of the final cadence of a piece of music.

The buoyant, affirmatory mood is developed further in the next stanza of the poem, which, according to Leavis, 'reverses the movement of the first', moving from an initial life-affirming mood to a final life-negating mood. In keeping with this, the foot reversal at the beginning of the first six lines of the second stanza continues the dactyl motif from the end of stanza 1:

/ X X /
O for a draught . . .

/   X   X / X /
Dance and Provencal song . . .

/   X X /
Cooled a long age . . .

/ X X / X
O for a beaker . . .

/ X X / X
Tasting of Flora . . .

/ X   X /
Full of the true . . .

The metre, then, has its own way of dramatizing Leavis's 'interplay of motions', and in particular, the change of mood and direction which takes place between the quatrain and the sestet of the first stanza.

4.5.3 The syntactic level

The first thing to notice, syntactically, is that the quatrain and sestet of stanza 1 each constitutes a single sentence. The major syntactic break of the stanza is therefore at the end of line 4, where Leavis notes that the 'Lethe-wards' movement ends. The structure of the first sentence is *progressive*, in that it consists of five clauses, each succeeding the other by a simple conjunctive link of subordination or coordination:

My heart aches,	(CLAUSE A)
and a drowsy numbness pains my sense,	(CLAUSE B)
as though of hemlock I had drunk	(CLAUSE C)
or emptied some dull opiate to the drains one minute past	(CLAUSE D)
and Lethe-wards had sunk.	(CLAUSE E)

48

It is not fanciful to suggest that this sentence structure is a syntactic enactment of the movement 'downwards', towards Lethe, as indeed is emphasized by its final word *sunk*. Psychologically, the sentence enables its interpreter to follow the line of least resistance: the end of each clause is, in Sinclair's terms,[15] a point of repose or release, a potential sentence-ending, for no clause contains anticipatory structural signals requiring interpretation in terms of a later clause. But at line 5, an element of *regressive* structure, of anticipatory tension, enters the syntax: '*Tis not* . . . looks forward, for its resolution, to the *but* . . . in the following line. A more striking case of syntactic suspense occurs in lines 7–10, where the subject of the final clause, *thou*, anticipates its verb, *singest*, which does not occur until nearly three lines later. Thus a syntactic expectancy is built up, to find its release in the last line, which in this respect, as well as metrically, becomes the climax of the sestet's 'affirmatory' movement.

We may correlate this mounting tension and its resolution with a progressive clarification of the contextual implications of the stanza in the last six lines. The first-person pronouns *my* and *I* are the only pronouns to occur in lines 1–4, which describe the poet's consciousness in a purely inward-looking, self-regarding way. In contrast, the only pronouns to occur in lines 5–10 are *thy, thine* and *thou*: the poet is now looking outwards, and addressing the external source of his ecstasies: the nightingale. But the identity of the poem's 'thou' is only gradually revealed; from the enigmatic references of lines 5–6, we move to the identification of 'thou' with the 'light-wingèd Dryad' in line 7, and finally with the 'singer' of line 10. The hidden addressee's nature, and hence identity, is at last clarified. The effect is of a progressive shift of focus from the poet towards the nightingale.

Thus in these three respects – metrically, syntactically and contextually – line 10 is the culmination of a tendency or movement which takes place in lines 5–10. By the end of the stanza, the 'pervasive sense of luxury', although still present in the phonemic patterning, has undergone a transformation into something vital and positive.

Although this analysis has been necessarily selective, it has illustrated, I hope, how Leavis's general critical judgment and interpretation of the poem can be supported, and to some extent deepened and clarified, by a more systematic scrutiny of its language than he himself felt it necessary to attempt.

First, close analysis bears out Leavis's impression of a 'fine organization', revealed in the way that patternings and tendencies on different linguistic levels work towards a common effect. Secondly, the balancing of the two contrasting parts of the stanza, representing the two main tensions of feeling in the poem, is also borne out by linguistic detail. Thirdly, analysis can show how those expressions which Leavis picks out as thematically significant are actually highlighted by linguistic means. In the case of *happy*, the phonemic make-up of the word, in contrast with the pervasive phonemic texture of lines 1–4, reinforces its mood-changing effect. Again, the keynote value of *light-wingéd* is foregrounded (a) by its innovatory status as a poetic neologism; (b) by its dactylic stress pattern (when in attributive position, as here); and (c) by the pattern of assonance (/aɪ/) and consonance (/t/ and /d/) which links it with the following word *Dryad*.

More generally, the linguistic analysis gives tentative clues to the explanation of vague aesthetic terms such as 'balance' (in the opposition between lines 1–4 and 5–10 in this stanza), and 'climax' (in the working of metrical and syntactic features, in alliance with the sense of the stanza, towards a resolution in the final line). In accord with Leavis's emphasis on 'dynamic "motions"', the analysis deals in dramatic concepts such as intensification and the heightening of tension, and not merely in the static, structural relations with which linguistic studies of poetry tend to be associated. Even that most general of aesthetic terms, 'unity', may gain some meaning from the observation of how, in this stanza, contrasting linguistic features predominate in opposed parts of the whole, and are reconciled in a final synthesis: just as some phonemic prominences of the opening quatrain return in the final tercet, so the rhythmic rallentando on *full-throated ease* recalls the metrical tempo of the quatrain, and the release of syntactic tension in line 10 brings back the tensionless character of the opening sentence.

4.6 Conclusion

My aim in this chapter has been to refute Youngren's contention that linguists are making a 'theoretical mistake' in claiming that linguistic analysis has an explanatory value for criticism. I have argued, and have tried to demonstrate, that the mistake lies only in claiming too much, and that linguistic stylistics has a proper role in providing a more secure basis for critical arguments from the text. My analysis of part of Keats's Ode goes some way, I hope, towards the fulfilment of this role, but is obviously incomplete and defective in various respects. In conclusion, I would like to add some further comments on the explanatory role to which I think stylistics should aspire, noting the ways in which my present analysis has fallen short of it.

First, let us distinguish again between the three chief sorts of statements which can be made about a literary text, or text-portion, T. A statement may be made about some linguistic property, some stylistic property or some aesthetic quality of T. A linguistic statement is either simple (e.g. 'T is a relative clause') or quantitative (e.g. 'T contains 5 relative clauses'). A stylistic statement is derived from linguistic statements about T, and generally asserts some respect in which T is in some relative or absolute sense abnormal ('T contains an unusually high frequency of short vowels', 'T contains such-and-such a regular pattern of repetition', 'T is ungrammatical in such-and-such a respect'). The applicability to T of an aesthetic statement (such as T is 'lively'), cannot be demonstrated, but can be given a reasonable justification in terms of the stylistic properties of T. But the relation between aesthetic properties and stylistic properties is not one-to-one, and therefore we cannot make such assertions as 'the liveliness of T is due to the high frequency of short vowels'. Instead, we must say that a given stylistic property s_i is potentially an exponent of a range of aesthetic values $a_m \ldots a_n$, and that a given aesthetic property a_i is expounded by the coincidence of a set of stylistic properties $s_m \ldots s_n$ within whose range it lies. Thus the aesthetic value of a stylistic property must be considered variable, and as dependent on other coexisting stylistic properties 'sympathetic' to that value. Aesthetic statements require the exercise of taste or discrimination by their user because the user has to evaluate the relative strengths of the stylistic properties (both of form and of meaning) contributing to this or that effect, and moreover has to choose between aesthetic terms with overlapping meanings (e.g. *languid, lethargic, lingering* might be, with slightly differing degrees of appropriateness, applied to the first four lines of the Ode).

Between the two most relevant levels of statement, aesthetic and stylistic, there is a third, interconnecting type of statement which asserts that in T, a given stylistic property s_i contributes to the expression of a given aesthetic property a_j. The main shortcoming of the preceding analysis is that the reader has been asked to take such statements (e.g. the statement that frequency of nasals, consonant clusters, etc., contribute to the 'languor') on trust. This is justifiable, to some extent, on the grounds that judgments of such statements tend to vary little from person to person, and have roughly the same status as the judgments of grammaticality, etc., on which linguistic descriptions are based. Ultimately, however, such statements have to be validated in terms of general theories of the psychological effects of stylistic features. Such theories, or 'rhetorics', although at present poorly developed, are open to empirical investigation. Thus, a rhetoric of metre has to include an account of the varying aesthetic effects of iambic, dactylic and other metrical patterns; a rhetoric of syntax has to include an explanation of the psychological effects of progressive as opposed to regressive syntactic structures. A more general concern of these rhetorics must be the investigation of linguistic mimesis: the phenomenon of form imitating or enacting content.[16]

Such considerations may seem to make the goal of a satisfactory stylistic explanation of critical judgments seem remote. Yet, even with their imperfections and limitations, the present techniques of stylistics allow us to strengthen the basis for critical argument, and reduce the critic's reliance on 'mere assertion of judgment'.

NOTE: I wrote this article after giving a paper on this subject to a number of stimulating and perceptive audiences during a tour of Dutch universities, in January 1976. I am grateful for their comments, and also for those of my departmental colleagues M.A. Beaken, G. Knowles and M.H. Short.

Notes

1. Richards (1970: 549) describes Jakobson and Jones's analysis of Shakespeare's 'Sonnet 129' as 'what may very well prove a landmark in the long-awaited approach of descriptive linguistics to the account of poetry'.
2. Youngren (1972: 141): 'This brief survey of recent attempts to apply linguistics to criticism will do to show not only the failure of these writers to come up with anything useful, but also the candour with which they have criticised each other . . .'.
3. The main contributions to this debate are reprinted as Chapters 4–6 in Fowler (1971).
4. Leavis (1936), Chapter 7 'Keats', especially pp. 244–50.
5. The term 'The New Stylistics' (which forms the title of the introductory chapter of Fowler, 1975b) is a useful one for referring to the cumulative body of writings applying the techniques of linguistics to literature over the last twenty years **(1955–75)**. As Fowler points out, however, this term does not designate a unified 'school of thought'. Fowler's chapter gives a brief review of the characteristics of 'the New Stylistics', and of the history of its relationship with literary scholarship. Earlier treatments of the same subject are given in the introductions to Fowler (1966a) and Fowler (1971).
6. Three papers by Sibley (1959, 1965, 1968) explore the nature of aesthetic concepts and the meaning of aesthetic terms and statements.
7. Sibley (1965: 138).
8. On the theory of foregrounding, see Mukařovský (1964) and, with reference to English poetry, Leech (1969: 56–9).
9. Spitzer (1948: 19–20).
10. This attitude is illustrated in the quotation in note 2 above, and the following from Bateson (1968: 182): 'Ultimately it is, I suggest, because of the verbal immobility, this failure to recognize that in literature language is for the reader a mere preliminary to style – and style itself is a preliminary to the literary response in its fullest sense – that the critic finds so little nourishment in modern linguistics in any of its forms. *Not here, O Apollo, are haunts meet for thee.*'
11. F.R. Leavis (1948: 74).
12. The transcription follows Gimson (1980 [1962]). The force of the analysis does not, however, depend on the choice of a particular system of transcription. Nor is what I have to say about the sound patterning of the stanza likely to be affected by the choice of a particular historical, dialectal, or stylistic variant in English pronunciation as a 'model' for the recitation of the poem. In this context, whether I ought to have attempted a reconstruction of the early nineteenth-century pronunciation of Keats is an interesting debating point, but no more.
13. In the table, affricates and diphthongs count as single phonemes. The percentages in the right-hand column, giving the frequency in English of certain phonemes and phoneme classes, are taken from D.B. Fry's phoneme count, as reproduced by Gimson **(1980: 149, 217–18)**.
14. It would be pointless to look for statistical significance here, since the psychological effect of a stylistically prominent feature depends, I assume, crucially on its interaction with other features having parallel aesthetic functions. I agree with

Halliday (1971: 344) that for literary stylistics 'a rough indication of frequencies is often just what is needed: enough to suggest why we should accept the analyst's assertion that some feature is prominent in the text, and allow us to check his statements'. **See, however, Chapter 11, in which I attempt to use statistical significance in support of statements about foregrounding in a text.**

15. Sinclair (1966: 72–4).
16. Epstein (1975) makes a promising start in the task of classifying and evaluating different kinds of linguistic mimesis.

CHAPTER 5

Stylistics

5.1 Introduction

In its broadest sense, stylistics is the study of *style*; of how language use varies according to varying circumstances: e.g. circumstances of period, discourse situation or authorship. A style X is the sum of linguistic features associated with texts or textual samples defined by some set of contextual parameters, Y. For example, Y may be a set of situational parameters such as the formality of the relation between addresser and addressee, the kind of communicative activity they are engaged in (e.g. scientific discourse), or the method by which communication is maintained (e.g. written correspondence). But traditionally and predominantly, stylistics has focused on texts which are considered of artistic value, and therefore worthy of study for their own sake. We may therefore begin by distinguishing *general stylistics*, the study of style in texts of all kinds, from *literary stylistics*, which is the study of style in literary texts, and is the main subject of this present chapter. The 'Y' mentioned above may be termed the *domain* of style, and it is essential to note that the domain can be more or less general. We may, for instance, be interested in the style of all novelists of the nineteenth century, or of only one of such novelists; we may wish to study all the novels of that writer, or only one. The most specific domain of style, and in many ways the most valuable starting point for stylistics, is the individual text or text extract.

Within the restricted area of literary stylistics, as outside it, there is room for differences of approach and purpose. We may distinguish *descriptive* stylistics (where the purpose is just to describe the style) from *explanatory* stylistics (where the purpose is to use stylistics to explain something). Again, within explanatory stylistics, we may distinguish cases where the explanatory goal is *extrinsic* (e.g. to find out the author(s) or the chronology of a set of writings), or *intrinsic* (where the purpose is to explain the meaning or value of the text itself). It is this latter type of study which is most common with literary texts, and which I shall illustrate here.

First, however, let us briefly consider general principles. The study of style is essentially the study of *variation* in the use of language. Over the whole range of language use, certain major parameters for classifying domains can be considered: e.g. the parameter of formality (slang, informal, formal, literary use, etc.), that of medium (especially spoken versus written language), and that of communicative function (advertising, scientific, legal, conversational use, etc.). In the most general sense, varieties of a language so defined constitute 'styles' (cf. Crystal and Davy 1969). It is a basic assumption of general stylistics that correlations can be established between situational domains (as defined above) and formal characteristics of language use. For example, in scientific English the passive voice occurs frequently and the imperative mood rarely, whereas in advertising English, the passive is rare and the imperative is common. Thus the stylistic features of a text may be seen as to a greater or lesser extent predictable from its situational parameters. The methods applied to general domains such as scientific or advertising usage may equally well be applied to more restricted domains, such as the essays of Bacon or the letters of Keats.

The concept of *deviation* (as the negative side, so to speak, of variation) is important to the study of style. To be stylistically distinctive, a feature of language must deviate from some norm of comparison. The norm may be an *absolute* norm, i.e. a norm for the language as a whole, or a *relative* norm, i.e. a norm provided by some set of texts which, for the purposes of the study, are regarded as comparable (e.g. the simple sentence structures of *As I Lay Dying* may be compared with the rest of Faulkner's oeuvre). Connected with this distinction is another one, between *determinate* and *statistical* deviation (Levin 1963). Statistical deviation is a quantitative measure of linguistic differences between the domain and the norm. The norm in this case must generally be regarded as a relative norm, as it is difficult to establish an absolute statistical norm for the language as a whole. (For features of very common occurrence, however, such as frequency of phonemes, of letters, or of frequent words, such an absolute norm can be usefully established.) Determinate deviation, on the other hand, is non-quantitative: in this sense the 'norm' is the language itself as a system composed of rules and categories and the deviation is observed as a discrepancy between what is allowed by the language system, and what occurs in the text. Determinate deviation therefore is a violation to some degree of the rules or constraints of the language code itself. This type of deviation is significant in the study of literary style, and especially in poetry (see Leech 1969: 36–71), as will be exemplified in sections 5.3 and 5.4.

The concept of deviation has not escaped criticism. As a statistical concept, it has been criticized because of the unclearness of the statistical concept of 'norm' as applied to style. The determinate sense of deviation has also been criticized: purely linguistic accounts of it in terms of grammaticality (see Lipski 1977) have failed to explain both the gradual nature of deviation, and the way in which it contributes to poetic meaning. There is no simple linguistic model of deviation, but understood informally, as the basis of surprising and creative manipulations of the language in literature, its role in stylistics is a useful if not indispensable one.

Another preliminary difficulty occurs over the concept of 'literary language'. Stylistics, as we have seen, generally assumes a predictable relation between situational parameters and the kind of language use associated with them. It is therefore often taken for granted that just as there is a special kind of language called 'scientific language', or 'advertising language', etc., so there must be a special kind of phenomenon called 'literary language'. This, in turn, leads to the assumption of a dichotomy between 'literary' and 'non-literary' language, which has been reinforced by formalist or structuralist theories that literature communicates in a totally different way from 'ordinary language' (see Pratt 1977: xi–37). One way to avoid this false dichotomy is to note that domains such as 'literature' do not have well-defined boundaries: it must be acknowledged that most texts are multifunctional, and that when we consider something to be 'literature' we do so on functional grounds, judging its artistic function to be important as compared with other functions (e.g. as propaganda or as biography) that it may have. It should also be noted that the literary use of language is characterized most typically by its avoidance of the predictable; and yet, on the other hand, that deviant and surprising uses of language are to be found not only in literature, but also in other domains such as joke-telling, advertising, and ordinary conversation. Thus the search for a set of criteria which, like a litmus test, will distinguish literary from non-literary language is futile.

To show how stylistic analysis of poetry works in practice, I propose to examine Shelley's *Ode to the West Wind*. My aim will be to demonstrate that a close examination of the language of the poem leads to a greater understanding of its meaning and value: i.e. to a greater *appreciation* of it as a work of art. I shall not be interested only in this poem, but also in showing, through this poem, how stylistics can be helpful in accounting for artistic notions such as unity, suspense and climax.

The method of stylistics, in these terms, is to relate features of linguistic description step by step to aspects of critical interpretation. The two activities of linguistic description and literary criticism are viewed as distinct, but complementary. If we start from the linguistic point of view, we have to *select* features of stylistic significance from the mass of data which might form part of a linguistic description. If we start from the literary critical point of view, we begin with some conception of the work's literary significance, and seek evidence for (or against) this significance in the linguistic details of the text. In either case, both points of view – linguistic and critical – must be simultaneously engaged if the analysis is to serve its explanatory purpose. My technique here, however, will be to begin with linguistic details and to work towards the literary interpretation, rather than vice versa.

5.2 The text: 'Ode to the West Wind' by Percy B. Shelley

Ode to the West Wind

I

O wild West Wind, thou breath of Autumn's being	1
Thou, from whose unseen presence the leaves dead	2
Are driven, like ghosts from an enchanter fleeing,	3
Yellow, and black, and pale, and hectic red,	4
Pestilence-stricken multitudes: O thou,	5
Who chariotest to their dark wintry bed	6
The wingèd seeds, where they lie cold and low,	7
Each like a corpse within its grave, until	8
Thine azure sister of the Spring shall blow	9
Her clarion o'er the dreaming earth, and fill	10
(Driving sweet buds like flocks to feed in air)	11
With living hues and odours plain and hill:	12
Wild Spirit, which art moving everywhere;	13
Destroyer and preserver; hear, oh, hear!	14

II

Thou on whose stream, mid the steep sky's commotion,	1
Loose clouds like earth's decaying leaves are shed,	2
Shook from the tangled boughs of Heaven and Ocean,	3
Angels of rain and lightning: there are spread	4
On the blue surface of thine aery surge,	5
Like the bright hair uplifted from the head	6
Of some fierce Maenad, even from the dim verge	7
Of the horizon to the zenith's height,	8
The locks of the approaching storm. Thou dirge	9
Of the dying year, to which this closing night	10
Will be the dome of a vast sepulchre,	11
Vaulted with all thy congregated might	12
Of vapours, from whose solid atmosphere	13
Black rain, and fire, and hail, will burst: oh hear!	14

III

Thou who didst waken from his summer dreams	1
The blue Mediterranean, where he lay,	2
Lulled by the coil of his crystalline streams,	3
Beside a pumice isle in Baiae's bay,	4
And saw in sleep old palaces and towers	5
Quivering within the wave's intenser day,	6
All overgrown with azure moss and flowers	7
So sweet, the sense faints picturing them! Thou	8
For whose path the Atlantic's level powers	9
Cleave themselves into chasms, while far below	10
The sea-blooms and the oozy woods which wear	11
The sapless foliage of the ocean, know	12
Thy voice, and suddenly grow grey with fear,	13
And tremble and despoil themselves: oh hear!	14

IV

If I were a dead leaf thou mightest bear;	1
If I were a swift cloud to fly with thee;	2
A wave to pant beneath thy power, and share	3
The impulse of thy strength, only less free	4
Than thou, O uncontrollable! If even	5
I were as in my boyhood, and could be	6
The comrade of thy wanderings over Heaven,	7
As then, when to outstrip thy skiey speed	8
Scarce seemed a vision; I would ne'er have striven	9
As thus with thee in prayer in my sore need.	10
Oh, lift me as a wave, a leaf, a cloud!	11
I fall upon the thorns of life! I bleed!	12
A heavy weight of hours has chained and bowed	13
One too like thee: tameless, and swift, and proud.	14

V

Make me thy lyre, even as the forest is:	1
What if my leaves are falling like its own?	2
The tumult of thy mighty harmonies	3
Will take from both a deep, autumnal tone,	4
Sweet though in sadness. Be thou, Spirit fierce,	5
My spirit! Be thou me, impetuous one!	6

Drive my dead thoughts over the universe,   7
Like withered leaves, to quicken a new birth;   8
And, by the incantation of this verse,   9

Scatter, as from an unextinguished hearth   10
Ashes and sparks, my words among mankind!   11
Be through my lips to unawakened earth   12

The trumpet of a prophecy! O, Wind,   13
If Winter comes, can Spring be far behind?   14

5.3 Stylistic analysis: deviation and foregrounding

Deviation provides us with a working criterion (though not an exclusive criterion) for the selection of those linguistic features which are of literary significance. Deviation is especially characteristic of poetic language: the poet deviates from 'expected norms' of linguistic expression. In other words, he exercises, in the broadest sense, 'poetic licence'. I shall call the type of deviation where the poet deviates from norms of the language as a whole *primary deviation*, to distinguish it from secondary and tertiary deviation to be considered in section 5.4.

Primary deviation takes two main forms:

(a) Where the language allows a choice, the poet goes outside the normally occurring range of choice; and
(b) Where the language allows a choice, the poet denies himself the freedom to choose, using the same item in successive positions.[1]

The first type of deviation can be readily exemplified from lines I 6–7:

Who chariotest to their dark wintry bed / The wingèd seeds, . . .

Here we find (i) lexical deviation, in the choice of the rare verb *chariotest*; (ii) collocational deviation, which can be most clearly displayed in the normalized form:

The *wind* (Subject) *chariots* (Verb) the *seeds* (Object) to their *bed* (Adverbial)

and (iii) the deviation of syntactic order (*hyperbaton*) in the sequence (abnormal for English) Subject + Verb + Adverbial + Object. The collocational oddity of the wind charioting the seeds to bed is the formal basis of a metaphor personifying the wind and the seeds. In this way, a formal deviation, or incongruous juxtaposition of words, is the basis for a semantic deviation, namely a poetic metaphor.

A simple example of the second kind of primary deviation is the alliterative pattern with which the poem begins: *O wild West Wind*. The poet selects on successive syllables the same consonant /w/. In this word-initial position, a large number of phonemes could have occurred; but the poet restricts his choice to just one of those phonemes: a pattern which is striking to the reader or listener, and is statistically unlikely to occur by chance. A less simple example, this time on the lexico-syntactic level, is the pattern of structural choices which is repeated in the first three stanzas. Elements from a small syntactic and lexical inventory are repeated, as is shown schematically below:

I O . . . Wind,	O + Vocative
Thou breath . . . ,	Vocative + Appositive
Thou, from whose . . .	Vocative + Relative Clause
O Thou, who chariotest . . .	O + Vocative + Relative Clause
Wild Spirit, which . . .	Vocative + Relative Clause
Destroyer	Vocative
hear, oh, hear!	Imperative + O + Imperative
II Thou on whose . . .	Vocative + Relative Clause
Thou dirge . . .	Vocative + Appositive
to which . . .	+ Relative Clause
from whose . . .	+ Relative Clause
Oh, hear!	O + Imperative
III Thou who didst . . .	Vocative + Relative Clause
Thou for whose path . . .	Vocative + Relative Clause
oh, hear!	O + Imperative

Although the pattern is not precisely regular, the above summary shows how the poet rings the changes on just five structural elements: the interjection *O*, the Vocative, the Appositive noun phrase, the Relative Clause, and the Imperative verb *hear*. In short, deviation can take the form either of abnormal *irregularity* (e.g. hyperbaton) or of abnormal *regularity* (e.g. syntactic parallelism and other kinds of schematic patterning).

Verse form (metre, rhyme scheme, stanza form) is itself a form of abnormal regularity. It is not, however, itself a form of stylistic variation, but rather a set of schematic structures which allow their own stylistic variation. Anyone who doubts that regular verse patterning is statistically unlikely should note how rarely prose writers produce lines of verse by accident, let alone whole stanzas of verse. It has been observed that Dickens, in many thousand pages of fictional prose, occasionally deviates into blank verse. Whether this was intended or not, it is to be expected that any randomly selected sequence of ten syllables in English will have a low probability of conforming to the alternating pattern of an iambic pentameter. (My estimate of this is a probability of 0.004, assuming, for simplicity, that rhythm is independent of other stylistic factors.) For a perfectly regular heroic couplet or rhyming quatrain to be produced by accident would be, in comparison with this, many times more unlikely, because of the double requirement that not only must the syllables arrange themselves in metrical lines, but also the line end must coincide with rhymes. When verse forms are occasionally produced inadvertently by prose writers, this is a matter for amusement and curiosity, an 'exception that proves the rule' that metrical form deviates from the expected norms of language use:

> There is no force, however great,
> Can stretch a cord, however fine,
> Into a horizontal line,
> Which is accurately straight.
>
> William Whewell, *Elementary Treatise on Mechanics*, 1819

The author of this quatrain, a philosopher, was so abashed when its unwanted 'poetic' quality was pointed out, that he insisted on changing it in a later edition of his treatise.

Foregrounding is a term (see Mukařovský 1958: 18ff) for an effect brought about in the reader by linguistic or other forms of deviation. The deviation, being unexpected, comes to the foreground of the reader's attention as a 'deautomization' of the normal linguistic processes (see Chapter 2, pp. 15–19). There is no requirement that foregrounding should be consciously noted by the reader.[2]

In addition to the normal processes of interpretation which apply to texts, whether literary or not, foregrounding invites an act of *imaginative interpretation* by the reader. When an abnormality comes to our attention, we try to make sense of it. We use our imaginations, consciously or unconsciously, in order to work out why this abnormality exists. The obvious question to ask, in the case of poetic deviation, is: What does the poet mean by it? In these imaginative acts of attributing meaning, or 'making sense', lie the special communicative values of poetry.

The *communicative values* of deviation are by no means random: they tend to fall into certain categories, of which the following seem to be the most important. We may perceive an effect of:

(a) *contrast*: e.g. the *paradox* of *Destroyer and Preserver* (line I 14).
(b) *similarity*: e.g. the similarity expressed through metaphor. In the metaphor already noted in I 6–7, the wind is likened to a charioteer, the seeds to passengers conveyed by the wind, and the earth to a bed.
(c) *parallelism*: e.g. the already noted lexico-syntactic parallelism of stanzas I–III conveys a semantic parallelism between

    I the wind's violent force on land (terrestrial nature)
    II the wind's violent force in the sky (aerial nature)
    III the wind's violent force in the sea (aquatic nature)

(d) *mimesis*: imitation or enactment of the meaning of the poem in its form, e.g. the initial /w/ sounds of *O wild West Wind*, together with the sibilants in the following line, *from whose unseen presence the leaves dead*, may possibly be taken as an instance of onomatopoeia, i.e. as an auditory representation of the sound of the wind. Although critics tend to dismiss such effects as trivial, if not illusory, we shall see below that mimesis can take more abstract and sophisticated forms, and can take a profound role in the elucidation of a poem's meaning and structure.

These interpretative values are not present in the text itself, but it is part of a reader's 'poetic competence' to look for such values. They are the basis for *local* acts of interpretation, and local interpretations in their turn contribute to the interpretation of the whole poem.

It would be possible to give a list of other linguistic deviations in the poem, but we now turn to deviations which are less directly manifested in language use.

5.4 Secondary and tertiary deviation

Secondary deviation is deviation not from norms of linguistic expression in general, but from norms of literary composition, of the 'poetic canon' (see Mukařovský 1958: 23), including norms of author or genre. This can also be called *conventional deviation* or *defeated expectancy*. Examples are:

(a) *metrical variation* is deviation from the metrical 'set', e.g. deviation from the Ode's implicit iambic pentameter pattern $X / X / X / X / X /$.
(b) *enjambment* (or 'run-on lines'), a lack of fit between metrical and syntactic units, such that a line end occurs at a point where there is no major grammatical boundary.

Metrical variation is pervasive in this poem: observe the comparative rarity of a regular iambic line such as I 12: *Wǐth lívǐng húes ǎnd ódǒurs pláin ǎnd híll*, in contrast to the irregularity of such lines as I 5 and I 6. *Pěstǐlěnce-strícken múltǐtùdes* has, in its initial stressed syllable, a strong onset, but then the polysyllabic words lend themselves to a speeding up of the rhythm (` indicating secondary stress), as befits a line describing dead leaves scattered before the wind. A similar effect is achieved in the succession of light syllables in *Whǒ chárǐǒtěst tǒ thěir* . . . , but then the juxtaposed accents of *dárk wíntrў béd* bring a sudden rallentando. In this way, metrical variation can contribute to the impression of the wind's unruly force.

A similar point may be made about the effect of *enjambment*, another prevalent feature of this poem. In I 6–7, for instance, the line boundary comes within the clause, at a point where a pause is not natural. To complete the sense of I 6 (*chariotest to their dark wintry bed*), we have to add the direct object by reading on (*the wingèd seeds*). A more extreme example is that of I 11–13, where a whole line (I 12) intervenes between *fill* and its direct object:

... and fill
...
With living hues and odours *plain and hill*.

In such cases, enjambment prevents the reader from reaching a point of repose: where the verse reaches a staying point, the syntax hurries us on (see Sinclair 1966). In this, enjambment reinforces the effect of metrical variation in suggesting the precipitate onward movement of the wind.

What is deviant, on the level of primary deviation, may become a norm for the purposes of secondary deviation. In this way, different levels of deviation may be recognized in poetry. Just as secondary deviation presupposes primary deviation, so it is possible for a tertiary deviation to build upon the norm of secondary deviation.

Tertiary deviation is deviation from norms internal to a text, and is for this reason also termed *internal deviation* (see Levin 1965). Like secondary deviation, it is a kind of defeated expectancy: a frustration of expectations which have been established in the poem itself. But unlike the other two levels of deviation, internal deviation is a dynamic phenomenon: it is identified by its contrast with the preceding context, and so what counts as internal deviation at one point in the text will not do so elsewhere. In fact, internal deviation often signals a point of climax. Consider the fourth stanza of Shelley's Ode. It marks a dramatic change in the pattern of lexico-syntactic parallelism we have observed (see section 5.3 above) in stanzas I–III. Instead of the elaborated vocatives of stanzas I–III, this stanza begins with a series of *if*-clauses. *If I were a dead leaf . . . /If I were a swift cloud . . .* But the climax of the poem's development does not arrive until IV 11 and IV 12, where, after just four extremely complex sentences in the whole poem up to this point, three very short sentences follow within two lines:

Oh, lift me as a wave, a leaf, a cloud!
I fall upon the thorns of life! I bleed!

This is a syntactic form of defeated expectancy, and is accompanied with a metrical example of the same phenomenon: for after persistent metrical variation, these lines return to the regular iambic rhythm, and to a match between line boundaries and sentence boundaries. Thus what is normal by the standard of secondary deviation is deviant by the standard of tertiary deviation.

The very end of the poem similarly achieves salience by internal deviation. There is a striking return to metrical regularity in the last line of all:

Ĭf Wíntĕr cómes, căn Spríng bĕ fár bĕhínd?

The line has a strict iambic rhythm, and moreover is syntactically self-contained, being a sentence in itself. These two factors help to explain why it seems to express a sense of repose and finality, after the restless movement of preceding stanzas. Its return to simplicity and order is like the perfect cadence at the end of a seemingly unfinishable Bach fugue.

The two passages I have cited as exemplifying internal deviation are not only among the most quoted lines of the poem, but interestingly also among its most criticized lines. Out of the context, they may strike the reader as banal: after all, the last line of the poem expresses the totally obvious platitude that spring follows winter. But an important effect of internal deviation is that it can make something which may seem trite in isolation into something peculiarly significant or expressive, by causing it to stand out against its context. Ezra Pound's observation is particularly apposite to this:

> Neither prose nor drama can attain poetic intensity save by construction, almost by scenario; by so arranging the circumstance that some perfectly simple speech, perception, dogmatic statement appears in abnormal vigour.
>
> (1934: 289)

This same observation may be applied to internal deviation in poetry.

5.5 Coherence of foregrounding (see Chapter 3, pp. 31–3)

According to Mukařovský (1958: 44), it is the 'consistency and systematic character of foregrounding' which is a special characteristic of poetic language. This means that in poetry, deviations are not just to be interpreted in isolation, but to be seen as forming a meaningful pattern in themselves. *Coherence of foregrounding* may be considered under two different headings:

(a) *Cohesion* between deviations occurring in different parts of the poem; and
(b) *Congruence* between deviations occurring concurrently, but at different linguistic levels.

These might be respectively described as 'horizontal' and 'vertical' coherence of foregrounded features in the text.

(i) Cohesion of foregrounding
Cohesion of foregrounding may be exemplified by reference to the parallelism of the three elements (Earth, Sky and Sea) in stanzas I–III. The

primary elaboration of this parallelism itself extends over three stanzas. But further, this same parallelism is resumed in the triple *if*-clause structure in IV 1–5: *If I were a dead leaf* . . . / *If I were a swift cloud* . . . / *A wave to pant beneath thy power* . . . And once again, the pattern recurs in a variant form in IV 11: *Oh, lift me as a wave, a leaf, a cloud!*

(ii) Congruence of foregrounding
On the *metrical* level, we have already noted the recurrent use of enjambment, and the effect this has in impelling the reader from one line to another without a rest.

(a) On the level of *rhyme*, Shelley uses an unusual and ingenious rhyme scheme in which each tercet (as in *terza rima*) shares a rhyme with the subsequent strophe: *a b a; b c b; c d c; d e d; e e*. This interweaving of rhymes prevents the rhyme scheme from reaching a point of finality until the final couplet. Each tercet is incomplete in itself, and 'looks forward' to the first line of the next stanza, which will supply the rhyme for its middle line.

(b) On the *phonemic* level, the line boundaries are often spanned by alliterative or other patterns:

I 2–3: . . . *dead* / *Are driven* . . . (alliteration)
I 4–5: . . . *hectic red* / *Pestilence* . . . (assonance)
I 6–7: . . . *wintry bed* / *the wingéd seeds* . . . (reverse rhyme)

Other examples: II 2–3, II 9–10, II 11–12, etc. In this way, the sense of 'onwardness' which is created in the verse structure is reinforced by interlinear bonds at the level of segmental phonology.

(c) On the *syntactic* level, the use of inverted or transposed word order (hyperbaton) repeatedly delays a major element of clause structure, such as a Subject or Object, so that the meaning of one line cannot be completed until a subsequent line is read. To the delay of the Object in I 6–7 and I 10–12, examples already noted, may be added a further, and more remarkable case of syntactic delay in II 4–9: *there are spread* / . . . / . . . / . . . / . . . / *The locks of the approaching storm.* The structure of this clause is unusual indeed, since after *there are spread*, three complex adverbials are interposed before we finally arrive at the logical Subject. The striking simile of the Maenad (a frenzied female Bacchanalian dancer) is posited before we know to what it is to be applied.

Such anticipatory use of syntax is also found in the larger structures of the first four sentences of the poem: those extending over stanza I, stanza II, stanza III, and the first ten lines of stanza IV. Not only are all these sentences exceptionally complex, but they postpone their main clauses to the end. In the first three sentences, the elaborated vocatives of lines 1–13 anticipate the main clause, the imperative (*hear,*) *oh, hear!,* in line 14. (Even here there is a further hint of incompletion in the syntactic ambiguity which allows us to read the imperative as being continued by the vocative of the next stanza.) In the fourth sentence, the *if*-clauses similarly build up syntactic suspense until the main clause is finally reached in IV 9–10.

(d) On the *discourse* level, there is yet one further layer of anticipatory structure, stretching over the whole poem up to the point (IV 11–12) which I have already described as the climax of the poem. Although stanzas I, II and III may be analysed as syntactically complete, they are not complete in a discourse sense, for they merely end with the invocation *Oh, hear!*, which indicates that the poet has something to say to the wind, and that this has not yet been said. Thus each of these stanzas anticipates a message which is stated, after long delay, in stanzas IV and V.

On these five levels, then, the poem foregrounds anticipation, the lack of finality. The reader's inclination to seek a point of rest is persistently frustrated, and so the poem dramatizes, in a number of interrelated ways, the sense of impetus and restlessness appropriate to its theme.

5.6 The poem's interpretation

In seeking patterns of coherence in foregrounding, we have already taken the most important step from stylistic analysis towards literary interpretation. Let us see now how cohesion and congruence of foregrounding can be brought together in a *holistic* interpretation and appreciation of the Ode.

First, however, we must give attention to an aspect of cohesion of foregrounding which has not yet been discussed: this is cohesion of metaphor. In stanzas I–III, two categories of metaphor are prominent:

(a) Metaphors which interassociate the three elements of Earth, Sea and Sky;
(b) Metaphors which animize or personify the phenomena of nature.

In the former category are:

(i) Metaphors which associate terrestrial and aerial nature:
    The wingéd seeds (I 7); *Driving sweet buds like flocks to feed in air* (I 11);
    Loose clouds like earth's decaying leaves are shed (II 2); *this closing night /*
    Will be the dome of a vast sepulchre (II 10–11); *Vaulted with all thy congre-*
    gated might / Of vapours (II 12–13); *solid atmosphere* (II 13).

(ii) Metaphors which associate aerial and aquatic nature:
    Thou on whose stream, mid the steep sky's commotion, / Loose clouds . . . are
    shed (II 1–2); *On the blue surface of thine aery surge* (II 5).

(iii) Metaphors which associate aquatic and terrestrial nature:
    old palaces and towers / Quivering within the wave's intenser day (III 5–6);
    All overgrown with azure moss and flowers (III 7); *the Atlantic's level powers*

/ *Cleave themselves into chasms* (III 9–10); *The sea-blooms and the oozy woods* (III 11); *The sapless foliage of the ocean* (III 12).

Perhaps the interassociation of the three elements is most forcefully conveyed by the complex metaphor in II 3, which involves all three:

Shook from the tangled *boughs* of *Heaven* and *Ocean*.

It can be argued, from these examples and others in stanzas I–III, that while the parallelisms show the wind's indomitable force equally at work in the three elements, the metaphors lead us to a vision in which all three elements combine and interrelate within the indivisible realm of nature, the dominion of the West Wind pictured as the universal force of destruction and regeneration.

This vision is easily related to the other category of metaphors: that of animation and personification. Such metaphors are numerous; in fact, there is one in practically every line of stanza I:

Thou breath of Autumn's being (I 1); *from whose unseen presence* (I 2); *like ghosts from an enchanter fleeing* (I 3); *Pestilence-stricken multitudes* (I 5); *Who chariotest to their . . . bed / The wingéd seeds* (I 6–7); *Each like a corpse within its grave* (I 8); *Thine azure sister* (I 9); *shall blow / Her clarion* (I 9–10); *(Driving sweet buds like flocks to feed on air)* (I 11); *With living hues and odours* (I 12); *Wild Spirit, which art moving . . .* (I 13); *Destroyer and preserver* (I 14).

Such an all-pervasive humanization of nature follows naturally from the initial conception of the wind as the breath, the animizing force, of all that is in the world. The overriding personification is that of the wind itself, to which the Ode is addressed as if in supplication to a deity. (Even the syntax of the elaborated vocatives followed by imperatives identifies the poem as a prayer.)

The thematic and stylistic change between stanzas III and IV is observed not only in the syntax, but also in the metaphors. The dominant trend of personification gives way to the opposite trend of depersonification, beginning in the hypothetical mood of *If I were*, and progressing to the passionate directness of the imperative *lift*:

If I were a dead leaf . . . (IV 1); *If I were a swift cloud* (IV 2); *A wave to pant beneath thy power* (IV 3); *Oh, lift me as a wave, a leaf, a cloud!* (IV 11).

The imperatives of depersonification continue into stanza V, but with an important alteration:

Make me thy lyre (V 1); *even as the forest is* (V 1); *What if my leaves are falling . . .* (V 2); *Be thou . . . / My spirit* (V 5–6); *Be thou me* (V 6); *Scatter, as from an unextinguished hearth / Ashes and sparks, my words among mankind!* (V 10–11).

Whereas in stanza IV the metaphors imply an equation of the speaker-poet with inert nature within the control of the wind, in stanza V they equate him with the wind itself, or with a vehicle of the wind's power. On the metaphorical level, then, the poem has the structure of an argument (it is indeed a dialectical argument in the form of thesis, antithesis and synthesis) as follows:

The wind embodies or symbolizes the cosmic force in nature (stanzas I–III).
But if so, how am I (man and poet) part of this natural world?
I cannot be like leaf, cloud, and wave, a part of passive nature (stanza IV).
Therefore let me be part of the active, inspiring part of nature: the force of the wind itself (stanza V).

Stanza by stanza, the dominant metaphorical structure is as in Figure 5.1:

STANZA I	STANZA II	STANZA III	STANZA IV	STANZA V
Personification	Personification	Personification	Depersonification	Depersonification
(LAND)	(SKY)	(SEA)	(Rejected)	(Accepted)

Figure 5.1 Metaphorical structure

The last stanza, appropriately enough, is marked by metaphors of music and poetry, for the poet, in keeping with the active role he assumes, represents himself as the musician, the lyre, and the prophet of the wind. From the despairing tone of the end of stanza IV, he moves to a triumphant affirmation of the poet's quickening power in the universe.

In its concluding lines, the poem becomes reflexive: Shelley prays that the 'incantation of this verse' (V 9) will itself fulfil the poet's role of manifesting the wind's force. Thus if the vindicating metaphor is to become a reality, the force of the wind must be enacted in the very sound and form of the poem. In this way, the foregrounding of anticipatory structure (discussed in section 5.5(ii)) and the foregrounding of metaphor (discussed in the present section) come together in the poem's interpretation. The overall coherence of foregrounding is established by the poet's acting out in the poem itself his declared role as mouthpiece of the wind, of godlike energy in nature.

5.7 Conclusion

A few concluding remarks may be added about the implications of a method of stylistic analysis which, like the one I have sketched, aims to make step-by-step connections between linguistic details and an integrated appreciation of the text.

 (i) The method demonstrates how stylistics extends linguistics beyond the sentence, to the description of structures or recurrent features which span sentence sequences, or even whole texts.

 (ii) One cannot use stylistic analysis as a means of evaluating a literary text. The method does not *result* in a value judgment, but rather *assumes* a value judgment, a kind of 'prejudice' in favour of the work being examined: it is this which sanctions the search for coherence in the text's interpretation. However, the method also provides the basis for a more explicit and reasoned assessment than could be obtained merely by an impressionistic reading.

(iii) Particularly through the concept of tertiary or internal deviation, the method enables us to see a linguistic basis for such critical concepts as 'climax', 'suspense', 'unity'. In the Ode we have noticed the achievement of suspense through anticipatory structuring. We have also observed two different kinds of climax: that in stanza IV corresponding to the dramatic notion of *peripeteia*, and that in stanza V corresponding to the dramatic notion of *denouement*.

(iv) The 'unity' of a poem, by this method, is not just discovered, but to some extent also invented. A sense of unity is arrived at through the interpreter's search for *maximum coherence* in the artistic features of the work, which in a poem means *maximum coherence of foregrounding*. This artistic coherence is essential to our view of what a poem is: in the poet J.V. Cunningham's words, 'It's the coincidence of form that locks in a poem'. But the coherence does not enable us to distinguish between poems and non-poems, for there is no independent criterion or set of criteria for judging that coherence of artistic forms and meanings exists in one text, but not in another. Stylistics cannot tell us that a text is literature; but once the text is accepted as literature, stylistics can teach us a great deal about it.

NOTE: I am grateful to Teun van Dijk and Michael H. Short for their comments on a draft of this chapter.

Notes

1. The second of these types of deviation largely corresponds to Jakobson's well-known criterion for the poetic function of language: 'The poetic function projects the principle of equivalence from the axis of selection to the axis of combination' (Jakobson 1960: 358).
2. Although foregrounding is a subjective phenomenon, empirical measures can be made in such a way as to confirm the presence of foregrounding. An important investigation of foregrounding from this point of view is van Peer (**1986**).

CHAPTER 6

Music in metre: 'sprung rhythm' in Victorian poetry

6.1 Introduction

My purpose in this chapter is twofold. First, I wish to present a particular view of metrical form in which the relation between rhythm in poetry and rhythm in music is explored. Secondly, I wish to use this view of metrical form as a means characterizing an era of English metrical history (roughly from 1850 to 1900) in which the musical principle in scansion was unusually important. By characterizing this period as a period of 'sprung rhythm', I am consciously extending the use of this phrase from Hopkins's own specialized use of it, and conveying my conviction that Hopkins's metrics, however idiosyncratic it may seem, represents a metrical trend typical of his period.

6.2 A multilevelled account of metre: four levels of metrical form

First, the metrical framework. Like language itself, metrical form can only be described as a multilevelled phenomenon. I shall discuss four levels of metrical form which are distinct but interrelated. But first let us see why a single-level view of metrics is inadequate.

A simple traditional idea – which may be termed 'naive metrics' – is that the purpose of metrical analysis is to assign a single analysis called a 'scansion' to a given piece of verse. 'Scanning' a line of verse, in this view, consists in deciding whether each of its syllables is stressed or unstressed, as in [1]:

```
      X    /   X  /   X   /   X  / X  /
```
[1] And sweet as those by hopeless fancy feign'd
                    (from Tennyson, 'Tears, Idle Tears')

Metre is therefore, within this view, a rhythmic parallelism whereby the same pattern of stressed and unstressed syllables is repeated sequentially (e.g. an iambic pentameter is a sequence of 5 iambic feet).

But, of course, we would not get far in scansion unless we allowed for deviations from this pattern. The following routine licences are allowed according to the conventions of *metrical variation*:

Inversion (the transposition of the positions of a stressed and an unstressed syllable)

[2a] X / → / X *or* / X → X /

Promotion (the placing of an unstressed syllable in the position of a stressed syllable)

[2b] X → /

Demotion (the demoting of a stressed syllable by placing it in the position of an unstressed syllable)

[2c] / → X

Such licences can only make sense if we postulate two levels of analysis, which have been called the levels of (i) metre and (ii) rhythm:

 (i) *Metre* has been called the 'metrical set' – i.e. the pattern of mathematical regularity that underlies the *rhythm.*
 (ii) *Rhythm* has been called (rather unnecessarily) 'prose rhythm', to indicate that it is the realization of metre in actual language: that the values which are given to syllables on this level have little to do with poetry but are simply the result of applying the rules of pronunciation of the language.

Thus, in this twofold analysis, metre is mathematical and rhythm is linguistic. Metre is the ideal pattern (say iambic pentameter) which is assumed by poetic convention; rhythm is the actual sequence(s) of stressed and unstressed syllables which the English language insists on. The routine licences of inversion, demotion, promotion, etc., define permissible relations between them.

But because there are two levels of analysis, scansion now requires two kinds of notation:

[3] (Metre)   w   s   w   s   w s   w   s   w   s
            Smit with the love of sacred song; but chief
    (Rhythm) /   X   X   /   X /   X   /   X   /

[4a] (Metre) w   s w s w   s   w   s   w s
            Nightly I visit nor sometimes forget
    (Rhythm) /   X X / X   \   /   X   X   /

Because it contains more instances of metrical licence, [4a] is more *irregular* than [3] – but both can be regarded as metrical. The assignment of /, X, and \ to syllables is determined by the rules of English pronunciation. For example, a polysyllabic word must be correctly stressed in order to reflect English pronunciation: (*vísit*, not *visít; forgét* not *fórget*); a monosyllabic noun (*song*) is normally stressed, whereas a monosyllabic preposition (*with*) is normally not stressed. Other words, such as the pronoun *him* or the auxiliary verb *can*, are neutral with respect to stress: they are stressed or unstressed according to meaning and context (and are marked \ above).

Key: w = 'weak', s = 'strong', / = stressed syllable, X = unstressed syllable, \ = neutral syllable (can be stressed or unstressed according to context)

Even two levels, however, are not enough. To present a realistic metrical analysis we have to recognize a third level, that of performance. I will mention three reasons for this. The most obvious need for this performance level arises where, as often happens, English pronunciation allows us to stress the same sequence of words, without any obvious preference, in more than one way. In such a case, a reading of the poem aloud requires a choice between alternative renderings:

       $_8$X   /$_9$
       $_9$/   X$_8$ X   /   X X X /   X   /
[5]   Shall I compare thee to a summer's day?

                                    (from Shakespeare, *Sonnet 18*)

The rhythm of this line may be said to be ambiguous, and the ambiguity is resolved on the level of performance. Secondly, words can in rather exceptional circumstances be given contrastive stress, upsetting the expected relativities of stressed and unstressed syllables:

<pre>
  / X   /   X   / X /   X
[6] If hate killed men, Brother Lawrence
    /   /   /   X / X /
    God's blood, would not mine kill you!
</pre>

In the first line of this passage from Browning's 'Soliloquy of the Spanish Cloister', the significant syllables are marked X, where *hate* and *men*, although nouns, are put 'in the shade', i.e. are downgraded in their stress value, by the contrastive stress on *killed*. In the second line, the relevant syllables, marked /, are upgraded rather than downgraded, being pronouns under contrastive stress. Here, *kill*, in contrast to *killed* in the previous line, is naturally downgraded, because it has already been mentioned, and so is 'given' information.

In this Browning passage, the contrastive stresses fit both the meaning and the metre, so they are not likely to be avoided in a careful reading of the poem. In other cases, the choice is more open:

<pre>
   X   /   X / X   /   X   / X   /
[7] No worst, there is none. Pitched past pitch of grief
                        (from Hopkins, 'No Worst, There is None')
</pre>

Contrastive stress on *is* fits in regularly with the metre, but the alternative reading X / *is none* is also acceptable. So again, the reader must make a choice.

Thirdly, having accepted performance as a separate level, we need not restrict any actual performance of the poem to a simple negative procedure of eliminating other natural English pronunciations in favour of the pronunciation chosen. There is also a more fundamental choice as to how far the reader should follow the natural linguistic rhythm rather than the rhythm which accords metre. An 'artificial' performance which slavishly follows the metre in defiance of linguistic rhythm will generally be regarded as unacceptable:

<pre>
   X   / X / X /   X   /   X /
[4b] Nightly I visit nor sometimes forget
</pre>

(from Milton, *Paradise Lost*, III)

73

(In [4b], *nightlý* and *sometímes* are blatantly given an unEnglish stress pattern.)

On the other hand, few people actually say a poem as if they were talking to a friend in the street, or for that matter as if they were reading from a novel. We may assume that the poet means us to 'hear' (so to speak) the interplay between the metrical set and the linguistic rhythm, and the degree to which the underlying metrical pattern is highlighted is a stylistic choice of performance in itself.

I have now distinguished three levels:

(a) Performance (individual, 'instantial') (least abstract)
(b) Rhythm   (linguistic, 'natural')
(c) Metre   (abstract, 'mathematical') (most abstract)

It may seem excessive to require a fourth level, but such an additional level is required, I believe, if we are to take full account of the chronometric aspect of metrical form and effect: i.e. rhythm in a musical sense. The key concept here is that of *isochrony*: the division of a piece of verse, in terms of psychologically perceived time, into equivalent units (or *measures*) marked off by a rhythmic 'beat'. All three levels (a) – (c) have a close interdependence with musical rhythm, but none of them exactly defines its nature.

To see this let us ask the questions:

(A) Does isochrony occur on the level (a) of performance?
No: we do not normally read poems in strict time, with equal intervals between stresses. We *may* read them in such a way, but that again would be a matter of the stylistic choice of the performer.

(B) Does isochrony occur on the level (b) of rhythm?
No: although the attempt to represent rhythm by 'musical scansion' has been quite widespread,[1] it ties the ordinary rhythm of speech more closely to chronometric values than is justified by phonetic evidence, and moreover, it does not allow for other factors (such as inherent length of syllables, the number of syllables intervening between stresses, and the incidence of tone unit boundaries) which disrupt the tendency to equalize intervals between stresses. There is some such tendency in the rhythm of the language, however, as we see in the contextual variations of accentuation which phoneticians have pointed out in such pairs as:

	X /		* / X / X*
[8a]	a princess	BUT:	Princess I-da
	X X /		* / X X / X*
	The laughing cavalier	BUT	the cavalier poets

A principle of rhythmic compensation, illustrated by these examples, helps to preserve isochrony in ordinary speech, evening out the number of syllables per stress, and also evening out the length of individual syllables.

The downgrading of the second of two adjectival modifiers is a further example of some such principle of rhythmic compensation:

/   X / X   /   X   /
[8b] a dear *old* lady   a nice *new* coat

This principle ensures that two stressed syllables are not juxtaposed, as they would be in the non-occurring: *cavaliér póets* or *a nice néw cóat.*

(C) Does isochrony occur on the metrical level (c)?
Metres do, indeed, tend to even out the intervals between beats (because they regulate the number of syllables intervening between stresses), and so metre increases the tendency to isochrony. But for a number of reasons it is necessary to postulate an independent level for musical scansion.

Before giving these reasons, I shall find it necessary to elaborate the notion of musical scansion.

(a) There is a tendency for beats to occur at regular intervals of time (the principle of isochrony).
(b) It is thus possible for the syllables of a piece of verse to be grouped in *measures* (or 'bars') in a musical sense; each measure beginning with a stressed syllable (where the *beat* occurs).
(c) Additionally, beats form a hierarchy of strength, based on hierarchical grouping of measures in twos or threes. Thus if a stanza consists of 16 measures, it will naturally break down in two 8-measure units (couplets). These will be further subdivided into four 4-measure units (lines), which will in turn be subdivided in eight 2-measure units (hemistichs):

[9] |||| 1 2 | 3 4 || 5 6 | 7 8 ||| 9 10 | 11 12 || 13 14 | 15 16 ||||

The binary pattern here is most dominant both in popular poetry and in popular music (being represented canonically by the ballad metre and the limerick metre), but there can also be less obvious and more sophisticated manifestations of musical scansion, as in Hopkins's 'The Wreck of the Deutschland'.

6.3 Why we need a separate level of musical scansion

The concept of musical scansion is independent of metrical set for the four reasons which I will now mention. First, musical scansion can include (as in music) rests, particularly rests at the beginning of a measure, referred to as

75

'silent beats'. In the past, silent beats have been introduced into the analysis of natural linguistic rhythm.[2] I would like now to suggest that that analysis is misleading and that only on this extra musical level have we the right to postulate silent beats. This is because linguistic rhythm is not strictly chronometric. Silent beats are important, however, in musical scansion, because they help to explain the natural appeal of popular metres such as the ballad metre and the limerick metre.[3]

Here is a typical limerick metre in musical scansion (the notation is based on that of Attridge 1982):

[10] o |||| B o o | B o o || B o - | - - o ||| B o o | B o o || B o - | - -
      o |||| B o o | B - o || B o o | B - o ||| B o o | B o o || B o - | - -

---

Key: B = beat, o = offbeat, - = rest, - | - = silent beat

Note that the end of each metrical line in the limerick metre [10] is marked by a rest in musical metre. The limerick metre, which appears highly irregular in *metrical* terms, is highly regular when it is analysed in musical terms.

The following is ballad metre in musical scansion:

[11] (o) |||| B o | B o || B o | B (o) ||| B o | B o || B - | -
      (o) |||| B o | B o || B o | B (o) ||| B o | B o || B - | -

There is partial, but not complete correspondence between line endings and major measure boundaries. Again, the ballad metre appears to be inexplicably irregular (with its alternation of four-stress and three-stress lines), until we realize that the end of each couplet is marked by a silent measure.

Thus terms such as tetrameter and pentameter, referring to number of feet per line, do not necessarily correspond to number of measures per line.

Secondly, metrical patterns consist of feet in which the unstressed syllables either precede or follow the stressed syllables, resulting in contrasts, for example, between iambic and trochaic metres. Such contrasts are not relevant to the level of musical scansion, and this is fortunate, since many English poems (particularly those of song or madrigal type) do not lend themselves to analysis in terms of feet. For example:

          s (w   s) (w   s)
[12a] Go not, happy day,
          ||| B o | B   o || B - | - - |||

          s (w   s) (w   s)
       From the shining fields,
       ||| B   o | B   o || B -| - - |||

                           (from Tennyson, 'Go not happy day'), *Maud* XVIII

```
        w    (s    w) (s      w)  (s   w)
[12b] The  mountain sheep are  sweeter,
        o   ||| B    o |  B   o || B   o | -
```

```
        w  w (s   w)  (s      w)  (s  w)
      But the valley sheep are  fatter
        o  o ||| B  o |  B    o || B o  |
```
                         (from Peacock, 'The War Song of Dinas Vawr')

(NOTE: The bracketing '(s w)' shows the putative grouping of syllables into metrical feet.)

In a foot-based analysis, this would leave an ungrouped syllable either at the beginning or at the end of each line, according to whether the metre were taken to be iambic or trochaic:

   (s w) (s w) s   *or*   s (w s) (w s)

Traditional foot-based scansion provides no non-arbitrary way of choosing between such competing analyses, which have no bearing on the meaning or performance of the line. But the musical scansion avoids this difficulty, by the simple expedient of abolishing feet.

Thirdly, *metrical feet* are normally based only on two-syllable or three-syllable units, whereas *musical measures* may consist of one, two, three, or four syllables.

Take this example of Tennyson:

```
(13)    Break, break,   break,
     ||||| B -   |  B  - || B  - | -
        At the   foot of thy crags, O   Sea!
        o   o ||| B  o  o |  B   o || B  - | -
        But the  tender  grace of a day that is  dead
        o   o |||| B o |  B   oo || B  o  o |    B
        Will  never come back to  me.
        o   ||| B o    o |  B   o | B - |- |||||
```
                              (from Tennyson, 'Break, Break, Break')

In the opening line, the repeated words obviously have to be given a 'beat' to themselves – hence forming one-syllable measures – and so each line counts as four measures. It would be difficult to deal with a line of this kind in terms of traditional metrical scansion: the wide variation in line length between three syllables and eleven syllables would lack explanation. As representatives of a popular verse tradition, many of Kipling's *Barrack Room Ballads* lend themselves to analysis in terms of *one* or *four* syllables.

```
        X   X   /  X   X   X   /  X   X   X     /   X   X  X       /
```
[14] For the temple-bells are callin', an' it's   there that I would be
```
      o    o ‖ B o    B    o| B  o  B   o  ‖   B    o B   o  |B —
```
(from Kipling, 'Mandalay')

For the four-syllable units in [14], traditional metrics supply the name 'paeonic foot', but the important point, not captured in metrical foot analysis, is that each four-syllable unit (measure) naturally subdivides itself into half measures, like a 4/4 time bar in music. This 4/4 rhythm is represented by | B o B o |, the third syllable being noted as a subsidiary beat.

But another factor which makes this resemble musical rhythm is the indeterminacy of the boundary between 4/4 and 2/4 time: in another Kipling example, we would prefer (because of the intrinsic stress of the intermediate beat) to say that in this case there are two separate measures which are nevertheless related as the bearers of main and subsidiary beats (in [15] the bold oblique / represents a strong accent):

```
        /    X   / X   /   X    / X  / X      /
```
[15] You're a better man than   I am, Gunga   Din
```
    | B      o ‖| B o|  B    o  ‖ B o  |B   o   ‖| B - | -
```
(from Kipling, 'Gunga Din')

This combination of two 'sub-measures' into one 'major' measure has sometimes been referred to as *dipody*. But there are other cases where the choice between the analysis in [14] and that in [15] is unclear; here, for example, is another line from 'Mandalay':

Ship me somewheres east of Suez, where the best is like the worst

We do not have to choose between the metrical patterns of [14] and [15] if we are thinking on the musical level. The choices which have to be made at the level of metrical feet obscure an important point: namely, that there is a common tendency, both in music and poetry, for subdivision to be based on duality. Here again, the musical level of prosody asserts itself.

Fourthly, where the poem maintains a strong pattern at the metrical level, the number of unstressed syllables between beats is normally constant with the line. At the level of musical scansion, this is not necessarily the case. Another Kipling ballad shows the variation of syllables per beat which could equally well be illustrated by many nursery rhymes or popular songs:

[16] There's a whisper down the field where the year has shot her yield,
```
      o o ‖ B o B o | B B o ‖ B o B o |B
```
and the ricks stand grey to the sun
```
      o o ‖ B   B   | B B o ‖ B - |  -
```

(from Kipling, 'The Long Trail')

This approaches classical Latin quantitative metre, in so far as syllables may be assigned the values long (—) or short (-) according to a notional division of each measure into half-measures. In this quantitative mode [16] could be transcribed as:

-- | - - - - | — - - | - - - - | —
   - - | — — | — - - | —

6.4 Sprung rhythm

In the preceding multilevelled account of metre, I have isolated a level of 'musical scansion' which at least in some kinds of poetry has an existence independent of other levels, in particular of the metrical level of analysis. Hence I have arrived at four potential levels for the analysis of metrical form in its broadest sense. The following is an augmentation of the three levels discussed in section 6.2:

(a) Performance   (individual, 'instantial')
(b) Rhythm   (linguistic, 'natural')
(c) Metre   (abstract, 'mathematical')
(d) Musical scansion (based on isochrony and a hierarchy of recurrent 'beats' and measures)

I hasten to add that this is not just a mechanical, intellectual exercise. I believe that these levels and their interaction can explain the subtlety and expressiveness of prosodic effects in poetry.

The thesis now to be argued is briefly as follows:

(a) The four levels are closely interrelated, and may all be said to have a role in the apperception of metrical form. But different fashions or trends in the use of metre show themselves in the extent to which one level is given more prominence than another. In some poems (Spenser's, for example) the metrical level is the primary level of organization; in others (e.g. Donne's) the realistic use of linguistic rhythm is more important; in yet others (e.g. perhaps Kipling's) the musical level is most salient.
(b) A more extreme experimental change in metrical taste may involve the disappearance of one level entirely. In free verse, there is no metrical level, and perhaps no musical level either.
(c) Hopkins's adoption of sprung rhythm is one such example of a radical change. It involved the abandonment of the metrical level (associated with standard metrics: the 'running rhythm' of the post-Spenserian tradition), and the adoption of musical scansion as a primary level of organization.

(d) In this, Hopkins's personal experiments were more radical and con-sciously systematic than those of his contemporaries; but the tendency to let musical scansion take the place of metrical scansion is found in many poets productive in the middle and later decades of the nine-teenth century, e.g. Browning, Clough, Swinburne, Hardy, Bridges.

(e) In a sense, such poets were not so much innovating, as drawing upon a tradition of popular metrics associated with ballads and songs. In fact, wherever poetry retains a close connection with music and popular verse, musical scansion tends to assert itself.

(f) The fact that Hopkins's was not an isolated metrical experiment sug-gested to me that his term 'sprung rhythm' might be fittingly extended to other poetry making use of musical scansion. The era of 'sprung rhythm', then, was an interestingly experimental period in the history of English metrics, preceding the more root-and-branch metrical innovations of Pound, Eliot and their contemporaries. The apparently sudden break with tradition by these twentieth-century poetic experi-menters had been (contrary to what is often supposed) heralded by a widespread innovative movement of the later nineteenth century.[4]

The above account (a) – (f) may seem to be at odds with Hopkins's own description of his metrical experiments. But I shall suggest that Hopkins did not have a full analytic understanding of his own practice (although what he says about metre in general shows great insight).[5] Hopkins's account of sprung rhythm relates it on the one hand to ordinary speech and on the other hand to music. He says of sprung rhythm:

[17] it is the rhythm of common speech and of written prose . . .
    it is the rhythm of all but the most monotonously regular music . . .
                        Hopkins, *Author's Preface*

These two statements are inconsistent. And, moreover, there are three aspects of Hopkins's description and practice which do not tally with the equation of sprung rhythm with ordinary speech rhythm.

First, Hopkins attaches importance to what he calls 'outrides' – that is, extrametrical (normally unstressed) syllables, which may be added as a 'licence', and are not part of the regular foot pattern. 'Outrides', however, are unnecessary within the framework of sprung rhythm since the number of syllables between stresses need not be limited. My suspicion is that Hopkins really felt outrides to be significant irregularities because they broke up the regularity of the musical beat.[6] When one adds too many syl-lables between beats, it becomes difficult to maintain a constant tempo. (In this respect, a reciter of a Hopkins poem may become like an amateur pianist, who has to slow down the tempo from time to time to cope with a rush of notes.) Thus 'outrides' are extrametrical only in terms of musical scansion.

Secondly, Hopkins's metrical practice in his poetry is not consistent with the equation of sprung rhythm with accentual metre:

[18] Márgarét , áre you gríeving
    ‖ B o | B - ‖ B   o | B   o
     Over   Goldengrove   unleaving?
    ‖ B   o | B   o ‖ B o | B o
     Léaves líke the things of man, you
    ‖ B - | B   o ‖ B   o | B   o
     With your fresh thoughts care for, can you?
    ‖ B   o | B   o   ‖ B o | B o
                                          (from 'Spring and Fall')

Hopkins's own accent on *–rét* seems to indicate his wish for this syllable to count as one of the beats of a four-beat (or four-accent) line. But *–rét* would not be stressed in ordinary speech (mɑːg(ə)rət is the RP pronunciation, not mɑːgərét), so the rhythm departs from that of ordinary speech. A way to make sense of this, despite Hopkins's own assertion that sprung rhythm is the rhythm of speech, is to suppose that some musical principle of isochrony here overrides the normal linguistic rhythm. The two levels of description are not incompatible: the unstressed syllable, preceding a pause marked by the comma, would naturally lengthen in performance, and could well coincide with the second beat of a 4-beat musical line just as the norm-ally unstressed *are* could fit the third position:

    / X X   /   X   / X
    Margaret, are you grieving
    ‖‖ B o | B - ‖ B   o | B   o ‖‖

That is, where the normal pronunciation and the musical rhythm are in conflict, it is the musical rhythm that defines the metre.

Thirdly, Hopkins's own description of the style of recitation appropriate to his poetry stresses its artificiality and music-like nature. On 'Spelt from Sibyl's Leaves' he says (Gardner 1953: 238–9):

[19] Of this long sonnet above all remember what applies to all my verse, that it is as living art should be, made for performance and that its performance is not reading with the eye but loud, leisurely, poetical (not rhetorical) recitation, with long rests, long dwells on the rhyme and other marked syllables, and so on. This sonnet should be almost sung: it is most carefully timed in *tempo rubato*.

This seems a fitting prescription for how a poem should be recited or read if it is assumed that the music equivalences are more important than the stressing of ordinary speech. (At the same time, Hopkins's sprung rhythm was able to retain the prosodic expressiveness of ordinary speech, being free from the straitjacket of conventional metre.) When we examine the poem itself, we find indeed that the eight beats per line are not always directly derivable from the ordinary spoken stress values. In particular, some normally stressed syllables must be subordinated to others if the eight-beat line pattern is to be sustained. The occasional lack of fit between the musical beat and the linguistic stress is the best evidence that Hopkins's poetry requires a level of musical scansion as well as a level of linguistic rhythm. Whereas the traditional post-Spenserian metrics requires the three levels of (A) performance (B) rhythm (C) metre, Hopkins's sprung rhythm also requires three levels, but they are slightly different: (A) performance (B) rhythm (D) musical scansion.

This is illustrated in [20] by the first eight lines of one of Hopkins's best-known poems in sprung rhythm, 'Felix Randal':

[20] Félix Rándal the   fárrier, O is he déad then? My dúty all énded
   ‖ B o | B o   o | B o o   o o o ‖ B   o   o | B o o | B o
   Who have watched his mould of man, big-boned and hardy-handsome
      o o ‖ B   o | B   o | B   o ‖   B   o | B o | B   o
   Pining, pining, till time when reason   rambled in it and some
   ‖ B o | B o   o | B   o ‖ B   o | B   o o o | B   o
   Fatal four disorders, fleshed there, all contended?
   ‖ B o | B   o| B o ‖   B   o | B o | B o
   Sickness broke him. Impatient, he cursed at first, but mended
   ‖ B   o | B   o   o | B o o ‖   B   o | B   o | B o
   Being anointed and all; though a heavenlier heart began some
   ‖ B o o | B o o | B   o   o ‖ B o o o | B   o | B o
   Mónths éarlier, since I had our swéet repríeve and ránsom
   ‖ B | B o o   o | B o   o ‖   B   o | B   o | B o
   Téndered to him.   Áh well, God rést him áll road éver he offénded!
   ‖ B   o   o o | B   o   o | B   o ‖ B   o | B o o o | B o

Here, as previously, I use the main features of Attridge's method of scansion. The accents over some vowels are from Hopkins's original; likewise the ties underneath certain words and syllables, signifying outrides. As each line has six beats, I have marked the fourth beat of each line as an extra strong one, corresponding to the beginning of the second half-line.

The occasional lack of fit is matched in the kinds of metrical variation we allow for standard metrics:

(a) *Demotion*: e.g. in line 2, the demotion *big* in *big-bonéd*, in line 8 demotion of *God* in *God rest him*.

(b) *Promotion*: e.g. promotion of *and* in line 3 *(and some)* necessary to achieve the rhyme with *handsome* in line 2 (cf. the promotion of *–et* in *Margarét*).

6.5 Conclusion

I have argued that, in a full account of English metre, four levels of metrical form are needed, although not all these levels will be prominent, or even active at all, in particular metrical styles. The four levels are (a) *performance*, (b) *rhythm*, (c) *metre* and (d) *musical scansion*. Whereas in mainstream accentual-syllabic metrics, attention needs to be given to (a), (b) and (c), metre having a central defining role, in Hopkins's sprung rhythm, attention is given to (a), (b) and (d), as the role of *metre* is backgrounded or suppressed.

My conclusion is that in his metrical experiments, Hopkins was not so much a precursor of the modern age, as a child of his own age. It was an age in which the parallels between music and poetic metre were explored with a new interest and adventurousness by many poets and especially by Hopkins, who went further than his contemporaries in the boldness of his thinking and the brilliant innovation of his practice. In the Appendix that follows, I give some further illustrations of musical scansion, showing how major poets of the later Victorian era followed a trend similar to that of Hopkins, particularly in varying the number of syllables per measure, following the principle of binarity, and making use of musically defined pauses.

Appendix: Further illustrations of musical scansion

showing examples of Victorian poetry with tendencies towards sprung rhythm

[1]   Oh, to be in England
    ‖ B   o | B   o ‖ B   o | -
    Now that April's there,
    ‖ B   o | B   o ‖ B - | -
    And whoever wakes in England
    | B   o ‖ B o | B   o ‖ B o
    Sees, some morning, unaware
    | B   o   ‖ B   o | B o ‖ B
    That the lowest boughs and the brushwood sheaf
      o o ‖ B o | B   o   o ‖ B   o | B
    Round the elm-tree bole are in tiny leaf,
      o   o ‖ B   o | B   o o ‖ B o | B
    While the chaffinch sings on the orchard bough
      o   o ‖ B   o | B   o o ‖ B   o | B
    In England – now!
    o ‖ B o | B ‖ - | -
                    (from Robert Browning, 'Home Thoughts from Abroad')

[2] These things, Ulysses,
‖ B   o | B o o
The wise bards also
 o ‖B   o | B o
Behold and sing
 o‖ B   o | B
But oh what labour!
  o ‖ B   o | B o
They too can see
 o ‖ B   o | B
Tiresias; – but the Gods
 o ‖Bo o ^ o   o | B
Who give them vision
  o ‖ B   o | B o
Added this law:
‖ B   o o | B

(from Arnold, 'The Strayed Reveller')
(^ signals an extra-musical pause)

[3]   Passing away, saith the World, passing away:
‖ B   o o |B   o o ‖ B | B o o ‖ B | - -
Chances, beauty, and youth, sapped day by day
‖ B   o | B   o o   ‖ B   o | B   o ‖ B| - -
Thy life never continueth in one stay
  o ‖ B | B o o ‖ B o o | B   o ‖ B | - -
Is the eye waxen dim, is the dark hair changing to grey
  o o ‖ B   o o | B   o o ‖ B   o | B   o o ‖ B| - -
That hath won neither laurel nor bay?
   o   o ‖ B   o o | B o o ‖ B

(from Christina Rossetti, 'Passing Away')

[4]   In a coign of the cliff between lowland and highland,
  o o ‖ B   o o | B   o o ‖ B o   o| B o
At the sea-down's edge between windward and lee,
  o o ‖ B   o | B   o o ‖ B   o   o| B
Walled round with rocks as an inland island,
‖   B   o   o | B   o o‖ B o | B o
The ghost of a garden fronts the sea.
  o ‖ B   o o| B o‖ B   o | B
A girdle of brushwood and thorn encloses
 o‖ B o o| B   o   o ‖ B o| B o
The steep square slope of the blossomless bed
  o ‖ B   o | B o o ‖ B o   o | B

Where the weeds that grow green from the graves of its roses
    o   o ‖ B   o   o |B   o   o ‖ B   o o |B o
Now lie dead.
‖ B   o |B ‖ - - | - -

(from Swinburne, 'A Forsaken Garden')

Notes

1. There is a long history of musical (or 'temporal') scansion of English verse. See particularly Lanier (1880) and Pope (1942) (on the metre of Old English poetry). Leech (1969: 103–30) also employs a musical notation for speech rhythm, and some of the ideas of this chapter are taken from that source. However, it is argued here that it is a mistake to conflate the levels of rhythm and musical/temporal pattern, a common error from which neither Hopkins (in his theorizing about sprung rhythm) nor Leech (1969) are free. For more recent examinations of temporal and musical concepts of rhythm, see Attridge (1982: 18–27, 80–108) and Cureton (1992: 12–13, 82–3, 87–8, 323–78).

2. Abercrombie's (1973 [1964]) use of silent beats in accounting for speech and verse rhythm was later adopted and extended by Halliday (1967, 1970a) in his modelling of English stress and intonation.

3. The argument (cf. Leech 1969: 113–14) is that these popular metres prove ill-accommodated to classical foot-based scansion. Yet they make good sense in terms of a regular underlying musical beat. Examples of each metre are:

Limerick:	*Ballad Metre:*
There was a young lady of Riga	They hadna sail'd a league, a league
Who rode with a smile on a tiger,	A league but barely three,
They returned from the ride	When the lift grew dark, and the wind
With the lady inside,	grew loud,
And the smile on the face of the tiger.	And gurly grew the sea.

   Anyone who has regularly sung or accompanied hymn tunes in 'common metre' (CM) will be familiar with the need to allow for a silent beat (representing a musical bar or half-bar) between the end of the second line and the beginning of the third line of each verse. CM is the hymnologist's term for ballad metre, as illustrated by William Cowper's well-known hymn 'God Moves in a Mysterious Way'.

4. In America, Walt Whitman's free verse, of course, antedated this development. It is interesting that Hopkins disassociated his own innovations from those of Whitman (see Martin 1991: 350–1), although both poets moved towards the abandonment of the mainstream metrical tradition through the freer use of speech rhythms.

5. 'Sprung Rhythm . . . is measured by feet of from one to four syllables, regularly, and for particular effects any number of weak or slack syllables may be used . . . In Sprung Rhythm, . . . the feet are assumed to be equally long or strong, and their seeming equality is made up by pause or stressing' (Hopkins, Author's Preface.) For further discussion, see Gardner (1949: 97–178).

6. 'An outriding foot is, by a sort of contradiction, a recognized extra-metrical effect; it is and is not part of the metre; not part of it, not being counted, but part of it by producing a calculated effect . . . ,' (Hopkins, Letter to Robert Bridges, 21 August 1877).

CHAPTER 7

Pragmatics, discourse analysis, stylistics and 'The Celebrated Letter'

The title of this chapter reads like one of those quiz questions 'What is there in common between A, B, C and D?' where, of course, the items compared must be as apparently dissimilar as possible. But the first three expressions in this title stand for areas of linguistic study which have a great deal in common – indeed, a reasonable complaint might be that they have far too *much* in common: such that even pragmaticians, discourse analysts and stylisticians (assuming such people exist) are unsure of their differences. The fourth part of this quadripartite titular conjunction is exemplificatory rather than explicatory. The aim of this chapter will be to expound the relation between three closely related fields of pragmatics, discourse analysis and stylistics by illustrative reference to Johnson's 'Celebrated Letter' to Lord Chesterfield (reproduced on pp. 97–8).

7.1 The close affinity between pragmatics, discourse analysis and stylistics: a goal-oriented framework

All three fields just mentioned have this in common: they investigate the nature and formal structure of language in use. There is a justifiable ex-pectation, then, that their domains will overlap, and that studies within these domains will contribute to one another. My own argument is that what binds these fields together is that they are all concerned with language as a purposeful phenomenon. The study of grammar – broadly conceived of as the system of rules and categories defining what is *possible* in a language – is thereby distinguished from these three areas dealing with how these rules and categories are *implemented* for communicative purposes.

In developing a goal-oriented approach to discourse (both literary and non-literary) I will be following my own particular bent, and I will have a considerable amount of explaining to do before we come to looking at Johnson's epistolary tour de force. My hope is that this ground-clearing will be an important clarificatory exercise in itself, not merely a long prelude to a necessarily somewhat cursory textual analysis.

First, in distinguishing pragmatics and discourse analysis it is valuable to start with Edmondson's 'componential' analysis:[1]

Field of study			Delimiting linguistic unit
Grammar	[–suprasentential]	[–use]	sentence
Text linguistics	[+suprasentential]	[–use]	text
Pragmatics	[–suprasentential]	[+use]	utterance
Discourse analysis	[+suprasentential]	[+use]	discourse

These distinctions are de facto, rather than justified by some overarching theory of how to study language. It just happens that people have engaged in studies which they have called 'text linguistics' and 'discourse analysis'; that those who claim to be studying grammar tend to limit their enquiries to what happens within sentences; that those who claim to be studying pragmatics tend to address their attention to a single utterance rather than, for example, a dialogue. But it is a matter for debate as to whether these four titles refer to well-defined and useful disciplines. (I would be sympathetic to some who argued, for example, that text linguistics is an ill-conceived branch of linguistics, on the ground that if one takes account of 'linguistics beyond the sentence', the only legitimate approach is [+use] rather than [–use].)[2] This might bring us to a more fundamentally contentious question: is there a legitimate distinction between studying language as an abstract system of possibilities ([–use]) and studying it as *parole*, in terms of particular realizations of those possibilities ([+use])? I believe that there is; but to avoid needless controversy, I will confine discussion strictly to the two terms in Edmondson's table which concern us: the distinction between pragmatics and discourse analysis.[3] Also, to prevent misapprehension, I will take it for granted that the association of *text* in the above sense with written language and of *discourse analysis* with spoken language is not essential, but only incidental: it happens to be easier to study language *as a system* by looking at specimens in the written medium;[4] but one can also study language *in use*, discourse, in the written medium – which is what I will shortly attempt to do with Johnson's letter.

Pragmatics may be understood as 'the study of meaning in speech situations', and the unit of pragmatics has been tacitly assumed (e.g. in the study of speech acts) to be the individual utterance: that is, when studying pragmatics, one is not normally concerned with more than one contribution to a conversation or discourse. The philosophical keystone of pragmatics is the Gricean understanding of meaning in terms of reflexive intention. Thus when a given speaker S says x, and means y by it, this may be interpreted roughly as 'S intended the utterance of x to produce some effect in an audience by means of the recognition of this intention.'[5] The intention to produce a given communicative effect is what, in a pragmatic framework, may be considered the meaning of x, and the hearer's recognition of the nature of this intention constitutes his interpretation of the utterance.

The philosopher's notion of communicative intention can be placed alongside the concept of goal-directed action, as employed in problem-solving studies in artificial intelligence.[6] In pragmatics, indeed, I find it better to talk of goals rather than purposes or intentions, because there is less likelihood of 'goals' being misinterpreted as implying conscious mental decisions. Consider the following as a perfectly commonplace example of *unconscious* goal-directed activity:

> Harry takes a packet of cigarettes out of his pocket, opens it, offers it to a friend, extracts a cigarette, puts the cigarette to his lips, takes a cigarette lighter out of his other pocket, lights the lighter, and uses the lighter to light the cigarette.

This is a complex and coordinated sequence of goal-directed actions, which a habitual smoker may nevertheless perform without any conscious or explicit planning. It is in such a broad understanding of human behaviour as goal-directed that we may claim that utterances are goal-directed, and that discourse itself consists of goal-directed activity.

Many discussions of 'intention' are hopelessly simplified: they tend to assume that the human mental apparatus is capable of containing only one intention at a time. But goal-directed activity is typically multiple in a sequential sense and in a simultaneous sense. Here, for example, is a so-called means-ends diagram representing the complex of actions described above:

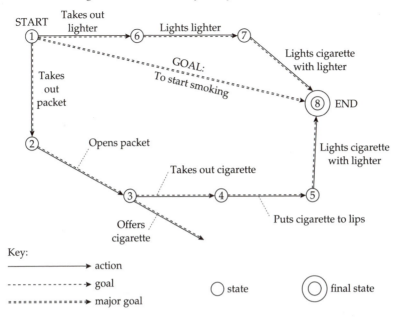

Figure 7.1 Goal diagram: lighting a cigarette

Even this is much simplified. But it illustrates the fact that goals combine *sequentially* (e.g. the initial goal of getting the cigarette lighter out of one's pocket is a means to an ulterior goal – that of gratifying an addictive need); and that goals combine *simultaneously* (e.g. Harry has the simultaneous goals of (a) smoking, and (b) staying on friendly terms with his interlocutor (by offering him a cigarette). The concept of goal-directed activity can now be further enriched by a distinction between

(a) *dynamic* goals: goals with the function of changing the environment (including the psychological state or attitude of the addressee);
(b) *regulative* goals: goals with the function of preventing the environment from changing (cf. Searle 1969: 33–42; Leech 1983: 36–40).

Dynamic goals are positive; regulative goals are negative. For example, Harry's offering a cigarette to his companion does not help him to achieve his ulterior dynamic goal (that of enjoying a smoke), but is a gesture of politeness which helps to ensure that when he smokes his own cigarette he does not therein offend another person. The appropriateness of the gesture depends, of course, on whether Harry believes the other person to be a smoker (of his kind of cigarettes). If his companion is a non-smoker, Harry might well make a different kind of gesture: a verbal gesture like *Do you mind if I smoke?*

All this begins to show an integrated role for language in the larger pattern of human goal-directed activity. In applying means-ends analysis to language, I am borrowing from practitioners of AI rather than of pragmatics;[7] but this framework can be reconciled to the thinking of linguistic philosophers such as Grice and Searle on the nature of communicative meaning.

First, let us consider Searle's description of communicative meaning in terms of speech acts. Searle's illocutionary acts[8] (e.g. acts of declaring, predicting, requesting, promising, thanking) may be seen as linguistic exemplars of what I have just called dynamic goals. Whereas Searle defined these meaningful acts in terms of conventional rules and conditions,[9] I see no problem in reinterpreting a promise, say, as a communicative action defined in terms of the speaker's goal of giving the hearer an assurance that the speaker will see to it that such-and-such will be the case; or of reinterpreting a request as a communicative act the purpose of which is to get the hearer to do a desired action. By calling these 'communicative acts', I mean that such acts are intended to achieve their goals by means of a linguistic or other code shared by speaker and hearer. If Harry, having mislaid his lighter, says *Could you give me a light?*, this may be interpreted as having the communicative (illocutionary) force of a request for an action which will enable him to smoke his cigarette. If he had just grabbed a box of matches from his companion, the intention and the result would have been the same, but this would not be a communicative act. A request is performed *by means of* the uttering of certain linguistic signals (e.g. words) with certain meanings; in its turn, a request is *a means to* a further action, namely, getting the hearer to provide a light. This way of looking at things leads to a further reinterpretation, in a goal-oriented perspective, of the three famous types of speech acts distinguished by Austin as locutionary, illocutionary, and perlocutionary acts.[10] (Compare this figure with that in Chapter 8, p. 110.)

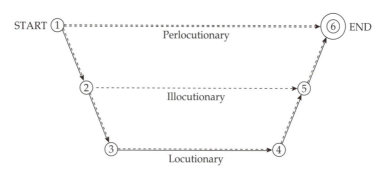

Figure 7.2 Locutionary, illocutionary and perlocutionary goals

As this diagram suggests, a locutionary act (the uttering of certain words, etc. with certain conventional meanings) is the means to a further goal of performing an illocutionary act, that is, conveying to the hearer a certain illocutionary force (e.g. the force of a promise, request, or declaration); and the illocutionary act is, in turn, the means to performing a perlocutionary act (such as persuading the hearer to do something). In the case we have just considered, uttering the words *Could you give me a light?* amounts to the locutionary act of asking whether, hypothetically, the hearer would have the ability to give the speaker a light; in doing this, Harry performs the further illocutionary act of requesting a light; and in doing this, he may, if he is lucky, manage to perform the perlocutionary act of prevailing on the hearer to provide a light. It is simpler and less problematic, however, to talk of a hierarchy of three different types of *goal*, rather than to talk of three different kinds of *action*.

If the Austin–Searle account of speech acts provides a prototype for dynamic communicative goals, the Gricean account of conversational implicature provides the paradigm for regulative goals.[11] Grice's Cooperative Principle (with its attendant Maxims) may be interpreted, in the present goal-directed framework, as follows. In order to maintain effective communication, users of language may be supposed to do their best to preserve certain regulative goals: they will try to be appropriately informative (Maxim of Quantity), truthful (Maxim of Quality), relevant (Maxim of Relation) and clear, orderly, and so on (Maxim of Manner). If a speaker manifestly appears not to observe these precepts of good communicative behaviour, then according to Grice, a reason may be that he intends the hearer to infer from his utterance some meaning additional to the conventional sense of the words and other signals he has uttered. But why should a speaker resort to such oblique methods of communication? Why, for example, instead of saying *Could you give me a light?*, does he not say more tersely and directly *Give me a light*? The answer lies in other regulative goals which he has to keep in view; for example, a request is inherently 'impolite' in requiring the hearer to do something not in the hearer's interests. It may also conflict with the regulative goals subsumed under Grice's Cooperative Principle: the need for politeness may lead one to abandon truthfulness, and to tell 'white lies'.

7.2 Politeness and irony in a multi-goaled view of communication

To Grice's Cooperative Principle we therefore add a second principle, the Politeness Principle, primarily expressed in the negative imperative 'Do not offend others', but also including the positive imperative 'Be nice to others'.

Politeness in communication requires us to adopt strategies of (a) maximizing 'polite beliefs' and (b) minimizing 'impolite beliefs'. *Polite beliefs* is the term conveniently used for beliefs (expressed or implicated) favourable to the other person or unfavourable to the speaker; and impolite beliefs are those which are unfavourable to the other person, or favourable to the speaker. There is therefore a basic asymmetry in polite conversation: whatever is a polite belief for the speaker is an impolite belief for the hearer. This can be illustrated with reference to the following Maxims of Politeness, which tend to go in pairs, and which are comparable to the Maxims of the Cooperative Principle:[12]

 (i) The TACT Maxim:
    (a) minimize the cost to *others*;
    (b) maximize the benefit to *others*;
 (ii) The GENEROSITY Maxim:
    (a) minimize the benefit to *self*;
    (b) maximize the cost to *self*;
(iii) The APPROBATION (or Flattery) Maxim:
    (a) minimize dispraise of *others*;
    (b) maximize praise of *others*;
(iv) The MODESTY Maxim:
    (a) minimize praise of *self*;
    (b) maximize dispraise of *self*;
 (v) The AGREEMENT Maxim:
    (a) minimize disagreement between *self* and *others*;
    (b) maximize agreement between *self* and *others*;
(vi) The SYMPATHY Maxim:
    (a) minimize antipathy between *self* and *others*;
    (b) maximize sympathy between *self* and *others*.

Of the two clauses of each maxim, the negative clause (a) is always more important than the positive clause (b). Each of the clauses above is an abbreviated form of one which should read something like: 'Minimize/maximize the expression of beliefs which involve . . .' The following *ceteris paribus* condition should be added to all clauses: '. . . in so far as this does not conflict with other communicative goals', for it is not suggested, by these maxims, that everyone behaves as a paragon of politeness. It is merely suggested that politeness is one of the major regulative goals of human communicative behaviour.

    Grice's justification of the Cooperative Principle was that it was a crucial part of the explanation of utterance meaning: namely, the explanation of conversational implicatures (whereby the speaker's communicative intentions may be inferred from what he says). On what grounds can the Politeness Principle be justified?

(1) The Politeness Principle helps to explain asymmetries in the acceptability of utterances; e.g. *What a marvellous dinner you cooked!* (which observes the Approbation Maxim) is obviously much more acceptable, in general, than *What a marvellous dinner I cooked!* (which contravenes the Modesty Maxim).

(2) It also helps to explain asymmetries in the interpretation of utterances; e.g. *Good luck!* is interpreted to mean 'I wish you good luck,' while *Bad luck!* is interpreted to mean 'I regret your bad luck'. (The opposite interpretations 'I regret your good luck' and 'I wish you bad luck' conflict with the Tact Maxim.)

(3) Without it, the Cooperative Principle is not fully explanatory. We need the Cooperative Principle to account for the indirect relation between what people say and what they mean. But it cannot in itself explain *why* people are so often indirect in the way they talk. For example, *You could type this letter for me* is more oblique, as a directive speech act, than *Type this letter*, and thereby appears to contravene the Maxims of Relation and Manner. It is only if we add that the speaker is trying to avoid breaking the Tact Maxim that this form of linguistic behaviour is fully comprehensible in a goal-oriented framework.

This last point amounts to saying that the Cooperative Principle must be supplemented by other principles, in particular the Politeness Principle, if it is to be satisfactorily applied to what have been called indirect illocutions or indirect speech acts.

To fit them into a goal-directed view of communication, it has been necessary to adapt the ideas of Austin, Searle and Grice somewhat freely. In particular, I would like to point out that from the present point of view, Searle's speech act theory is too regimented. He claims that using language is a matter of 'performing speech acts according to constitutive rules'; whereas for me, the principles and maxims of communicative behaviour are (in Searle's terms) regulative rather than constitutive rules. That is, these maxims or principles are capable of being violated without abnegation of the kind of activity in which the speaker is engaged; they can be observed or contravened to varying degrees; one principle or maxim may conflict with another; and one may be adhered to at the expense of another. All these factors are typical of goal-directed behaviour. For Searle, on the other hand, performing a promise or a request, for example, is a matter of observing categorical rules. For him, it is possible to set up a classification of speech acts in which differences between different illocutionary acts can be clearly determined.[13] For him, describing the communicative meaning of an utterance is primarily a matter of deciding into which illocutionary pigeonhole it fits.[14] Searle cannot, therefore, easily cope with utterances with multiple goals, such as the following:

Considering that I am hostage, I should say that I have been treated fairly.

Language in Literature

This utterance was reported as being said to a reporter by an American hostage in Iran. Because of its complex goal structure, it is arguably more typical of human communication than a performative utterance (such as *I promise to pay you £5*) of the kind which has been treated as canonical by speech act philosophers. We could say that this utterance has meaning in terms of a number of competing goals:

(i) the goal of satisfying a demand by the news media for news of some kind (in accordance with the Maxim of Quantity);
(ii) the need to reassure relatives and the American public that things were not so bad as they could be;
(iii) the desire to avoid offending one's captors, and thereby (perhaps) delaying the hostages' release.

These goals are combined in a way which makes the force of the whole utterance indeterminate and subject to negotiation. Searle's model, which implies that there is a set of labels such that one or another of those labels can be appropriately attached to each utterance, is notably unsubtle and inadequate here.

In the present model, the meaning of utterances is not a matter of 'performing speech acts according to constitutive rules', but rather a matter of problem-solving. From the speaker's point of view, problem-solving is appropriately represented by means-ends analysis; the problem to be solved is how best to achieve one's goal(s) by communicating one's meaning to the hearer. From the hearer's viewpoint, problem-solving is a different kind of activity – interpretative rather than communicative; the problem to be solved is: given the speaker said *x*, what did the speaker intend to convey by *x*?

Having outlined a particular view of pragmatics, I have now to argue the applicability of this general approach – namely, a goal-directed approach – not only to pragmatics, but also to discourse analysis and to stylistics. Following Edmondson's distinction, discourse analysis can be regarded simply as a projection of pragmatics into a suprasentential time dimension; so it is difficult, if one has accepted the goal-oriented view of pragmatics, not to accept a similar view of discourse analysis. An interactive element is already implicit in the Cooperative Principle: e.g. the Maxim of Relation ('Make your conversational contribution relevant') invites a goal-directed interpretation as 'Make your conversational contribution such as contributes to the conversational goals either of yourself or of your interlocutor.' As with other Maxims, the Maxim of Relation, so understood, is a matter of degree, of how directly an utterance can be related to the perceived goal(s) of discourse; and these, of course, are judged in the light of preceding discourse. Even in the following exchanges there is an element of indirectness:

(1) A: Do you have any matches?
     B: Yes; *here you are.* (Gives matches)
(2) A: Did you eat all those muffins?
     B: Yes – *I was so hungry.*

In (1) B replies not merely to A's overt question (for which *Yes* would be an adequate answer), but to the assumed goal of A's remark – to obtain matches. Similarly, in (2), B replies not merely to A's question, but to the accusation it obliquely implies. Many aspects of conversation can be seen, in this way, as bridging the gap between overt meanings by responding to the import of another person's remark in a goal-oriented sense. A special polite conventionalization of this is an 'anticipatory illocution', e.g. an indirect request, such as *Could you stand over there a moment?*, where the question about possibility is relevant only as a means to an unspoken end, an ulterior goal – that of getting the hearer to perform the action indicated.

Any goal-oriented model of discourse analysis will have to handle the following distinctions which are fairly routine aspects of discourse:

(a) dynamic and regulative goals (see p. 89);
(b) coexisting goals (which may be in competition or in conflict);
(c) subordinate goals and superordinate goals (one serving as a means to another);
(d) long-term goals (persisting through a whole discourse or section of discourse) and short-term goals (which may, for example, be confined to a single sentence or utterance);
(e) major goals and minor goals (i.e. some goals are more important than others).

An example of the last factor – the relative importance of goals – is the coexistence in private letters of a phatic goal (that of keeping in touch) and an informative goal (that of telling one's correspondent the news about one's current life). It is a common experience that the latter goal is less important than the former.

Earlier models of discourse analysis tended to suffer, like speech act theory, from an over-regimented view of human communicative behaviour. J.R. Searle's discrete classifications of speech acts may be compared, in this respect, with Sinclair and Coulthard's (1975) pioneering analysis of discourse into units on hierarchic and taxonomic principles.[15] Similar assumptions about the analysis of texts were made by text grammarians (such as van Dijk 1972)[16] in early attempts to model text grammar on sentence grammar. Perhaps understandably, these models were based on the assumption that techniques of grammatical analysis could be adapted to apply to larger-than-sentence units. While some types of discourse (e.g. the classroom discourse analysed by Sinclair and Coulthard) are relatively regimented and conventionalized, and therefore lend themselves to this kind of treatment, the less tightly organized features of discourse (e.g. indeterminacy, competing goals, negotiated meaning) also have to be accounted for, and this can only be done within a more freely constructed, goal-directed model of discourse.

Irony is a good example of a discourse phenomenon which requires analysis in terms of a multiple-goal model. We can consider Grice's Maxims of Cooperation and the Maxims of Politeness (listed on p. 92) as representing independent goals in communication. But they often conflict with one another: e.g. we often cannot be tactful while being informative and truthful. We can solve this problem by sacrificing one principle to the other: we can be offensively frank, or we can be evasively or dishonestly polite. But irony offers a cleverer way out of this dilemma – that of conveying an offensive meaning (the covert meaning of the irony) while maintaining a pleasant façade of overt meaning. We thus have our cake and eat it.

Irony is the supreme device of prose literature, and irony is also pervasive in Johnson's letter, to which we shortly turn. But before doing so, we must consider the relation between discourse analysis and literary stylistics. I will argue that although these 'sub-disciplines' have grown up in different intellectual surroundings, the latter is nothing but a special case of the former. The goal-oriented framework applicable to pragmatics and to discourse analysis is also applicable to stylistics, which may be regarded simply as the variety of discourse analysis dealing with literary discourse. Just as pragmatics relates the propositional meaning of an utterance (its 'sense') to its implicit meaning (its 'force'), and just as discourse analysis relates the text to its discoursal functions, so the main business of stylistics is to relate the literary work, as a text, to its artistic function or significance – to its meaning in the fullest sense.[17]

The mention of 'goals' or 'intentions' in a literary context inevitably recalls the debate over the intentional fallacy.[18] Should we argue, with the intentionalists, that a work cannot be interpreted without reference to the author's intention, or should we argue, with the anti-intentionalists, that the meaning of the work lies in what can be recovered from the text itself? A goal-oriented approach to literary meaning appears, by definition, to align itself with the intentional fallacy, and yet I would argue that in fact it achieves a proper reconciliation of these opposing points of view. Let us refer back to the earlier description of the interpreter's task, in pragmatics, as problem-solving. The address of a commonplace remark such as *You could have warned me!* interprets it by working out, or reconstructing, what the speaker's communicative intentions or goals might reasonably have been; and the same may be said of the reader's immeasurably more complex problem-solving task in interpreting a work of literature. The evidence of communicative intentions is to be found largely, perhaps even exclusively, in the text itself: in this sense, the literary text is self-revealing. But the notion of 'meaning', for a literary work as for any other text, makes sense only in terms of what its originator must have 'meant' (i.e. 'intended') by it. Stylistics reconciles the autonomy of text with the intentionality of meaning.

7.3 Samuel Johnson's 'Celebrated Letter' as a demonstration text

There is, therefore, in our approach as interpreters, a natural continuity between literary and non-literary discourse – a continuity which denies the practicality of a strict division between the two. This may help to justify my choice of a 'demonstration text' which inhabits the middle ground between literature and the world of social linguistic transactions. In this case, we do have external evidence of the author's communicative intentions from the report of Johnson's own account in Boswell's *The Life of Johnson*. Chesterfield had offended Johnson first by failing to offer patronage when Johnson, impecunious and comparatively unrecognized , addressed to him the *plan* of his *Dictionary*, and secondly by apparently angling for the dedication of the *Dictionary* when, after Johnson's prodigious labours, it was close to completion. Johnson explained the motivation for his letter as follows:

> Sir, after making great professions, he had, for many years, taken no notice of me; but when my Dictionary was coming out, he fell a scribbling in 'The World' about it. Upon which, I wrote him a letter expressed in civil terms, but such as might shew him that I did not mind what he said or wrote, and that I had done with him.[19]

In its surviving form, the letter reads as follows:[20]

TO THE RIGHT HONOURABLE THE EARL OF CHESTERFIELD
February 7, 1755.

MY LORD.
I have been lately informed, by the proprietor of the World, that
two papers, in which my Dictionary is recommended to the publick,
were written by your Lordship. To be so distinguished, is an honour, which, being very little accustomed to favours from the great, I
5   know not well how to receive, or in what terms to acknowledge.
When, upon some slight encouragement, I first visited your
Lordship, I was overpowered, like the rest of mankind, by the
enchantment of your address; and could not forbear to wish that
I might boast myself *Le vainqueur du vainqueur de la terre*; – that I

10   might obtain that regard for which I saw the world contending; but I
found my attendance so little encouraged, that neither pride nor
modesty would suffer me to continue it. When I had once addressed
your Lordship in publick, I had exhausted all the art of pleasing which
a retired and uncourtly scholar can possess. I had done all that
15   I could; and no man is well pleased to have his all neglected, be it
ever so little.

Seven years, my Lord, have now past, since I waited in your
outward rooms, or was repulsed from your door; during which time
I have been pushing on my work through difficulties, of which it is
useless to complain, and have brought it, at last, to the verge of
20   publication, without one act of assistance, or one word of encouragement, or one smile of favour. Such treatment I did not expect, for I
never had a Patron before.

The shepherd in Virgil grew at last acquainted with Love, and
found him a native of the rocks.
25   Is not a patron, my Lord, one who looks with unconcern on a man
struggling for life in the water, and, when he has reached ground,
encumbers him with help? The notice which you have been pleased
to take of my labours, had it been early, had been kind; but it has
been delayed until I am indifferent, and cannot enjoy it; till I am
30   solitary, and cannot impart it; till I am known, and do not want it. I
hope it is no very cynical asperity not to confess obligations where
no benefit has been received, or to be unwilling that the Publick should
consider me as owing that to a Patron, which Providence has
enabled me to do for myself.
35   Having carried on my work thus far with so little obligation to any
favourer of learning, I shall not be disappointed though I should
conclude it, if less be possible, with less; for I have been long
wakened from that dream of hope, in which I once boasted myself
with so much exultation,

My Lord,
Your Lordship's most humble,
Most obedient servant,
SAM. JOHNSON.

To explain the effectiveness of this masterly put-down, we have to recognize,
within the present goal-directed framework, that it has more than one purpose. It was important that the letter should administer its rebuff with full
effect, and that at the same time it should be expressed (as Johnson himself
put it) 'in civil terms', i.e. (as I would prefer to say in the present context) that
the Politeness Principle should be observed. These two goals – the dynamic
goal and the regulative goal – are explicit in Johnson's remark to Boswell.
But yet a third, aesthetic motive may also be acknowledged: the letter was

meant to be admired as a thing in itself. And again there is some external evidence that points to this conclusion: the letter was preserved (Johnson dictated it twice and corrected it in his own hand) and was later published.

More relevant to our present concern is the way in which these three goals are evident in the letter itself:

(a) the goal of 'civility' is evident in the veneer of politeness that is maintained throughout;

(b) the goal of castigating the Earl is seen in the covertly insulting implications which one finds, with increasing force, throughout the letter;

(c) the artistic goal shows itself in Johnson's cleverly parallelistic and climactic use of language, and particularly in the way the second, offensive goal makes itself felt more and more strongly as the letter progresses, until the *coup de grâce* is administered at the end.

To gain the effect of leading the reader up the garden path, Johnson starts the letter as if it were a conventional expression of gratitude to a prestigious benefactor. The Approbation Maxim is uppermost in the italicized words of 'To be so *distinguished*, is an *honour*, which, being very little accustomed to *favours* from the *great* . . .' and Chesterfield must have read up to this point with complacency. There is also a decorous hint of the Modesty Maxim in Johnson's claim to be unable to reply adequately to this favour. These two maxims are in competition, one being balanced against the other. Almost from the start, we meet a note of ambiguity. Does his pose of inadequacy mean that Johnson lacks social graces, or that the distinction the Earl has conferred on him is of dubious value? At this point Chesterfield could have felt some unease.

The second paragraph continues the game of keeping the reader in two minds. The adjective of '*slight* encouragement' (l. 6) might indicate fitting meekness ('Who am I to expect more than *slight* encouragement from such as you?'), but on the other hand may suggest a criticism of the Earl. The continuation of this sentence reads like conventional flattery, but again mixed with some self-deprecation. 'I . . . could not forbear to wish that I might boast myself . . .' – the negatives and modalities apologetically admitting to a mild degree of self-esteem. A suggestion of more overt criticism emerges in the following sentence (ll. 10–14): 'I found my attendance so little encouraged . . .' etc. But the use of passive verbs (*encouraged, neglected*), with the omission of the agent, blunts the implication of blame, since the author of the 'neglect' is hinted at, but not mentioned. When the passive voice is continued in ll. 17–22 ('was repulsed from your door') the tone of complaint becomes unmistakable. But Johnson keeps up the dual stance by modestly pretending that his disappointment was due to the naive expectations of a 'retired and uncourtly scholar': 'Such treatment I did not expect, for I never had a Patron before.'

This mock innocence sharpens into bitter sarcasm as Johnson offers (ll. 25–7) an absurdly disparaging definition of a patron. But as elsewhere, he relies upon implicature rather than open accusation. Why should Johnson offer such a definition? Evidently because he wishes Chesterfield to admit that this metaphor of 'a man struggling for Life' applies to his treatment of Johnson. Such inferences have to be drawn via the Maxim of Relation. There is no 'you' or 'me'. The syntax further mitigates the force of the rebuke by casting the definition in the form of a negative question: 'Is not a Patron, my Lord . . . ?' By this device, Johnson appears to defer to his Lordship's superior opinion; but he might equally be challenging his correspondent to deny something which is satirically assumed to be self-evident. The strategies which render criticism oblique continue to be remarkably varied. We have (i) the counterfactual condition '. . . had it been early, had been kind' (l. 28), implying the Earl's *un*kindness; (ii) the evasive passive which returns again with 'it has been delayed . . .' (ll. 28–9); (iii) the indefinite third-person reference which evades direct reference to the Earl ('to a Patron', 'to any favourer of learning'); and the thicket of negatives beginning at line 31 ('*no* very cynical asperity'; '*not* to confess', '*no* benefit', and '*un*willing'), camouflaging Johnson's denial of Chesterfield's claim to receiving the dedication of his *Dictionary*. But the last stratagem of indirectness is the most injurious of all. Still keeping up appearances, Johnson appears to sign himself in the displayed conclusion 'Your Lordship's most humble/Most obedient servant'; but a second glance shows that he does no such thing – he actually declares that the time for such humility and obedience is past. By a *trompe l'oeil* trick, the letter has finally turned the tables on the conventional patron–protégé relationship, saying in effect 'The decorums of a commoner's address to a nobleman no longer count, for I have finished with you, my Lord!'

The rhetorical skill which I said was part of Johnson's design is clear not only in the way the hostility of his attack sneaks up on Chesterfield, culminating in the devastating rebuff of the last few lines, but also in the details of the syntax, where Johnson's well-known partiality for parallelism shows itself restrained but effective. Consider the following examples:

[1] . . . I waited   in   your outward rooms
    or was repulsed   from   your door

(ll. 17–18)

[2] without one   act   of   assistance
             one   word   of   encouragement
        or   one   smile of   favour

(ll. 20–21)

[3] until	I	am	indifferent	and	cannot enjoy	it
till	I	am	solitary	and	cannot impart	it
till	I	am	known	and	do not want	it

(ll. 29–30)

The expected rhetorical ordering is one in which the second and/or final element of the structure achieves an effect of climax. Johnson follows this, and strengthens his animadversions by so ordering the parallelisms that the most damaging point is saved to the end. Thus it is bad enough, in [1], that Chesterfield kept Johnson waiting in his 'outward rooms', but it is even worse that he 'repulsed' him 'from (his) door'. More subtly, in [2], the ordering seems to go from the strongest to the weakest point, but in fact it goes from the weakest to the strongest, because the preceding *without* indicates a negative, and the most damning observation is that the Earl did not even deign 'one smile of favour', which would have cost him nothing. In [3] the reason for the ordering is less obvious again, but I take it that Johnson saves 'till I am known, and do not want it' as his punchline, because this is the most damaging and belittling thing *he* can say to *the Earl* – spurning his patronage as worthless.

In this letter, the three goals of (a) affronting the Earl, (b) remaining 'civil', and (c) producing a piece of epistolary art seem to be well balanced. The letter seems to have been successful in its time, for Chesterfield, always the gentleman, accepted the rebuke. More importantly, the letter, two-and-a-half centuries after it was written, still evokes admiration for its own sake. It has become a piece of literature, or (in Boswell's phrase) a 'Celebrated Letter'.

7.4 Conclusion: there is no dichotomy between literary and non-literary texts

This leads us back to a general assessment of how a goal-oriented view of discourse applies to literature. Goal-orientation always implies value: i.e. a text is valued to the extent that it demonstrates skill or artistry in achieving its assumed goals. But a literary work (according to a well-known view which has recurred in various guises)[21] has an immanence of purpose and value. The goal is in the creation of the work itself, and in nothing beyond the work: a poet writes a poem in order to write a poem. This view has been rightly criticized to the extent that it proposes a clear-cut distinction between literary and non-literary texts. But we have seen that goals may be manifold, and that one goal may be subordinate to another coexisting goal. On this basis, then, there is no reason for a dichotomy between the immanence of the author's goal in literature, and the extrinsic nature of the author's goal in non-literary discourse. There can be many different ways in which literary objectives are combined with non-literary objectives, and one of them is illustrated by Johnson's letter.

NOTE: I am grateful for Felicity Rosslyn's advice during the writing of this paper.

Notes

1. For the explanation of these four categories, see Edmondson (1981: 3–4).
2. R. de Beaugrande and W. Dressler (1981: 33) argue that texts must be studied in their context of communicative use, rather than in terms of their constituent elements such as morphemes and sentences.
3. The separation of pragmatics from grammar is widely accepted. This question is discussed in Leech (1980: 1–29).
4. The tendency to associate the grammatical system with written language is observable, for example, in the description of syntax in terms of '*left*-branching', '*left*-dislocation', '*right*-branching', '*right*-dislocation', etc. Moreover, the sentence, as a principal unit of grammatical description, is difficult, if not impossible, to isolate in impromptu speech. See Svartvik (1982) on the segmentation of impromptu speech.
5. See Grice (1957); also, with particular reference to communicative intention in pragmatics, Bach and Harnish (1979: 12–15).
6. This type of goal-oriented approach has been applied to pragmatics by Parisi and Castelfranchi (1982); and to text analysis by de Beaugrande and Dressler (see note 2 above). The possibilities of a goal-oriented approach to discourse analysis are explored in P. Poulter, 'A goal-oriented approach to discourse analysis', unpublished MA dissertation (1982), University of Lancaster.
7. See Newell (1973).
8. See Searle (1969: ch. 3) and Searle (1975). I here assume the critical attitude to Searle described in Leech (1983: 20–4 and 174–95).
9. See Searle (1969: 33–42), and for a contrary view, Leech (1983: 22–3).
10. See Austin (1962: 98–132). Searle in his *Speech Acts* (1969) does not recognize Austin's distinction between locutionary and illocutionary acts.
11. Grice (1975) 'Logic and conversation'.
12. The maxims of the Politeness Principle are described and illustrated in Leech (1983: 131–9, 149).
13. J.R. Searle (1975: 355–68).
14. Searle (1975: 369) does, on the other hand, acknowledge an 'enormous unclarity' in the identification of illocutionary act categories.
15. See Sinclair and Coulthard (1975: 19–60); also the discussion of this and other 'categorical' discourse analysis models in Edmondson (1981: 54–74). Sinclair and Coulthard's model has been modified in Coulthard and Brazil (1979).
16. De Beaugrande and Dressler (1981: 14–29) discuss the development of text grammar as an attempt to apply grammatical techniques to larger-than-sentence units.
17. This view of the goal of stylistics is presented in Leech and Short (**2007**[1981]:12–14**)**. One may, however, extend the scope of stylistics more broadly, to include explanatory studies of style where the goal is not intrinsic (to explicate the literary

work itself) but rather extrinsic (e.g. to investigate the work's authorship, date of composition, etc.). **(See Chapter 5, pp. 54–5, on intrinsic and extrinsic goals.)**

18. See Wimsatt and Beardsley (1954[1946]) on 'the intentional fallacy', in Wimsatt (1954: 1–30). A number of positions in this controversy are presented in Newton-de Molina (1976). In particular Hirsch's contribution 'In defense of the author' contrasts with that of Wimsatt in the same volume.

19. *Boswell's Life of Johnson*, ed. George Birkbeck Hill, rev. L.F. Powell, 6 vols. (Oxford: Clarendon Press, 1934), I. 259–60.

20. *Boswell's Life*, I, 261–3.

21. Most famously, in Jakobson's definition of the poetic function of language as a 'set towards the message' Jakobson (1960). See also Widdowson (1975: 51), **quoted in the discussion of autotelism in Chapter 8 (p. 115)**.

Stylistics and functionalism

8.1 Roman Jakobson: a formalistic functionalist

In his admirable critique of Jakobson's 'Closing Statement' of the 1958 'Style in Language' conference, Derek Attridge[1] has already discussed the model of linguistic functions presented by Jakobson in that memorable paper. The sections in which Jakobson discussed the functions of language also, naturally enough, form the pretext (or pre-text) for this chapter, which is on the theme of stylistics and functionalism.

These two terms 'stylistics' and 'functionalism' I will define simplistically for the present purpose as follows: stylistics is the study of style (particularly in literary texts, and more particularly, with a view to explicating the relation between the form of the text and its potential for interpretation).[2] Functionalism (in the study of language) is an approach which tries to explain language not only internally, in terms of its formal properties, but also externally, in terms of what language contributes to larger systems of which it is a part or subsystem. Whether we call these larger systems 'cultures', 'social systems', 'belief systems', etc. does not concern me. What is significant is that functionalist explanations look for relations between language and what is not language, whereas formalist explanations look for relations between the elements of linguistic text itself.

It is commonly assumed, as I have just assumed, that functionalism is defined by contrast with its opposite, formalism. It is strange, then, that Jakobson, who provides us with one of the best-known classifications of language functions, should also, in his analyses of literary texts, be the most successful and influential practitioner of formalism. The basis of this paradox lies in Jakobson's well-known definition of the poetic function as 'the set (*Einstellung*) towards the *message* itself, focus on the message for its own sake' (Sebeok 1960: 356). It will be remembered that Jakobson's typology of functions attributed a different function to each of the six components in an archetypal linguistic situation. Think of such a situation as one in which an ADDRESSER sends a linguistics MESSAGE to an ADDRESSEE. Jakobson goes on:

> To be operative the message requires a CONTEXT referred to . . . ; a CODE fully, or at least partially, common to the addresser and addressee . . . ; and finally, a CONTACT, a physical channel and psychological connection between the addresser and the addressee, enabling both of them to stay in communication.
>
> (Jakobson 1960: 353)

The six functions associated with these elements of the communicative situation are named by Jakobson as follows:

addresser	EMOTIVE	context	REFERENTIAL
addressee	CONATIVE	message	POETIC
contact	PHATIC	code	METALINGUAL

By thus relating language to its communicative setting, he was in a *general* way providing a linguistic model which is functionalist in the sense I have specified. But the poetic function was an exception – for he represented the poetic function as the special case where the linguistic artefact has no function beyond itself, where (as it were) language turns in on itself.

8.2 A goal-oriented multifunctionalism

As Attridge points out, the notion of a 'set towards' one aspect of the communicative situation – a focus or *Einstellung* – has implications of a psychological or social nature. But, rather than pursue this, let me reveal something of my own 'focus', prejudice – call it what you like – by adopting the commonplace idea that a 'function' presupposes some kind of orientation towards a goal (see Chapter 7, pp. 86–91). For example, we use language conatively *in order to* influence the addressee in some way; our emotive use of language *serves to* express our opinions or attitudes; the phatic use of language is *a means to* establish or maintain contact with one's interlocutor.

These expressions which imply goals, ends or objectives, do not have to suggest that there is a conscious purpose or precisely definable intention – in fact, in many cases it would be misleading to make any such suggestion. But I see no difficulty in assuming, as a general postulate, that functionalism implies goal orientation. Thus one may reinterpret Jakobson's poetic function as follows: whereas in relation to other functions, a message/text is seen as a means to an end, in relation to the poetic function, a message/text is regarded as an end in itself. It is 'autofunctional' or, to use a technical term, *autotelic*.

Moreover, function involves value. Whereas in relation to other functions, messages/texts are evaluated in terms of their efficacy in attaining extrinsic goals, in relation to the poetic function, they are evaluated by criteria intrinsic to themselves.

There are two further points to make about this concept of function, if its importance for the study of poetic language is to be appreciated.

First, a given utterance or text *may* have, and in general, *will* have, more than one function. Multifunctionalism is the norm. This point has been emphasized by Jakobson (1960), as it has been by Halliday (1970a, 1973), and by others who have provided functional typologies of language. It has also been emphasized (and Jakobson himself is particularly insistent on this) that one function may be placed in a subordinate relation to another, such that, for example, an utterance which is dominantly conative – like an advertisement or a political slogan – may be secondarily referential or secondarily poetic. Within this framework, poetry (or literature – there is no need to distinguish between these two terms here) is definable as that kind of text in which the poetic function is dominant over others. But the framework allows for texts which combine a dominant poetic function with subsidiary functions of another kind: for example, a love poem is not only poetic, but also emotive/expressive; a didactic poem is not only poetic, but also conative. Jakobson's functional model therefore exonerates him from the worst consequences of what Mary Louise Pratt (1977) has called 'the poetic language fallacy' – the presumption of a linguistically definable dichotomy between 'literary language' and 'ordinary, non-literary language'. The functional model, on the contrary, makes the quality of literariness depend on the evaluation or interpretation of the text by readers, by a social or linguistic community: 'poeticalness (says Jakobson) is ... a total re-evaluation of the discourse and all its components whatsoever' (1960: 377).

8.3 Typologies of language function and kinds of meaning

My second point is that there is an important interconnection between function and meaning. This applies to an individual utterance if we adopt Grice's (1957) explication of non-natural meaning: meaning understood as the speaker's intention that the utterance should produce some effect on an audience by means of the *recognition of this intention*. What from the speaker's viewpoint is function or communicative intention becomes from the hearer's viewpoint significance, or interpretation. There is a parallel to be drawn here between Jakobson and a contemporary of his who came from a different intellectual tradition, and whose perspective on poetic language was so different – I.A. Richards. Richards's four kinds of meaning, enunciated in his *Practical Criticism* (1929) overlap strikingly with Jakobson's functions:

sense: what is said, the state of affairs presented
         (cf. Jakobson's referential function)
feeling: attitude to what is said
         (cf. Jakobson's emotive function)
tone: attitude towards the hearer
         (cf. Jakobson's conative function)
intention: the author's aim, the effect he is endeavouring to promote
           (tone and intention can be seen as subdivisions of Jakobson's
           conative function).

Furthermore, like Jakobson, Richards stresses relations of dominance or subordination between the categories: 'now one, now another of the functions may become predominant' (1929: 183). (Notice how easily Richards moves between the terminology of meaning and the terminology of function.) Richards's description of the addresse*r*'s end of the process of communication is easily seen as a metaphor for the multifiunctionality of language: 'Whether we know and intend it or not, we are all jugglers when we converse, keeping the billiard-balls in the air when we balance the cue on our nose'.[3] Despite Richards's assimilation of the poetic function to the emotive function, there is enough similarity between Jakobson's and Richards's schemes to suggest the value of a more general comparison between various schemes of linguistic functions. In view of the apparent lack of constraints on the various functions of language that one might dream up, there is a surprising and reassuring degree of similarity between the various schemes proposed. Figure 8.1 attempts to represent their common ground, although it must necessarily do so only roughly:

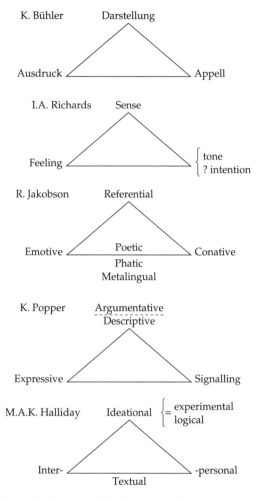

Figure 8.1 Different classifications of the functions of language

I have been inclined to wonder whether Jakobson's scheme has any supe-riority over other schemes, in spite of its enduring popularity. It is tempting to suppose that the appeal of his scheme is in its tidy symmetry, and in the attractive idea (which so far as I know lacks any intrinsic justification) that every major aspect of the communication situation has its corresponding function. But at least the close correspondence between three of his functions and parts of other schemes makes me believe that there is some genuine substance underlying the superficial attraction. These three functions – the referential, emotive and conative functions – are those which, together with his colleagues of the Prague School, he borrowed from the more traditional scheme of Bůhler (1965 [1934]), which also formed the basis for that of Bůhler's student Karl Popper, and more indirectly for that of Halliday.

Very briefly, let me pick out some significant differences between the various schemes, taking Bůhler and Jakobson as points of reference. I used to think that Jakobson's metalingual function (for which he gives only one example – that of the dictionary definition) was the least well motivated of his six functions, useful only for maintaining the symmetry of the scheme. Surely, I thought, metalanguage is just a special case of the referential function of language, in which the object of reference is language itself. But then it occurred to me that if one interpreted metalanguage broadly enough, this could correspond to Popper's argumentative function, or to Halliday's logical function (which he defines as a subfunction of the ideational function). For Popper, the functions of language are important in explaining the evolution of the human mind, and particularly the development of scientific thought. He sees the functions as forming a hierarchy, leading from the primordial 'expressive function', which human language shares with all animal behaviour, to the most advanced 'argumentative function', which enables us to interconnect logically, and reflect on, our descriptions of the world, and hence to criticize and to evaluate them. If we allow metalanguage to include the meta*semantic* activity of manipulating propositional meaning, with its descriptive values of truth and falsehood, then the metalingual function takes on the importance assigned to the argumentative function by Popper. Similarly, Jakobson's metalingual function can be associated with Halliday's logical subfunction. Halliday draws the distinction between his experiential subfunction (corresponding, I suppose, to Popper's descriptive function) and his logical subfunction (exemplified by the logical connectives *and* and *or*) as follows (1979: 73):

> In the experiential mode, reality is represented more concretely, in the form of constructs whose elements make some reference to *things* . . . In the logical mode, reality is represented in more abstract terms, in the form of abstract relations which are independent of and make no reference to things.

Three further distinctive features of Halliday's scheme of functions deserve comment.

First, Halliday stresses that the functions of language are integrated within the grammar: that they are manifested in the organization of the language in terms of system and structure. He thus achieves a kind of synthesis of function with form: functions determine not only how we use the language, but how the language itself is constructed.

Secondly, Halliday recognizes that the emotive and conative functions cover the same ground – that the resources of language we use to express our own emotions and attitudes are to a large extent the same as those which we use to influence the emotions and attitudes of others. Hence he subsumes the addresser-oriented and addressee-oriented functions under the single heading of the 'interpersonal function'.

Thirdly, having thus subtracted one term from Bühler's triad, he adds another term, and ends up with a new triad consisting of the ideational, interpersonal and textual functions. The new term in the model – the textual function – is the area in which Halliday has probably contributed more than in any other, in explicating (under the inspiration of Prague School functionalism) such notions as theme and rheme and given and new. And yet one can argue that the textual function is not really a function of language in the strict sense of 'relating language to what is not language' at all: Halliday recognizes its special status by calling it an 'enabling function' (1970b: 143, 165).

8.4 Functionalism in terms of a threefold hierarchy

In the study of pragmatics (Leech 1983: 59), I have tried to reinterpret Halliday's three functions as a hierarchy of instrumentality. A linguistic event of communication can be described as constituting a transaction between addresser and addressee on three different planes: an interpersonal transaction (or discourse), an ideational transaction (or representation) and a textual transaction (or text)[4] (see Figure 8.2).

But these planes of instantiation are ordered in such a way that the discourse is enacted *by means of* the representation, and the representation is conveyed *by means of* the text. Each plane has the *function* of transmitting the

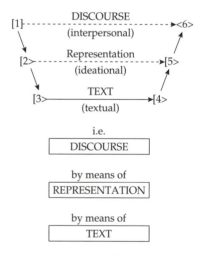

Figure 8.2 A layered view of the functions of language

plane or planes above it. Mick Short and I have explored the application of this kind of model to literature in our book *Style in Fiction* (2007 [1981]). Thus a work of fiction can be considered as a text – as a linguistic object consisting simply of words in a particular order on the page; it can also be considered as a representation of a reality – or rather, in the case of fiction, of a mock reality. The text is the means of conveying that mock reality to the reader, although in principle it might be conveyed by another means, such as a film, or strip cartoons. The discourse is the work of fiction in its fullest sense, as a transaction between the author and the reader, subsuming the various sub-discourses (e.g. the discourses of fictional characters) it may contain, including the authorial attitude to elements of the fiction and to the reader.

But before considering the implications of this model for stylistics, I would like to say a little about its application more generally. A functional model of language is naturally to be associated with a functional model of language use, i.e. with a theory of rhetoric.[5] Each of the planes, therefore, has its own principles of effective communication: there is an interpersonal rhetoric, an ideational rhetoric and a textual rhetoric.[6] We can take Grice's Cooperative Principle (Grice 1975) as the canonical example of ideational rhetoric, with its maxims of informativeness, of truthfulness, of relevance and of clarity. The interpersonal rhetoric, concerning relations between the addresser and addressee, contains maxims of politeness, as well as second-order reflections of politeness or impoliteness, such as irony and banter. The textual rhetoric contains such maxims of well-behaved text as end focus and end weight – placing the information focus and the grammatically heavy elements towards the end of the information unit. It also contains maxims of economy of expression, and clarity of expression, operative, for example, in the choice between pronominalization, ellipsis, and lexical repetition. The claim is not that speakers and writers invariably obey these maxims: indeed, it is essential to note that the maxims place conflicting claims upon the user. Rather, the claim is that by assuming that the goals of the addresser include reasonable adherence to these maxims, the addressee interprets infringements or floutings of them by making certain inferences, drawing certain conclusions, about what the addresser intends to communicate. Hence we explain a wide range of implicit or indirect meanings which arise in discourse interpretation. Here again we note that a functional orientation at the addresser's end leads to attribution of meaning at the address*ee*'s end.

The addressee draws different kinds of conclusions. Consider a simple conversational example: a knock on the door is followed by NOW *what does he want?* On the textual plane, the fact that the emphasis falls on *now* means that end focus has not been observed, and this in turn implies that the following part of the utterance is what the speaker takes as 'given'. This leads to the conclusion that on a previous occasion, a similar action (knocking at the door) was performed by the same person for a certain purpose. On the

111

ideational (or referential) plane, the fact that 'he' is mentioned without further specification implies that there is sufficient contextually shared knowledge to enable the addressee to understand which person is meant by the addresser: and so, on this basis, the addressee can draw a conclusion about the person's identity. On the interpersonal plane, both these 'lower level' inferences may contribute to an understanding of the speaker's motivation, which in this case is not, presumably, to elicit information (despite the interrogative form of the sentence), but to express annoyance: the utterance is a complaint or grumble. In such conversational examples, a great deal depends on a shared context that speaker and hearer can take for granted, and since factors such as degree of shared knowledge may be unclear to both parties, there is considerable latitude for alternative interpretations and *mis*interpretations.

This is a different conception of multifunctionalism from Halliday's; but it leads me to declare support for Halliday's demonstration, in his study of Golding's *The Inheritors* (Halliday 1971) and elsewhere, that there is no discontinuity, in functional terms, between everyday communication and literature. The same methods and principles of interpretation apply to both. In particular, multiplicity and indeterminacy of meaning are characteristic of both literature and conversation; and in both literature and conversation, as readers or hearers, we have to engage our minds fully (in terms of background knowledge, intelligence and imagination) to reconstruct the addresser's intention as well as we can.

We may now illustrate the three planes of rhetoric and interpretation by reference to literary examples.

8.5 Applications to literature

The TEXTUAL PLANE can be illustrated by the varied meanings we can attach to the author's sequencing of elements and to lexical repetition. The sequencing of elements in fiction often assumes chronological ordering of events in the narrative; but it can also suggest 'psychological ordering', that is, the order in which impressions or elements of knowledge are apprehended by some fictional observer; or it can suggest what one may call 'rhetorical ordering' – i.e. the order in which the author intends impressions to be registered, for maximum effect, in the mind of the reader.

In this passage from Conrad's *The Secret Agent*, the psychological interpretation of sequencing seems to be dominant:

> She saw there an object. That object was the gallows. She was afraid of the gallows.

> (Chapter 12)

The three sentences trace the step-by-step dawning of grim realizations in the mind of Mrs Verloc after her murder of her husband. In the following sentence from Dickens's *Little Dorrit*, on the other hand, the dominant value of ordering appears to be that of rhetorical arrangement, so that the reader (having been temporarily taken in by Mrs Sparkler's seeming sincerity) may savour the step-by-step progression towards an ironic climax at the end of the sentence:

> Mrs Sparkler, who was not unfeeling, had received them [the tidings of death] with a violent burst of grief, which had lasted twelve hours; after which she had risen to see about her mourning, and to take every precaution that could ensure its being as becoming as Mrs Merdle's.
>
> (Book 2, Chapter XXIV)

Lexical repetition, when it is a refusal to pronominalize, is at face value an offence against the maxim of economy of expression, and so acquires a stylistic significance of its own. Something of the multiple values attaching to repetition is suggested by the Conrad example. The repetitions of *object* and *gallows* clearly have an emotively intensifying effect. But with *gallows* there is also an apparent offence against the maxim of end focus, since the word's second occurrence is necessarily 'given', and should therefore be defocused: *'She was aFRAID of the gallows'*. There is, however, a way in which we can motivate this apparent double infringement of textual maxims: we can suppose that *gallows* is used with two different meanings, and hence with two different emphases: a double take as in *'That object was the GALLOWS. She was afraid of the GALLOWS.'* The first 'gallows' is a visible object; the second 'gallows' is an institution, with all its associations of fear, shame and death.

My next example from Dickens's *David Copperfield* illustrates the attribution of meaning through IDEATIONAL and INTERPERSONAL rhetoric, and how this, like textual rhetoric, can manifest ambiguity:

> Three years. Long in the aggregate, though short as they went by. And home was very dear to me, and Agnes too – but she was not mine – she was never to be mine. She might have been, but that was past!
>
> (Chapter 58)

The question here is: to whom do we attribute the meanings expressed in the passage? Is it to the implied authorial consciousness of the mature David, looking back on his youth? Or is it to the young David, suffering the pangs of love, whose thoughts are here being reported in free indirect speech?

If it is the mature autobiographer's voice anticipating the future, then we find out later, when David does marry Agnes, that we have been conned. So retrospectively, to avoid imputing narratorial inconsistency to the mature

David (and by implication to Dickens), we should conclude that it *was* free indirect speech, reporting the fallible consciousness of the younger David. But perhaps the ambivalence is important at this stage in the story: it enables Dickens to avoid the opposite pitfalls of letting us know too much too soon, and being too blatantly guilty of misleading us. Here, therefore, we see Dickens balancing the competing demands of (a) the ideational rhetoric (how to give us knowledge about the fiction), and (b) the interpersonal rhetoric (how to position the narrator with respect to the fiction and the reader).

These quotations illustrate functional stylistics as an explication of a literary work in which, not satisfied with a study of just the formal linguistic features, we seek an interpretation of linguistic features in terms of stylistic or functional values. These values we attribute to the work in our endeavour to explain *why* the author used this or that form of expression.

8.6 Jakobson's poetic function revisited: autotelism

Returning to Jakobson, we have seen that in spite of his functional model of language in general, his definition of the poetic function required him to take a formalist approach to poetic language in particular. In Jakobson and Jones's (1970) analysis of Shakespeare's *Sonnet 129*, for example, there is an impressive and meticulous attention to the formal patterning of the text, but no explanation of how significances are to be read into such patterns (see Attridge 1987: 25). There is instead an unargued assumption that complexity of patterning is self-justifying; that virtuosity is its own reward. Criticisms of this formalistic approach have been many – see, for example, Fowler (1975a).

From a functional point of view, the observation of formal structures, e.g. of parallelism, is merely the first step towards an exegesis of the text. Consider these syntactic parallelisms from Eliot's *Prufrock*:

After the novels, after the teacups, after the skirts that trail along the floor –

To have bitten off the matter with a smile,
To have squeezed the universe into a ball
To roll it towards some overwhelming question,
To say: 'I am Lazarus, come from the dead . . .'

The significance lies not in the structural equivalences themselves:

the novels = the teacups = the skirts that trail along the floor

but in the fact that these equivalences challenge us to find some common factor of meaning linking apparently unconnected phenomena.

Hence the 'set towards the message', as a definition of the poetic or literary function of language, is too limiting, if the 'message' is understood simply as a text in a formal sense. But this does not mean we have to throw away Jakobson's definition entirely. Perhaps is should be reinterpreted in a truly functional sense, as the 'set towards the discourse' – the discourse being, as I have stated it, the literary work in its fullest sense: an interpersonal transaction between author and reader, including all three planes of discourse, representation and text.

This redefinition corresponds to a view which has been expressed by Widdowson (and in somewhat similar terms by many others) that a literary discourse is situationally autonomous, or autotelic. Widdowson says (1975: 51):

> a piece of literary discourse is in suspense from the usual process of social interaction whereby senders address messages directly to receivers. The literary message does not arise in the normal course of social activity as do other messages, it arises from no previous situation and requires no response, it does not serve as a link between people or as a means of furthering the business of ordinary social life.

This discoursal autonomy, or autotelism, explains why when we appraise a discourse as a piece of literature, we discount the reality of its interactants. For the rhetoric of fiction, as Booth describes it (1961: 71–6, 137–8), the implied author and implied reader are more relevant to our understanding of a narrative than the real author or reader. Similarly, for a lyrical poem, the persona the poet presents (real or fictional) is more relevant than the poet's own biographical self.

This autotelism on the discourse plane corresponds with a parallel autotelism on the plane of representation. The domain of reference represented in a literary work need not correspond at all points with historical reality – it may, in fact be a fictional *mock* reality. So whereas, for example, an autobiography is valued in part in relation to historical truthfulness, an autobiographical novel is not answerable to any such constraint.

Is there any parallel autotelic function on the third functional plane, the textual plane, that of the literary text as a formal object? I would argue that there is, and that it lies in the principle of iconicity which assumes, in literature, an importance far beyond that which it has in everyday language. A literary work, in its textual form, is what Epstein (1975) calls a 'self-reflexive artefact': its very physical substance imitates or enacts the meaning that it represents. I have already mentioned an example of this in textual sequencing: chronological sequencing mimics the order of events in a fiction; psychological sequencing mimics the order of impressions in the mind of some character or narrator. Thus sequencing, although it is recognized as such on the textual plane, can directly dramatize the ideational and interpersonal functions of the work. Whereas iconicity has a relatively minor role in everyday language use, in literature it comes into its own as an important communicative device.

The autotelic character of literature does not mean that the normal functions of language are suspended. It means, rather, that the other functions are subsumed under, or subordinated to, the autotelic function. In fact, these other functions are put to work more strenuously in literature, in that all interpersonal, ideational and textual interpretations have to be extrapolated from the literary work itself: there can be no reliance on the specific contextual knowledge which is so important for conversational interpretation.

In view of what I have said about the diversity and ambivalence of functional interpretation, the autotelic quality of literature means that literature can become an experimental arena for possible discourse, possible experiential worlds, possible texts. Literature can be an 'adventure playground' within which the human communicative–interpretative faculty can be explored without a hindrance of real-life consequences.

One aspect of this exploration is that literary language can be superficially *dys*functional in striking ways, without adverse effects. Dysfunctional features, e.g. distortions of linguistic norm, obscurities and ambiguities, challenge the reader to find new avenues of interpretation. Jakobson's definition of literary form in terms of patterns of equivalence plays down the important role of deviation from linguistic and other norms in literature: deviation being a negative characteristic of poetic language only so long as one confines oneself to form rather than function.

8.7 Conclusion

It seems clear that since the 1958 'Conference on Style' (see note 1, this chapter), linguistics and stylistics/poetics have moved from a predominantly formalist or structuralist climate of thought to a predominantly functionalist one. This trend has advanced alongside the development of such fields as pragmatics, text linguistics, discourse analysis and social semiotics – where the emphasis has shifted away from language as a formal system towards language in use in society. But it may be felt, with some justice, that what we have gained by extending the frontiers of the subject in this way has entailed a sacrifice of rigour; functional stylistics still relies too heavily on selective and subjective judgment.

So, looking ahead rather than back, let us foresee an era in which the processes of interpretation are subjected to more careful study within the framework of 'descriptive rhetoric'. Grice's exploration of conversational implicature is one area where progress has been made in this direction, but there are many more areas (for example, in the study of iconicity) where knowledge is lacking, and where, to explain interpretations, we rely on impressions and guesswork. If progress leads us to overcome these weaknesses, we may look forward to a time when the combination of insight with rigour (which Jakobson admirably demonstrated within a formalist paradigm) will do justice both to literary works themselves as linguistic artefacts, and to the partly shared, partly variable processes of interpretation whereby readers find meaning in them.

Notes

1. Derek Attridge's paper, 'Closing statement: linguistics and poetics in retrospect', was published as Chapter 1 of the book *The Linguistics of Writing*, edited by Fabb et al. (1987), containing the proceedings of a conference at Strathclyde University in 1986, in which the present chapter first appeared. The conference was seen as a sequel, after more than twenty-five years, to a 'Conference on Style' held in Indiana in 1958, whose proceedings were published in Sebeok (1960), entitled *Style in Language*. The most influential paper in the earlier conference had been Roman Jakobson's famous 'Closing Statement', often referred to by participants in the later conference.
2. See the more detailed discussion of 'style' and 'stylistics' at the beginning of Chapter 5 (pp. 54–5).
3. The connection between Jakobson and Richards is worth exploring further. Richards was the first contributor to that *Style in Language* volume to which Jakobson contributed his 'Closing Statement', and was the only contributor to that symposium older than Jakobson himself. Ten years later, in his late seventies, Richards became a belated but enthusiastic convert to the linguistic analysis of literature, on reading Jakobson and Jones (1970), which he reviewed in the *Times Literary Supplement* (Richards 1970).
4. The distinction between 'discourse' and 'text' here corresponds to that of Widdowson (1975: 6).
5. Notice that the term *rhetoric* has a very different emphasis in this chapter from that in Chapter 2. In Chapter 2, the traditional study of rhetoric, with its emphasis on figures of speech, was in focus. Here, the term *rhetoric* applies more generally to (the study of) the effective use of language – that is, the use of language directed towards the attainment of the author's communicative goals.
6. See also Leech and Short (2007: 108–9, 168–9); and Chapters 7 and 10 of this book. In my *Principles of Pragmatics* (Leech 1983: 16) I did not distinguish between interpersonal and ideational rhetoric, treating the latter (as represented by Grice's Cooperative Principle) as part of the former.

CHAPTER 9

Pragmatic principles in Shaw's *You Never Can Tell*

9.1 Introduction

The notion of poetic *foregrounding*, as a touchstone of literary effect through the use of language, has been inherited from the Russian Formalists via the Prague School structuralists (see van Peer 1986: 1–24). With such a background, it is not obvious that this concept can be revealingly applied to the study of literary discourse in relation to its context – whether we are concerned with the fictional or real-world context of a work of literature.

I shall argue in this chapter, however, that foregrounding – significant literary 'deviation' against the background of a non-literary norm – is just as applicable to the pragmatic study of language in context as to other, more formal, aspects of language. Consider those well-known classical devices of literary expression, the apostrophe (*Death be not proud*) and the rhetorical question (*Was marriage ever out of fashion?*). In spite of their hackneyed literariness over the centuries, they still clearly gain their effect through a mismatch between language and context: in the former case, the abnormality of addressing an inappropriate addressee; in the latter case, that of asking a question where no informative reply can be forthcoming.

But my plan now is for a more extended examination of contextual incongruity in literature, with reference to George Bernard Shaw's comedy *You Never Can Tell* (1898). In this, I hope to show how the concept of foregrounding has a broader application than has been generally appreciated. We think of its application most centrally to poetry (where abnormalities in the use of language are most obvious), and less centrally to prose style (see, for example, Leech and Short 2007: 39–41, 110–16). Its application to drama has on the whole been neglected, except where dramatic language is seen to have its own counterpart of poetic deviation, in the discoursal incongruities and inarticulacies of the theatre of the absurd. (Of relevance here are the stylistic studies on Pinter and Ionesco respectively in Short 1989b: 156–61 and Simpson 1989.)

You Never Can Tell, on the other hand, is more fittingly described as a comedy of manners: almost all its major characters are associated with comic exaggerations of conversational behaviour. To reveal the richness and significance of this behaviour, I will have recourse to a theory of pragmatics which seems to be well equipped for this purpose: namely, the Gricean model based on the Cooperative Principle (Grice 1975), augmented by the Principle of Politeness as presented in Leech (1983: 104–51).[1]

9.2 The plot of Shaw's *You Never Can Tell*

First, it will be necessary to sketch the plot of the play, and to introduce its main characters.

> In this, one of Shaw's earliest and most popular comedies, Valentine, a young dentist, has just set up in practice at a seaside resort. Here he meets the Clandon family, consisting of Mrs Clandon, a strong supporter of women's rights, and her three children, Gloria, Dolly, and Philip. [The latter two are 17-year-old twins.]
>
> Mrs Clandon has long since left a dictatorial husband, and has brought up her children in Madeira under a name other than that of their father. However, when Valentine arrives for lunch, Mrs Clandon discovers to her dismay that his landlord, Mr Crampton, is her former husband. Dolly and Philip appeal to William, a tactful waiter, who gently informs Mr Crampton that he is dining with his family after 18 years of separation. Valentine, in love with Gloria, proposes marriage. Mr M'Comas, Mrs Clandon's solicitor, calls on Mr Crampton, who is resentful of his family's casual attitude. He believes that they and Valentine are plotting to annoy him, and demands the custody of the younger children. M'Comas engages the services of Bohun, a famous barrister, and arranges for a conference with Crampton that evening.
>
> The hotel is giving a fancy-dress ball, and Bohun arrives in costume. It turns out that he is the son of William, who has discovered that his son's successful career hampers him as a waiter, and so spells his name 'Boon'. Bohun straightens out Crampton's difficulties with his family, and Valentine's engagement to Gloria is accepted. All ends happily.
>
> (Summary from Haydn and Fuller 1978: 810–11)

9.3 Pragmatic principles and pragmatic deviation

To characterize deviations from 'normal' conversational behaviour, we have first to characterize 'norms'. The constituent maxims of Grice's CP (Cooperative Principle), and the constituent maxims of the PP (Politeness Principle) provide a relevant framework: Grice's Maxims of Quantity (informativeness), Quality (truthfulness), Relation (relevance) and Manner (clarity, etc.) are well known. Although the Maxims of the PP (Leech 1983: 131–42) are less well known, they will not be repeated here, as they have already been spelt out in Chapter 7 (p. 92). They consist of the Tact Maxim and the Generosity Maxim, the Approbation Maxim and the Modesty Maxim, the Agreement Maxim and the Sympathy Maxim.

A number of points should be made about these maxims: like the maxims of the CP, the maxims of the PP are (a) associated with pragmatic scales or gradients, (b) capable of being infringed, namely, governed by a *ceteris paribus* condition, (c) capable of conflicting with one another, and with the maxims of the CP. These maxims, like those of the CP, are purely descriptive: postulated for the purpose of explaining observed behaviour (e.g. accounting for communicative indirectness, asymmetries of speaker-reference vs. addressee-reference, pragmatic 'paradoxes', gradations of linguistic politeness, pragmatic unacceptability). It should also be explained that in the wording of the maxims, 'maximize benefit to *others*', etc. describe linguistic (rather than social) imperatives, which should be more carefully worded: 'maximize the expression of beliefs implying benefit to *others*' etc.

I assume, as part of this principle-constrained theory of pragmatics, that humans carry around with them a conception of what is a norm (in part societal, in part personal) of cooperative or polite behaviour for a given conversational situation. These norms are variable according to who the speakers are; what the social relations between them are; what the situational background is in terms of the kind of activity they are engaged in; what goods or services are being transacted; what the background presumptions regarding the rights and obligations of individuals are, and the relative weightiness of various rights and obligations, goods and services. I also assume that manifest deviations from such norms are recognizable, even though such deviant linguistic behaviour might be totally normal in a different situation.

9.4 (Un)cooperative and (im)polite behaviour in the play

Some of these maxims, and some rather obvious violations of them, can be illustrated from the play itself. First the Maxim of Quality (truthfulness). At the beginning of the play, the twins (Dolly and Philip) are being treated by the novice dentist, Valentine. At this stage, we do not yet know their names:

[1] DENTIST. . . . Why didn't you let me give you gas?
     YOUNG LADY. Because you said it would be five shillings extra.
     DENTIST. [*shocked*] Oh, don't say that. It makes me feel as if I had hurt
       you for the sake of five shillings.
     YOUNG LADY. [*with cool insolence*] Well, so you have.

(I, 212)[2]

Dolly's last, blunt remark is typical of her, in that she speaks the truth
(Maxim of Quality) at the expense of politeness (Maxim of Approbation).
Where the CP and the PP conflict (e.g. where to speak the truth would cause
offence), human beings tend to take refuge in craven compromise. We tell
'white lies', or we tone down the assertion of any truthful utterance that
might hurt or challenge the interlocutor (e.g. when asked by our dinner
hosts if we enjoyed the meal, few of us would say no, even if that would be
true). Dolly suffers from none of these niceties. She and her brother have
been brought up by their 'advanced' mother abroad, far away from the
evils, but also the civilities, of English society.

Similarly, Dolly believes in the Maxim of Quantity (informativeness) at all
costs: she does not believe in withholding her own 'private' information
from others, or in allowing others to withhold *their* information from her. So
she fires a series of personal questions at the dentist:[3]

[2] THE YOUNG LADY. . . . your rooms. Are they expensive?
     DENTIST. Yes . . .

(I, 212)

[3] THE YOUNG LADY. . . . I suppose you havent been here long?
     DENTIST. Six weeks. Is there anything else youd like to know?
     THE YOUNG LADY. [*the hint quite lost on her*] Any family?

(ibid.)

Here is another respect in which politeness and cooperativeness conflict.
Individuals' 'ownership' of information is analogous to their ownership of
property. It is not normally acceptable (in the English society portrayed in
the play) to ask other people to give you details of their private lives, any
more than it is acceptable to ask them to give you their private possessions.
But for Dolly, the Maxim of Quantity is clearly supreme: or rather, she
defines the Maxim ('make your contribution as informative as is required')
for her own purposes, rather than for others'. She demands personal information from a stranger, blindly unaware of the power of the Tact Maxim
to conceal information in British society (and more particularly in late
Victorian upper-middle-class society).

The Maxim of Quantity, however, can also be violated. This is shown later on in the opening scene of the play, when Valentine (the dentist) expresses himself tautologically:

[4] VALENTINE. . . . But – and now will you excuse my frankness? [*They nod*]. Thank you. Well, in a seaside resort theres one thing you must have before anyone can afford to be seen going about with you; and thats a father, alive or dead.

(I, 217–18)

Naturally, everyone has a father – alive or dead – so Valentine's statement is necessarily, hence vacuously, true. Such a tautology overtly transgresses the Maxim of Quantity, because tautologies convey no information. But, of course, one interprets Valentine's remark, like many tautologies, as implicitly informative: it implies that the supremely middle-class, supremely respectable society into which the twins have strayed is one in which appearances matter. 'Having a father' means having a respectable background. The twins lack such a requisite: their mother (Mrs Clandon) refuses even to mention the husband she abandoned, because of his gross and tyrannical behaviour, many years ago.

Another ironical tautology is uttered by the male twin, Philip, when Mrs Clandon joins her children in the dentist's surgery:

[5] PHILIP. . . . Now my knowledge of human nature leads me to believe that we had a father, and that you probably know who he was.
MRS CLANDON. [*her agitation rising*] Stop, Phil. Your father is nothing to you, nor to me. [*Vehemently*] That is enough.
GLORIA. [*advancing*] Mother: we have a right to know.

(I, 224)

Mrs Clandon's reply to her son is significant, again, in terms of the CP: in spite of her 'liberated' views on every other topic, she exercises an embargo on information about her estranged husband. She justifies her violation of the Quantity Maxim by an apparent violation of the Quality Maxim: it is obviously untrue that a father is 'nothing': but by this hyperbolic literal untruth, Mrs Clandon implies that no information worth the name is being withheld. In adding 'That is enough', she also appears to proclaim her particularly restrictive application of the Quantity Maxim, clearly at odds with that of her children. Thus her implication is not accepted by her elder daughter, Gloria – a comely, somewhat priggish paragon of female independence – who at this point claims the children's right to freedom of information on this matter of personal importance.

Here, we have an inversion of the situation in examples [2] and [3] – where one character denied to another the right to withhold information personal to the latter. Here, one character claims from another the right to obtain information personal to the latter (and in fact to both). The Maxim of Quantity, we discover, is intimately bound up with the rights and obligations of individuals in relation to such informational 'property'.

The third maxim of CP, Grice's Maxim of Relation (relevance) is, like the others, most noticeable when it is manifestly violated. In the following exchange, Dolly and her sister are doing their best to make polite conversation to a middle-aged man, Mr Crampton, who is Valentine's uncouth and unaccommodating landlord:

[6] DOLLY. [*suddenly, to keep things going*] How old are you, Mr Crampton?
GLORIA. [*hastily*] I am afraid we must be going, Mr Valentine.

(I, 231)

I called this an 'exchange', but actually Gloria's remark has no overt connection with that of Dolly. In other words, Gloria appears to break the Maxim of Relation. Grice's argument in favour of the Maxim of Relation, however, is that we *infer* relevance where none appears on the surface; thus we infer, from Gloria's interruption of the conversation, that she is trying to combat the embarrassment of her sister's tactless question. As often happens, a superficial violation of the CP is explicable as an attempt to mitigate impoliteness (i.e. to observe the PP).

However, Gloria's ploy fails, and after the interruption Mr Crampton answers Dolly's question, only to be thrown by a further instance of her rudeness (breaking the Maxim of Approbation in favour of the Maxim of Quality):

[7] CRAMPTON. . . . . So you want to know my age, do you? I'm fifty-seven.
DOLLY. [*with conviction*] You look it.

(I, 231)

The positive side of the PP is amply demonstrated by the benignly ingratiating behaviour of the waiter William, who is a model of politeness in every sense. At the beginning of Act II, he is talking to Mrs Clandon's old friend and solicitor, Mr M'Comas, who has arrived at her hotel from London to see her (I quote Shaw's detailed description of William on his first entry, to give the flavour of his character, which has a key role in the play):

[8] WAITER. Quite sure, sir. She expects you at a quarter to one, sir. [*The gentleman, soothed by the waiter's voice, looks at him with a lazy smile. It is a quiet voice, with a gentle melody in it that gives sympathetic interest to his most commonplace remark: and he speaks with the sweetest propriety, neither dropping his aitches nor misplacing them, nor committing any other vulgarism. He looks at his watch as he continues*] Not that as yet sir? 12.43, sir. Only two minutes to wait, sir. Nice morning, sir!

GENTLEMAN. Yes: very fresh after London.

WAITER. Yes, sir: so all our visitors say, sir. Very nice family, Mrs Clandon's sir.

(II, 238)

The last sentence, praising Mrs Clandon's family for no particular reason other than phatic communication, is an example of the Approbation Maxim. The preceding remark *Only two minutes to wait, sir* illustrates the Tact Maxim – minimizing the cost of waiting for his interlocutor. The Agreement Maxim appears in the *Yes* and *Yes, sir* of both men, and in William's 'phatic' remark *Nice day, sir*. (Phatic communion is essentially a way of seeking ground for agreement on matters on which disagreement is virtually impossible.) There is, further, a hint of the Modesty Maxim in the waiter's addition: *so all our visitors say, sir*. Since Mr M'Comas has made a complimentary remark about the seaside resort where the waiter works, the waiter is obliged in modesty to attribute his agreement to the opinions of others. A further sign of politeness in the waiter's behaviour is his excessive use of respectful vocatives – here *sir*.[4]

It is noteworthy that William's behaviour, in vocatives as in other respects, is the opposite of that of the twins, who scandalize their mother by their overfamiliar use, in addressing Mr M'Comas, of his first name *Finch*. William's behaviour is the comical extremity of *over*politeness, whereas that of Dolly and Philip is the extremity of *under*politeness (not to be confused with *im*politeness, since the twins appear to cause offence in all innocence of the norms required). These are, therefore, two contrasting examples of exaggerated conversational behaviour – and it is significant that William and the twins are on the best of terms throughout the play, since William's departure from the norm in one direction compensates for the twins' departure in the other.

In this case, and in the play more generally, it is important to note that the conversational singularities of different characters are related to one another in a system of similarities and contrasts. This will be elucidated in due course (pp. 127–32), and summarized in table form. But first, some observations on the general significance in *You Never Can Tell* of the Maxims of Quality and Quantity.

9.5 Quality and quantity: rights and obligations

A recurrent problem for the play's characters is how to deal with unpleasant truths. For example, when Dolly and Philip demand to know who their father is, Mrs Clandon passes the buck to M'Comas, who has the unpleasant duty

of informing them that their father is none other than the objectionable
Fergus Crampton:

[9] MRS. CLANDON. [*earnestly, even a little peremptorily*] Dolly: Mr
M'Comas has something more serious than that to tell you . . .
MR M'COMAS. [*nervously*] . . . I was hardly prepared – er –
DOLLY. [*suspiciously*] Oh, we dont want anything prepared.
PHILIP. [*exhorting him*] Tell us the truth.
DOLLY. [*emphatically*] Bald headed.
M'COMAS. [*nettled*] I hope you intend to take what I have to say
seriously.

(II, 243)

The twins (believers, as we have seen, in freedom of information) see nothing problematic about telling the truth outright, 'bald headed'; their elders,
on the other hand, appear to regard this attitude as frivolous: truth, when
unpalatable, should be told indirectly, if at all.

Ironically, when the truth is out, M'Comas is blamed for his role as
breaker of bad news:

[10] PHILIP. Mr M'Comas: your conduct is heartless. Here you find a family
enjoying the unspeakable peace and freedom of being orphans. We
have never seen the face of a relative: never known a claim except the
claim of freely chosen friendship. And now you wish to thrust into
the most intimate relationship with us a man whom we dont know –
DOLLY. [*vehemently*] An a w f u l old man. [*Reproachfully*] And you
began as if you had quite a nice father for us!
M'COMAS. . . . . what right have you to choose your own father?

(II, 242)

M'Comas's reply to this unjust accusation is a rhetorical question which
confronts them with another recurrent theme of the play, interrelated with
that of information and truth: the theme of rights and responsibilities. In
effect, he is saying that, although the twins may have a right to information,
they have no right to change truth into falsehood.

When Mr Crampton is about to join the party, another awkward question
of truth-telling arises: who is to tell him that these unspeakably unman-
nered children, Dolly and Philip, are his own offspring?

[11] GLORIA. Which of us is to tell him the truth? . . .
MRS CLANDON. Finch, you must tell him.
DOLLY. Oh, Finch is no good at telling things. Look at the mess he
made at telling us.

(II, 245)

(Dolly, like Philip, shows herself to be a more modern equivalent of the king who executes the messenger bringing ill tidings.) Finally, a solution is found:

[12] PHILIP. . . . Mr M'Comas: this communication should be made, should
      it not, by a man of infinite tact?
      M'COMAS. It will require tact, certainly.

(II, 246)

The obvious candidate is the waiter:

[13] PHILIP. William: you remember my request to you to regard me as
      your son?
      WAITER. [*with respectful indulgence*] Yes, sir. Anything you please, sir.
      PHILIP. William: at the very outset of your career as my father, a rival
      has appeared on the scene.
      WAITER. Your real father, sir? . . .

(ibid.)

William finds the ideal way of telling Mr Crampton the bad news, by treating it as a joke. Talking of Philip, he says:

[14] WAITER. [*smoothly melodious*] Yes, sir. Great flow of spirits, sir. A vein
      of pleasantry, as you might say sir . . . The young gentleman's latest
      is that youre his father, sir.
      CRAMPTON. What!
      WAITER. Only his joke, sir, his favourite joke. Yesterday *I* was to be his
      father. . . .

(II, 248)

In this way, he exploits the previous joke (a licensed suspension of the Maxim of Quality) about his own paternity of the twins, and conveys the truth without causing offence, by appearing to tell an innocuous falsehood. Manifestly, William is an ingenious communicator: skilled in upholding the PP without sacrificing the CP.

The recurrent comic dilemma of truth and information (how do we uphold both the Maxim of Quality and the Maxim of Quantity?) interacts with the dilemma of how to uphold both the CP and the PP. This, in turn, raises the problem of how to reconcile rights with responsibilities. Whereas the twins assert their right to *know*, Mrs Clandon asserts her right to withhold *private* knowledge. Mr Crampton asserts his right to consideration as a (long-lost) parent, and the twins assert their right to choose their own parent. The assertion of a right frequently imposes a responsibility on others. So Mrs Clandon reluctantly accepts the responsibility to make sure her children know the truth. Mr Crampton (later in the play) asserts his right to parental respect, although he has assumed none of the responsibilities of parenthood. In the last act the twins beguile him into the discovery that to be truly considered a father, one has to grant one's children the right to be themselves.

9.6 Pragmatic abnormalities of character

Like William and the twins (see [9.4] above), the other characters exhibit deviant conversational behaviour with respect to the CP and the PP. Let us consider first Mr Crampton, whose 'deviation' appears to be a cynical distrust of others' words: in terms of pragmatic principles, he rejects the CP in interpreting the utterances of others, taking to extremes the well-motivated assumption that the PP must make the CP unreliable. Hence he repeatedly reads impolite meanings into other people's words, obsessively seeking causes for grievance under the polite or innocent surface of what is said. Thus, after meeting her husband for the first time in eighteen years, Mrs Clandon finds that breaking the ice can lead to immersion in cold water:

[15] MRS CLANDON. . . . . Fergus: you are greatly changed.
  CRAMPTON. [*grimly*] I daresay. A man does change in eighteen years.
  MRS CLANDON. [*troubled*] I – I did not mean that. I hope your health
      is good.

(II, 251)

In a similar fashion, Crampton succeeds in offending M'Comas, who is doing his limited best to keep the conversation alive at the lunch table:

[16] M'COMAS. We are getting on very nicely after all.
  DOLLY. [*critically*] After all! After all what, Finch?
  CRAMPTON. [*sarcastically*] He means that you are getting on very
      nicely in spite of the presence of your father. Do I take your point
      rightly, Mr M'Comas?
  M'COMAS . [*disconcerted*] No, no. I only said 'after all' to round off the
      sentence. I – er – er – er
  WAITER. [*tactfully*] Turbot, sir?

(II, 253)

William, again, shows his supreme tact by intervening just where the conversation is grinding to a disastrous halt. But Crampton has more pretexts for displeasure: on the sensitive matter of vocatives (see note 4), he quarrels with the twins for addressing him as 'Mr' – as a stranger (which, of course, he is):

[17] CRAMPTON. ... M i s t e r Crampton! What right have they to talk to me like that? I'm their father: ... have I no rights, no claims? [*Frantically*] My own children! M i s t e r Crampton! My –
VALENTINE. Come, come! theyre only children. She called you father.
CRAMPTON. Yes: 'goodbye, father'. Goodbye! Oh yes: s h e got at my feelings: with a stab!

(II, 259)

As this extract shows, Crampton perversely finds further fault when it is pointed out that his elder daughter Gloria did call him 'father'. Still on the subject of names, he takes umbrage once again on discovering that the daughter he named 'Sophronia' was renamed 'Gloria' by her mother. (The right of parents to name their children is one which few people, even today, would challenge.)

[18] GLORIA. Then my mother gave me a new name.
CRAMPTON. [*angrily*] She had no right to do it!

(II, 264)

Here once more, we note a key connection between impoliteness and the upholding of one's own rights at the expense of those of others.[5] Where normal behaviour is to look for implied *polite* meanings in what others say, his conversational pathology consists in finding *offensive* meanings where none was presumably intended.

We turn now to the pragmatic peculiarity of Gloria herself, which is her refusal to accept the patronage, or compliments, of others:

[19] VALENTINE. [*Pretending to forget himself*] How could that man [i.e. Crampton] have so beautiful a daughter!
GLORIA. ... That seems to be an attempt at what is called a pretty speech. Let me say at once, Mr Valentine, that pretty speeches make very sickly conversation ...

(II, 267)

The duel of love between Gloria and Valentine depends on a double irony: Valentine, the philanderer, finds himself in love, so that his flattery of Gloria is sincere in spite of himself. On the other hand, Gloria, who has been taught by her mother to be immune to such male blandishments, rejects his flattery, only to be utterly taken in by his cunningly sincere insults:

[20] VALENTINE. ... Youre a prig: a feminine prig: thats what you are. [*Rising*] Now I suppose youve done with me for ever ...
GLORIA. [*with elaborate calm, sitting up like a High-school-mistress posing to be photographed*] That shews how very little you understand my real character. I am not in the least offended.

(II, 269)

Flattery and insult are defined conversationally in terms of the Maxim of Approbation. To insult is to violate the maxim; to flatter is to obey the maxim, perhaps to the extent of violating the Maxim of Quality. Gloria's response – to reject a compliment and accept an insult – is an inversion of normal conversational practice. She has acquired (under her mother's tutelage) a strong commitment to a woman's right to independence, especially from the opposite sex. Hence, while a man's praise is suspect, a man's dispraise may reasonably be respected as genuine.

Her mother, Mrs Clandon, an author of books on modern parenthood, prides herself on granting independence to her children, whose privacy she respects by never asking them questions. Thus, back in Act I, she reproaches Philip for questioning her on the matter of the twins' paternity, and rebukes Dolly for her habit of asking personal questions, even of the stranger Valentine:

[21] MRS CLANDON. . . . Phil: I never ask you about your private concerns. You are not going to question me, are you?

(I, 224)

[22] DOLLY. [*eagerly*] Oh, tell us. How long has he given you to pay?
MRS CLANDON. [*distracted by her child's manners*] Dolly, Dolly, Dolly, DEAR! You must not ask questions.
DOLLY. [*demurely*] So sorry. Youll tell us, wont you, Mr Valentine?

(I, 227)

Mrs Clandon's vehemence in these matters reflects her strong conviction that *personal* information is not free, but belongs to the individual. However, that conviction is comically overruled when she finds her own curiosity and concern about Gloria's involvement with Valentine getting the better of her desire not to interfere:

[23] MRS CLANDON. . . . My dear?
GLORIA. . . . Yes.
MRS CLANDON. You know I never ask questions.
GLORIA. . . . I know, I know.

(III, 273)

Mrs Clandon's broad hint that she would like information without breaking her non-questioning rule is ignored by her daughter, who takes her remark 'You know I never ask questions' at its face value. This is an ironic inversion of the situation in [22], where Dolly apologizes for asking questions, but then elicits the information from Valentine nonetheless!

Valentine, in his turn, has a strange pragmatic eccentricity for a practised philanderer: an embarrassing predilection for telling the truth (observing the Maxim of Quality):

[24] GLORIA. . . . Is it true? Did you ever say that before? Did you ever feel that before? For another woman?
VALENTINE. [*bluntly*] Yes.

(III, 282)

In spite of such unpromising exchanges, the love match between Gloria and the impecunious Valentine prospers. Yet, even pressure from the family solicitor fails to deter Valentine from disarmingly and outrageously telling the truth:

[25] M'COMAS. . . . Miss Clandon: it is my duty to tell you that your father has also persuaded himself that Mr Valentine wishes to marry you –
VALENTINE. [*interposing adroitly*] I do.
M'COMAS. [*huffily*] In that case, sir, you must not be surprised to find yourself regarded by the young lady's father as a fortune hunter.
VALENTINE. So I am. Do you expect my wife to live on what I earn?

(III, 286)

(Note that Valentine not only tells a 'bare-faced truth', but also does so cleverly, in a way that reinterprets fortune hunting as a generous act, for the benefit of *others* rather than *self*.)

Improbable as the match between Gloria and Valentine seems, there is a good pragmatic reason behind it: Valentine's eccentricity (for a lover) of being a slave to the Maxim of Quality helps him to win Gloria's heart because it is the antithesis of her own eccentricity – a marked aversion to compliments, even when sincere.

The last two characters to be considered are the two lawyers – the solicitor M'Comas and the barrister Bohun. M'Comas is the least appealing character, in many ways a stock Shavian Aunt Sally.[6] In spite of his earlier reputation for advanced ideas, he is an ageing mouthpiece for conventional Victorian values. If he has an eccentricity, it is the eccentricity of his type: a tendency to take offence (thus frustrating the function of the PP) at the unconvention- alities (especially an unconventional devotion to the Maxim of Quality) of younger characters. This characteristic of M'Comas has been sufficiently illustrated in [9], [10] and [25].

The particularly infuriating eccentricity of Bohun is his habit of assuming control over the conversation, and denying conversational rights to others. This kind of conversational impoliteness may be appreciated by observing that turn-taking in conversation is a matter of exercising and granting rights to the 'conversational floor'.[7] To interrupt others, to usurp their conversa- tional ground, is a kind of rudeness akin to taking something that belongs to another person. Hence, in the real world, claiming the floor, particularly by interruption, is often accompanied by apologies, hedges and indirect requests: 'If I may put in a word here – . . .', 'Could I just say . . .', etc. Bohun, however, assuming the bullying, railroading manner of a stage advocate even in private conversation, dominates the floor, and has no compunction about refusing conversational rights to others:

[26] BOHUN. . . . In this family, it appears the husband's name is Crampton: the wife's, Clandon. Thus we have on the very threshold of the case an element of confusion.
VALENTINE. . . . But it's perfectly simple –
BOHUN. [*annihilating him with a vocal thunderbolt*] It is. Mrs Crampton has adopted another name. That is the obvious explanation which you feared I could not find out for myself. You mistrust my intelligence, Mr Valentine. – [*stopping him as he is about to protest*] no: I don't want you to answer that: I want you to think over it when you feel your next impulse to interrupt me.

(IV, 300)

His tactics are similarly domineering in persuading Mr Crampton that he would not benefit from claiming custody of the twins:

[27] BOHUN. . . . Now, Mr Crampton, . . . You think youd like to have your two youngest children to live with you. Well, you wouldn't [*Crampton tries to protest*] no you wouldnt: you think you would; but I know better than you . . .

(IV, 305–6)

Conversely, when Mrs Clandon, representing more normal conversational behaviour, apologizes for interrupting Bohun, Bohun brushes her apology aside, refusing to give the customary 'minimizing' response such as *Not at all*:

[28] MRS CLANDON. I am afraid we interrupted you, Mr Bohun.
BOHUN. [*calmly*] You did.

(IV, 303)

A further aspect of Bohun's pragmatic eccentricity is his tendency to make assertions about matters which are private or internal to other characters, or else are already known to them (to adopt a distinction of Labov and Fanshel 1977, he turns A events into A/B events). For example, in [26] he prohibits Valentine's intervention on a matter about which Valentine, not he, is informed, and insists instead on making the statement 'Mrs Crampton has adopted another name' himself. In [27] he suppresses Crampton's attempt to interrupt his own predictions of Crampton's present and future states of mind. This extreme form of conversational arrogance falls foul of the CP both by informing people of what they may be expected to know already (Maxim of Quantity) and by making claims about others' personal lives, apparently without adequate evidence (Maxim of Quality). Bohun's behaviour, in this respect, invites contrast with that of Mrs Clandon, who (as we noted earlier, p. 122) asserts her right to withhold personal information from the people (her children) most entitled to know it.

9.7 A system of pragmatic contrasts

The following table is a summary of the pragmatic deviances of the various characters as they have been noted above. This table suggests certain ways in which the characters naturally form pairs, in terms of their deviation from pragmatic norms. The relations may be either of repulsion or attraction, helping to explain why the plot of *You Never Can Tell*, as expressed through dialogue, is one of repulsion and attraction between different conversational 'styles' and the characters associated with them.

The Twins:	overrating CP (Quality, Quantity) and correspondingly undervaluing the PP
William:	overrating PP (without sacrificing CP)
Valentine:	overrating Quality (willing to sacrifice PP)
Gloria:	underrating PP (unwilling to sacrifice CP?)
Mrs Clandon:	overrating the children's right to independence and underrating Quantity
Mr Crampton:	underrating the children's right to independence, overrating PP and underrating CP in others' language
M'Comas:	taking offence (negative infringement of PP) especially at others' overrating of CP
Bohun:	giving offence (positive infringement of PP) and misconstrual of CP

However, the table oversimplifies, particularly in suggesting a stereotyping of character, whereas in the play itself there is character development, as the participants in the comedy learn through experience the mistakes associated with their particular pragmatic abnormalities.

Each character, except the irrepressible twins (and to a lesser extent M'Comas) finds that the eccentricity leads to discomfiture: each meets his or her 'come-uppance' before the end of the play. Bohun, the most stereotyped character of all, meets his severest come-uppance when Dolly quells him in the way he has quelled other conversational participants:

[29] DOLLY. [*striking in as Bohun, frowning formidably, collects himself for a fresh grapple with the case*] Youre going to bully us, Mr Bohun.

BOHUN. I –

DOLLY. [*interrupting him*] Oh yes, you are: you think youre not; but you are. I know by your eyebrows.

(IV, 306)

Correspondingly, William's discomfiture is acute when he is asked to sit down and behave as if he were an equal, rather than as an inferior, caring for the rest of the company.

[30] WAITER. [*earnestly*] Oh, if you please, maam, I really must draw the line at sitting down. I couldn't let myself be seen doing such a thing, maam: thank you, I am sure, all the same. [*He looks round from face to face wretchedly, with an expression that would melt a heart of stone.*]

(IV, 299)

Mrs Clandon and Crampton, as we have seen, are both mortified by their children's uncontrollable ability to set at nought their own ideas of 'polite' or 'correct' behaviour. Gloria and Valentine, on the other hand, are mortified by the experience of being in love with one another – their betrothal (at the end of the play) signalling their complete surrender to the fate of being under the control of the opposite sex: a bitter pill indeed for Gloria who has seen herself as the model of 'independent womanhood', and for Valentine who has vaunted himself 'the Duellist of Sex'.

9.8 'You never can tell'

The title of the play is a catchphrase used by William, the waiter, as the panacea for all future ills. In Act II, he uses the phrase to soothe the disconsolate Crampton, whose daughter appears likely to marry the penniless Valentine:

[31] WAITER. [*philosophically*] Well, sir, you never can tell. Thats a principle of life with me, sir, if youll excuse my having such a thing, sir. [*Delicately sinking the philosopher in the waiter for a moment*] Perhaps you havent noticed that you hadnt touched that seltzer and Irish, sir, when the party broke up. [*He takes the tumbler and sets it before Crampton*] Yes, sir, you never can tell. There was my son, sir! Who ever thought that he would rise to wear a silk gown, sir? And yet, today, sir, nothing less than fifty guineas. What a lesson sir!

(II, 261)

This apparently empty phrase sounds the consolatory note of the waiter's character: this nonpareil of politeness, submerging his own desires and interests in those of other characters, resolves the enmities and tensions exhibited through the conversational deformations of other characters. His 'overpoliteness', counteracting the 'underpoliteness' of other characters, finds a favourable resolution of all difficulties in the vague sentiment that the future is unpredictable, and things may well turn out better than you feared. So, at last, under William's ministrations, Crampton and Mrs Clandon are mollified; the children are reconciled with their father, and Gloria and Valentine bury their antipathies in a marriage which, nevertheless, promises to be less than blissful. The play ends with William's last words of comfort to Valentine:

[32] VALENTINE. [*collapsing on the ottoman and staring at the waiter*] I might as well be a married man already.

WAITER. [. . . *with ineffable benignity*] Cheer up, sir, cheer up. Every man is frightened of marriage when it comes to the point; but it often turns out very comfortable, very enjoyable and happy indeed, sir – from time to time. *I* never was master in my own house, sir: my wife was like your young lady . . . But if I had my life to live twice over, Id do it again: Id do it again, I assure you. You never can tell, sir: you never can tell.

(IV, 316)

Notes

1. An alternative pragmatic framework for analysing politeness in terms of 'face needs' is that of Brown and Levinson (1987), which has been applied to the analysis of drama by Simpson (1989).
2. Quotations and their page references are taken from Shaw, G.B. (1898), *Plays Pleasant*, Harmondsworth: Penguin Edition (1946). Ellipses indicate where I have omitted words from the original text. The singularities of Shaw's spelling have been retained.
3. Examples of characters' conversational behaviour shown in this text are illustrative of a tendency which I regard as to some extent typical. A more thorough analysis than has been undertaken here would contain a quantitative survey of pragmatic features as observed in the speech of different characters throughout the play.
4. Positions on the scale of Politeness (and on a closely related scale of respect/ deference) are often signalled by the use of vocatives and other forms of personal reference (see Ervin-Tripp 1972, Quirk et al. 1985: 773–5, Leech and Short 2007: 248–50). In *You Never Can Tell*, deviation in the use of vocatives is at various points a clear manifestation of pragmatic foregrounding . William's excessive use of vocatives as markers of respect is noted not only in [8] above, but in the following exchange, in which his *maam* contrasts with Mrs Clandon's familiar use of the first name *William*:

MRS. CLANDON. We shall have two more gentlemen at lunch, *William*.
WAITER. Right, *maam*. Thank you, *maam*.

(II, 239)

Note also how Dolly's outrageous addressing of M'Comas by his first name, *Finch*, is gently reproved by her mother's substitution of the more respectful form *Mr M'Comas*:

> DOLLY. [*to Mrs Clandon*] Has Finch had a drink?
> MRS CLANDON. [*remonstrating*] Dearest: Mr M'Comas will lunch with us.
>
> (II, 242)

Mrs Clandon's use of *dearest* above also brings to mind the power of familiar vocatives (in Mrs Clandon's case somewhat overused) to indicate loving family relationships. In this connection, we have seen Mr Crampton's sense of insult, in [7], when his own daughter addresses him with respectful distance as *Mr Crampton*. In the last Act, the reconciliation between Crampton and his children is correspondingly indicated by the familiar vocatives *my boy* (used by Crampton to Philip) and *dad* (used, overfamiliarly, by Philip to his father):

> CRAMPTON. [. . . *with an attempt at genial fatherliness*] Come along, my boy. Come along [*He goes*]
> PHILIP. [*Cheerily, following him*] Coming, dad, coming.
>
> (IV, 309)

In contrast, William continues to use the deferential *sir* to his own son Bohun, pointedly refusing to claim familiarity with someone so much above him in social station.

5. On the relevance to politeness of rights and responsibilities, see Thomas (1995: 124, 131).
6. M'Comas bears a close similarity, in this respect, to the ageing 'advanced thinker' Roebuck Ramsden in Shaw's *Man and Superman*.
7. On turn-taking and its relevance to politeness, see Sacks, Schegloff and Jefferson (1974) and Leech (1983: 139–42).

CHAPTER 10

Style in interior monologue: Virginia Woolf's 'The Mark on the Wall'

10.1 Introduction

This chapter examines Virginia Woolf's 'The Mark on the Wall', an early and apparently slight piece which E.M. Forster felt (in *Two Cheers for Democracy*, 1951: 255), for all its admirable qualities, seemed 'to lead nowhere'. On the other hand, I have long felt there is something special about 'The Mark on the Wall' – and part of its special quality is its seeming inconsequentiality (together with the emblematic inscrutability of the mark on the wall itself – which turns out to be a snail!). Lytton Strachey wrote to Leonard Woolf: 'How on earth does she make the English language float and float?'[1] – a remark which seems peculiarly appropriate to this work. And retrospectively, in a letter of 1931, Virginia herself wrote: 'I shall never forget the day I wrote "The Mark on the Wall", written all in a flash, as if flying after being kept stone breaking for months'.[2] The speed and spontaneity expressed through the style was apparently part and parcel of the composition process. At the same time, 'The Mark' has been called 'a manifesto of modernism',[3] and has the characteristic modernist openness to multiple interpretations.

As part of this multiplicity, there is a problem about what to call 'The Mark on the Wall'. As an exercise in stream-of-consciousness writing, is it a story? An essay? A diary entry? A literary experiment? Is it a piece of impromptu writing as a form of therapy (Virginia Woolf was recovering from a bout of severe mental illness at the time)? Part of its innovative (creatively foregrounded) quality lies in this blurring of the dividing lines between genres, and indeed the blending of several opposites we usually treat as distinct (such as fact and fantasy; inner and the outer experience; the specific and the universal; the precise and the imprecise). The analytic framework I shall use is loosely based on the one put forward in Leech and Short, *Style and Fiction* (2007 [1981]: 95–116) – which in turn is modelled on some aspects of Halliday's functional theory. This can be thought of as adopting a combination of formal and functional types of statement (see pp. 104ff), and using a tripartite hierarchy for each. From the formal point of view, we look at the three main coding levels of linguistic analysis: graphological/phonological, lexigrammatical and semantic. From the functional point of view, we interpret each of the formal levels in terms of three functional tiers: constructing a *text* (textual function), conveying a *representation* of some reality (ideational function) and communicating a *discourse* (interpersonal function). These correspond to the three 'macro-functions' of Halliday (1973), but only in a loose sense. As I see it, although both formal and functional triads form hierarchies, they are different – one being a coding (i.e. encoding or decoding) hierarchy, and the other an interpretative hierarchy (cf. Figure 8.2 in Chapter 8, p. 110).

Formal hierarchy	Functional hierarchy
SEMANTIC LEVEL	INTERPERSONAL FUNCTION (conducting a **discourse**)
encoded as	*rendered by means of*
LEXICOGRAMMATICAL LEVEL	IDEATIONAL FUNCTION (conveying a **representation**)
encoded as	*rendered by means of*
GRAPHO/PHONOLOGICAL LEVEL	TEXTUAL FUNCTION (constructing a **text**)

At the end of this chapter I will come to a strange conclusion: that this model of stylistic analysis, although revealing for this purpose, does not really *work* for the text under examination. I will argue that the three functions – although they need to be clearly distinguished for the purpose of analysis – in practice undergo a merger in this interior monologue mode of writing. In this way the foregrounded nature of stream-of-consciousness writing is recognized and clarified.

I will base most of my analysis on the following opening passage of 'The Mark on the Wall', which in many ways can be seen as representative of the whole work.

Extract A   *The Mark on the Wall*

Perhaps it was the middle of January in the present year that I first   1
looked up and saw the mark on the wall. In order to fix a date it is   2
necessary to remember what one saw. So now I think of the fire; the   3

steady film of yellow light upon the page of my book; the three   4
chrysanthemums in the round glass bowl on the mantelpiece. Yes, it   5
must have been the winter time, and we had just finished our tea,   6
for I remember that I was smoking a cigarette when I looked up   7
and saw the mark on the wall for the first time. I looked up through   8
the smoke of my cigarette and my eye lodged for a moment upon   9
the burning coals, and that old fancy of the crimson flag flapping   10
from the castle tower came into my mind, and I thought of the   11
cavalcade of red knights riding up the side of the black rock. Rather   12
to my relief the sight of the mark interrupted the fancy, for it is an   13
old fancy, an automatic fancy, made as a child perhaps. The mark   14
was a small round mark, black upon the white wall, about six or   15
seven inches above the mantelpiece.   16

How readily our thoughts swarm upon a new object, lifting it a   17
little way, as ants carry a blade of straw so feverishly, and then   18
leave it . . . If that mark was made by a nail, it can't have been for   19
a picture, it must have been for a miniature – the miniature of a   20
lady with white powdered curls, powder-dusted cheeks, and lips   21
like red carnations. A fraud of course, for the people who had this   22
house before us would have chosen pictures in that way – an   23
old picture for an old room. That is the sort of people they were –   24
very interesting people, and I think of them so often, in such queer   25
places, because one will never see them again, never know what   26
happened next. They wanted to leave this house because they wanted   27
to change their style of furniture, so he said, and he was in process   28
of saying that in his opinion art should have ideas behind it when   29
we were torn asunder, as one is torn from the old lady about to   30
pour out tea and the young man about to hit the tennis ball in the   31
back garden of the suburban villa as one rushes past in the train.   32

But for that mark, I'm not sure about it; I don't believe it was   33
made by a nail after all; it's too big, too round, for that. I might get   34
up, but if I got up and looked at it, ten to one I shouldn't be able to   35
say for certain; because once a thing's done, no one ever knows   36
how it happened. Oh! dear me, the mystery of life; the inaccuracy   37
of thought! The ignorance of humanity! To show how very little   38
control of our possessions we have – what an accidental affair this   39
living is after all in our civilization – let me just count over a few of   40
the things lost in one lifetime, beginning, for that seems always the   41
most mysterious of losses – what cat would gnaw, what rat would   42
nibble – three pale blue canisters of book-binding tools? Then there   43
were the bird cages, the iron hoops, the steel skates, the Queen Anne   44
coal-scuttle, the bagatelle board, the hand organ – all gone, and   45
jewels, too. Opals and emeralds, they lie about the roots of turnips.   46
What a scraping paring affair it is to be sure! The wonder is that   47

I've any clothes on my back, that I sit surrounded by solid furniture   48
at this moment. Why, if one wants to compare life to anything, one   49
must liken it to being blown through the Tube at fifty miles an hour   50
– landing at the other end without a single hairpin in one's hair!   51
Shot out at the feet of God entirely naked! Tumbling head over   52
heels in the asphodel meadows like brown paper parcels pitched   53
down a shoot in the post office! With one's hair flying back like the   54
tail of a race-horse. Yes, that seems to express the rapidity of life,   55
the perpetual waste and repair; all so casual, all so haphazard . . .   56

But after life. The slow pulling down of thick green stalks so that   57
the cup of the flower, as it turns over, deluges one with purple and   58
red light. Why, after all, should one not be born there as one is born   59
here, helpless, speechless, unable to focus one's eyesight, groping at   60
the roots of the grass, at the toes of the Giants? As for saying which   61
are trees, and which are men and women, or whether there are such   62
things, that one won't be in a condition to do for fifty years or so.   63
There will be nothing but spaces of light and dark, intersected by   64
thick stalks, and rather higher up perhaps, rose-shaped blots of an   65
indistinct colour – dim pinks and blues – which will, as time goes   66
on, become more definite, become – I don't know what . . .   67

And yet that mark on the wall is not a hole at all. It may even be   68
caused by some round black substance, such as a small rose leaf,   69
left over from the summer, and I, not being a very vigilant house-   70
keeper – look at the dust on the mantelpiece, for example, the dust   71
which, so they say, buried Troy three times over, only fragments of   72
pots utterly refusing annihilation, as one can believe.   73

In a full stylistic analysis, we would undertake a detailed analysis both of the three levels of coding, and of the three planes of functional interpretation. But every linguistic aspect of a text can be viewed formally as well as functionally, so this would seem tediously repetitive. Consequently, the analysis offered here deals mainly with the functional planes, and I will deal with the formal levels cursorily, treating them mainly as an initial platform on which to build the functional account. Both formal and functional analyses – for obvious reasons of space – will be selective rather than comprehensive.

10.2 The formal levels of phonology, lexigrammar and semantics

10.2.1 The phonological level

Characteristic of literary tradition are examples of phonological (including prosodic) repetition which appear to have an expressive function in the text. Note the effect of consonant and vowel repetition (alliteration and assonance) in the following passage – where the pronunciations of the underlined letters form part of a repetitive pattern:

[1] and that old <u>f</u>ancy of the <u>c</u>rimson <u>fl</u>ag <u>fl</u>apping from the <u>c</u>astle tower <u>c</u>ame into my mind, and I thought of the <u>c</u>aval<u>c</u>a<u>d</u>e of <u>r</u>e<u>d</u> knights <u>r</u>i<u>d</u>ing up the <u>s</u>i<u>d</u>e of the bl<u>a</u>ck ro<u>ck</u>. (ll. 10–12)

It seems that Woolf is aiming here at a poetic effect consonant with the romantic daydream sparked off by pictures in the fire. Note also the effect of the rhythmic repetition (a snatch of poetic metre) in the following:

[2] X / X / X / X / X / X /
    the steady film of yellow light upon the page (ll. 3–4)

where the evenly-paced iambic rhythm seems to reinforce the 'steadiness' of the light; and in the following:

[3] X   X   / X X / X X / X X / X
    With one's hair flying back like the tail of a race-horse (ll. 54–5)

where the triple-time rhythm (see pp. 47–8) appropriately suggests head-long movement.

10.2.2 The lexigrammatical level

On the lexigrammatical level, the most striking feature of 'The Mark on the Wall' is that it contains many stylistic features of impromptu conversation. Interior *monologue* might be considered a misnomer, since the representation of thought inevitably seems to contain *dialogic* elements[4] – a topic I will return to in section 10.6.

A number of features of conversational[5] syntax contribute to the spontaneity of interactive talk and here conjure up a sense of the human voice and the human mind acting in real time. At the same time – since conversation is a patently unregulated form of discourse – they also contribute to the impression that the narrator herself is undertaking a somewhat impulsive, impromptu exploration of 'reality', dwelling on the accidental and haphazard nature of existence:

1. **Interactional features** such as questions, response forms, exclamations and discourse particles, are typical of spoken dialogue, where one speaker is responding to another, or inviting such a response:

[4] Why, after all, should one not be born there as one is born here . . . ?
    (Question) (ll. 59–61)

[5] Yes, it must have been winter time . . . (Response form) (ll. 5–6)

[6] How readily our thoughts swarm upon a new object . . . (Exclamation) (l. 17)

[7] Oh! dear me, the mystery of life . . . (Discourse particles, interjections) (l. 37)

[8] . . . let me just count over a few of the things lost in one lifetime . . . (First-person imperative) (ll. 40–41)

2. **Minor sentences** are independent ('stand-alone') constructions without a finite verb. There are many examples of such constructions in the text:

[9]   A fraud, of course . . . (l. 22)

[10] But after life. (l. 57)

[11] Oh! dear me, the mystery of life; the inaccuracy of thought! The ignorance of humanity! (ll. 37–8)

3. **'Right dislocation'** (End dislocation) occurs when a stand-alone phrase follows a clause in which a pronoun 'stands proxy' for the phrase. It occurs quite naturally in colloquial speech:

[12] That is the sort of people they were – very interesting people, < . . . > (ll. 24–5)

4. **'Left dislocation'** (Front dislocation) is like 'right dislocation', except that the stand-alone phrase precedes the clause:

[13] Opals and emeralds, they lie about the roots of turnips. (l. 46)

5. **Progressive structure** is the kind of syntactic structure where clauses are strung out one after the other, in accordance with the 'add on' principle of everyday speech (see Leech and Short 2007: 183–5 and Biber et al. 1999: 1068–9):

[14] Yes, it must have been the winter time, and we had just finished out tea, for I remember that I was smoking a cigarette when I looked up and saw the mark on the wall for the first time. (ll. 5–8)

The underlined words here are linking words (subordinating or coordinating conjunctions) which simply connect one clause to another as if they were beads strung together.

6. **Parenthetical sentences** are inserted into a sentence of which they are only loosely a part, breaking up the linearity of the text as the speaker/ narrator spontaneously digresses. One test of parenthetical structures is that they can be omitted without affecting the structure and sense of the rest of the main sentence:

[15] To show how little control of our possessions we have – <u>what an accid-
      ental affair this living is after all our civilization</u> – let me just count over
      a few of the things lost in one lifetime, . . . (ll. 38–41)

7. **Parataxis** (or asyndeton) is the linking of equivalent structures without
any connective. It is like coordination, but the coordinating words (*and, or,
but* or *nor*) are omitted, and the effect is somewhat different. It is as if the
speaker is latching on to one idea after another, without any overt connection between them:

[16] It's <u>too big, too round</u> for that. (l. 34)
[17] Yes, that seems to express <u>the rapidity of life, the perpetual waste and
      repair; all so casual, all so haphazard</u> . . . (ll. 55–6)

8. **Anacoluthon** is a kind of grammatical mismatch, where a sentence begins
with one pattern, and then switches to another pattern:

[18] . . . <u>and I, not being a very vigilant housekeeper</u> – look at the dust on
      the mantelpiece, for example, the dust which, so they say, buried Troy
      three times over, only fragments of pots utterly refusing annihilation,
      as one can believe. (ll. 70–73)

Obviously, unlike most published texts, conversation is not carefully
planned and edited. Instead, it reflects the inconsequential, spur-of-the-
moment, production of language online. The cumulative effect of such a
range of conversational features – as well as other features not noted here –
gives to Woolf's style a lively, engaging immediacy. However, because of
poetic qualities, of which some have been noted and others will be noted
later, this conversational tone is far away from the ordinariness of conversation. One could say it is poetic matter using a conversational manner.

10.2.3 The semantic level

On the semantic level, we are interested in the way Woolf selects meanings,
to create a particular way of experiencing life, a particular 'mind style'
(Fowler 1977: 76, Leech and Short 2007 [1981]: 150–67). I will mention only
one or two examples, to prepare the way for consideration of the representation plane later.

   Colour terms occur often: *yellow (light), crimson (flag), red (knights), black
(rock), white (powdered curls), green (stalks).* These are just a sample of how
colourful is the impression we get of the world of outer reality or the world
of inner imagination as Woolf depicts them. This impression is also a lively
one, invigorated by the frequent use of verbs of motion such as *flapping*
and *riding.* Verbs of sudden or lively motion come thick and fast in certain
passages, such as the one describing life as a headlong journey:

[19] ... *blown* through the Tube at fifty miles an hour – *landing* at the other end without a single hairpin in one's hair! *Shot* out at the feet of God entirely naked! *Tumbling* head over heels in the asphodel meadows like brown paper parcels *pitched* down a shoot in the post office! (ll. 50–54)[6]

Another class of verbs of unusual frequency is that of psychological (including perceptual) verbs, such as *looked up, saw, remember, saw, think* – these are the first five verbs in the story, apart from the copula *to be*. This interspersing of physical motion verbs and psychological verbs, I find, evokes a particular kind of reality, in which physical and mental life – the mind and the body – are continually interacting with one another. This is more clearly enunciated in the combination of metaphor and simile which introduces the second paragraph:

[20] How readily our thoughts swarm upon a new object, lifting it a little way, as ants carry a blade of straw so feverishly, and then leave it . . . (ll. 17–19)

Here the mind's train of thought is explicitly likened to the 'feverish' swarming of ants. Note that Woolf portrays the stream of consciousness, here and elsewhere, to be active and adventurous: the term 'stream of consciousness' in this respect may give a misleading impression of passive drift. The interior monologue of thought, like the spontaneous speech of conversation, takes place in real time, and is impelled by its own momentum – asking questions, seeking and giving answers to problems, interrupting its own train of ideas, launching new topics.

10.3 A digression on the stream of consciousness

Before turning to the three functional planes of the model sketched in section 10.1, it is as well to consider the concept of **stream of consciousness** more carefully.[7]

The free flow of thoughts and impressions is something each of us experiences, and yet what we each experience in this way is ineffable, incommunicable. As Dorrit Cohn (1978) paradoxically puts it: 'The life-likeness of fiction < . . . > depends on what writers and readers know least in life: how another mind thinks, another body feels.' The reason for this is that the stream of conscious impressions we experience is not experienced in words: although some of it may be realized linguistically, much of it (sensory impressions, feelings, images, for example) lies beyond the explicit formulations of language, which can only capture the inner life of the mind through the second-hand or indirect means of description and figurative expression.

Representing this purely subjective stream of consciousness through language, therefore, is a piece of imaginative artifice. As an attempt to verbalize the non-verbal, stream-of-consciousness writing is comparable to the Shakespearean soliloquy. Making it seem 'real' to the reader means overstepping the limits of ordinary language – in short, it requires foregrounding, such as is found in poetry. The use of metaphor and simile in examples [19] and [20] above are vivid examples of this.[8] Other foregrounded devices take the form of ellipsis and disjunctivity, considered in sections 10.4–10.5 below.

10.4 The textual function

Text is a linear phenomenon. On the textual plane, we are interested in explaining the linear composition of the text: its TEXTURE.[9] But it is important to see linearity in terms of the way the sequence is partitioned into larger segments such as sentences or 'sense groups', and the way salience, or prominence, is given to some parts of the sequence rather than others. Three s-words – SEQUENCE, SEGMENTATION and SALIENCE (cf. Leech and Short 2007: 169–81) – form a useful mnemonic for what we are dealing with on the textual level. Let us see how these three factors operate in the very first sentence and what follows it.

[21] Perhaps it was the middle of January in the present year that I first looked up and saw the mark on the wall.

The first sentence is a carefully balanced and articulated statement, rather like the initial exposition of a theme in music. The construction is that of a cleft sentence (a sentence in two parts as in *It was X that Y*), in which the pivotal point (before *that*) occurs exactly – if we count words – in the middle, at the point marked FULCRUM:

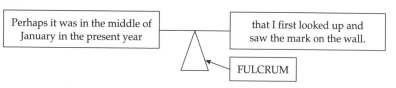

Figure 10.1 The first sentence

The first half of the sentence begins with a modality indicator (*perhaps*), then moves in sequence through a reference to a past time (*in the middle of January in the present year*), an event involving the narrator (*I first looked up and saw . . .*) and finally, an object (*the mark on the wall*), which, because it has end focus in the sentence, bears the major emphasis, as regards informational salience, of the sentence. (In reading aloud, this is where the main nucleus of the intonation contour would naturally occur.) The information loading of the sentence progresses from 'given information', what is relatively familiar, as we see from the mention of 'the present year', to what is relatively new and unexpected information – at least, to the reader. This gives appropriate salience on first mention, of course, to 'the mark on the wall' as the recurrent theme (*leitmotiv*) of the story. It is sometimes useful, though, to explore the effect of a piece of text by comparing other means of expressing the same meaning (see Hoover 2004), and this I shall briefly do now.

Clearly the effect would have been diminished by rearranging the sentence thus:

[22] Perhaps I first looked up and saw the mark on the wall in the middle of January of the present year.

(This shifts the end focus from the 'mark' to the past-time component, and removes the balancing, double-focusing effect of the cleft sentence.) Or thus:

[23] Perhaps it was the mark on the wall that I first looked up and saw in the middle of January.

(This completely changes the effect by altering the focus of the cleft sentence, so that the OBJECT rather than the TIME is focused.) This second stylistic variant is thought-provoking, though, for it invites us to ask why Woolf chose the cleft sentence construction, placing the cleft focus not on the 'mark', but on the time, thus giving the sentence two distinct (and differently signalled) points of salience. Part of the answer, presumably, is that she had two distinct points to make in the same sentence. For us, the readers, it is necessary to fasten on the significance of 'the mark on the wall' as the theme of the text. But for the 'voice', the author's inner persona (whom I will call the *narrator*), it is also important to reconstruct the time. For her, the 'mark' is what is important. But what troubles her, in her retrospective reverie, is when (and hence how and why) it first made its appearance – something likely to throw light on the nature of the mark itself. Note that the two points could have also been made by putting the time phrase in first position, without using the framing effect (*It was . . . that*) of the cleft sentence:

[24] Perhaps in the middle of January in the present year I first looked up and saw the mark on the wall.

But this would have left unclear the source of the narrator's puzzlement, the locus of uncertainty. The framing effect of *Perhaps it was . . . that* makes it clear that the modal adverb *perhaps* applies to the time of discovery. The cleft sentence construction also has another effect. By the implication of given-ness, signalled by the 'presupposition' part of the cleft sentence, ... *that I first looked up and saw the mark on the wall*, Woolf subtly puts us in the middle of an 'evolving discourse situation', as we tune in to the voice of a narrator recalling a prior experience, a landmark in the memory.

Too much attention may have already been given to the first sentence. But, before moving on, let us notice the very first word of all, which itself has a kind of salience as the text's starting point. *Perhaps* is a word of doubt already signalling that we are not dealing with an omniscient author, but with a narrator who is uncertain about the realities of the world she wishes to explore.

Considering texture will also lead us to note how the phrase 'the mark on the wall' recurs in line 8, this time in a medial position in the sentence, since it is no longer (for the purposes of this text) new information. Instead, the position of end focus is now occupied by *for the first time*, elaborating on the unobtrusive medial adverb *first* in the opening sentence, and giving more prominence to the initial discovery of the mark, as the clue that might resolve the narrator's puzzlement:

[25] I looked up and saw the mark on the wall <u>for the first time</u>.

If we compare this with the first sentence, the reversal of focal and non-focal elements seems to be motivated by contrastive emphasis: the implication[10] is that the narrator has noticed the mark on the wall not just once, but a number of times. This in turn leads to part of the 'pre-history' of the narra-tive which will have implications for what follows: the repeated return of the narrator's attention to the mark in the rest of this story will seem simply a continuation of what has happened before.

A further recurrence of *the mark* in lines 12–13 signals another shift in attention:

[26] Rather to my relief the sight of <u>the mark</u> interrupted the fancy ...

The 'mark on the wall', now abbreviated as a thing taken for granted, occurs even more unobtrusively here in a medial and subordinate position. But in further repetitions, in lines 19, 33, and 68, the 'mark' keeps cropping up in the initial topic position, as its thematic role is restated:

[27] If <u>that mark on the wall</u> was made by a nail ...
[28] But <u>for that mark</u>, I'm not sure about it ...
[29] And yet <u>that mark on the wall</u> is not a hole at all ...

There are nine occurrences of the word 'mark' in the extract quoted, and several more instances of this return to the 'mark on the wall' in the part of the text not quoted. Finally, in the conclusion to the story, the 'the mark on the wall' is given solitary exclamatory emphasis in a sudden denouement:

Extract B
– but something is getting in the way . . . Where was I? What has it all been about? A tree? A river? The Downs? Whitaker's Almanack? The fields of asphodel? I can't remember a thing. Everything's moving, falling, slipping, vanishing . . . There is a vast upheaval of matter. Someone is standing over me and saying:
   'I'm going out to buy a newspaper.'
   'Yes?'
   'Though it's no good buying newspapers . . . Nothing ever happens. Curse this war; God damn this war! . . . All the same, I don't see why we should have a snail on the wall.'
   Ah, the mark on the wall! It was a snail.

In the very last line of the text, as in the first sentence, the 'mark on the wall' makes its appearance again, leading to the anticlimactic disclosure 'It was a snail'.

Segmentation: variation in sentence length
In this section on texture, some attention has been given already to two of the trio of s-terms: *sequence* (the order in which elements occur), and *salience* (focus and defocusing, which are themselves largely dependent on sequencing). It is time to say something now about *segmentation*: the most obvious device of segmentation in a written text is punctuation, particularly a full stop (or an equivalent question mark or exclamation mark) signalling a sentence break. If we trace the length of sentences through the quoted passages, we notice a great deal of variation, which relates to the expressive effect of those sentences. Particularly at the beginnings of paragraphs, as if the narrator is launching abruptly into a new domain, sentences tend to be short:

[30] But after life. (l. 57).

or else made up of short staccato units:

[31] But for that mark, I'm not sure about it; I don't believe it was made by a nail after all; it's too big, too round, for that.

Elsewhere, in the middle of elaborative episodes, sentences can be exceptionally long, as the narrator launches into a fresh flight of fancy, piling up impressions in a higgledy-piggledy manner:

[32] To show how very little control of our possessions we have – what an accidental affair this living is after all in our civilization – let me just

count over a few of the things lost in one lifetime, beginning, for that seems always the most mysterious of losses – what cat would gnaw, what rat would nibble – three pale blue canisters of book-binding tools? (ll. 38–43)

In the final few lines of the text, already quoted as Extract B, there is a veritable torrent of brief interrogatives of which a sample is: *Where was I? What has it all been about? A tree? A river? The Downs? Whitaker's Almanack? The fields of asphodel? I can't remember a thing* – and so on. This spate of minisentences ends abruptly in the last two brief sentences already quoted: *Ah, the mark on the wall! It was a snail.*

We can sense from these examples that variations in sentence length have dramatic potential. In ordinary prosaic writing, it is often a good idea to construct sentences of roughly average length – say, around 18 words plus or minus 5 – rather than to indulge in hugely elaborated sentences (which tend to be difficult to unravel) or overly short sentences (which tend to disconnect the thread of ideas). In literary writing, on the other hand, unusually long or unusually short sentences will draw attention to themselves (i.e. will be foregrounded), having rhetorical effect. Consider the loss of effect, for example, if the final two sentences of the text had been collapsed into a single more orthodox sentence: *Ah, the mark on the wall was a snail.* For Woolf, it seems, unusually long sentences contribute to dramatic build-up and involvement, whereas unusually short sentences contribute to a sense of sudden change, of revelation, of finality.[11]

10.4.1 Repetition

Another aspect of sequence and segmentation which calls attention to itself is repetition; in direct contrast to variation, which is the sequential exploitation of difference, repetition is the sequential exploitation of sameness. The management of variation and repetition is one of the requirements of composition for any speaker or writer. But when there is more repetition than necessary, we do feel the need for an explanation, a 'warranty' for it. We wonder, for example, why the narrator insists on repeating so often *the mark*, or its lengthier equivalent *the mark on the wall*, even though there is no other 'mark' in the text, so that *the mark* should be a sufficiently explicit expression. The effect is similar to the repetition of a *leitmotiv*, or a recurrent snatch of thematic melody, in different positions and different guises in a musical work. The sequence of short sentences at the end, culminating in the last two abrupt sentences, including 'the mark', is again reminiscent of musical effect: where (a device of Beethoven's) a convulsive sequence of repetitious phrases or chords, partially repeating an earlier theme, brings a work to a climactic conclusion. Tempting as it is to see such musical analogies in Woolf's writing, here the analogy is only partial, since the effect of this repetition in 'The Mark on the Wall' is not so much symphonic as bathetic (section 10.4.2). How could a mere mark on a wall, whatever its origin, achieve such importance as is suggested by the rather obsessive repetition of the phrase in this story?

Interestingly, the banal-seeming phrase *the mark on the wall* is itself invested with some repetitive musical quality. The two parallel nominal phrases *the mark* and *the wall* form a weak parallelism (*the* X [*on*] *the* Y), and are symmetrically placed around the pivotal syllable *on*. The weak parallelism is made slightly stronger by the fact that X and Y are both monosyllabic nouns. Although this patterned structure of *the mark on the wall* is only mildly foregrounded, it does seem to give the phrase a certain inflated dignity, increased by its repetition. For example, if *the mark on the wall* were replaced throughout by something like *that mark* (*Ah, that mark! It was a snail*) – the effect would again be diminished.

However, the repetitiveness of the final passage (quoted above in Extract B), is not just a matter of repeating *the mark on the wall*: there are also consecutive forms of repetition of grammatical and lexical structure, belonging to a long rhetorical and literary tradition as types of parallelism (see Chapter 2, pp. 21–2). Examples – with the repetitions underlined – are:

[33] <u>Where</u> was I? <u>What</u> has it all been about? [Repetition of *wh*-questions]
[34] <u>A</u> tree? <u>A</u> river? [Repetition of <u>a</u> + noun as a question]
[35] Curse <u>this war</u>; God damn <u>this war!</u> [Repetition of verb + <u>this war</u>]

Examples of parallelism in the text are frequent, and occur with greater density than could be supposed to occur by accident. Another example, this time from the first few lines of the text, is:

[36] the steady film of yellow light upon the page of my book;
    the three chrysanthemums in the round glass bowl on the mantelpiece.
    (ll. 3–5)
[37] what cat would gnaw, what rat would nibble, (ll. 42–3)

Here it is not the repetition of words that is striking, but the repetition of grammatical structures. In [36] the pattern (*the* + modifier + noun + prep. + (*the*) + adj. + noun + prep. + *the* + noun . . .) has the effect of underlining the meticulous factual detail summoned up by the narrator's memory. In [37] the pattern is more compact (*what* + noun + *would* + verb), and is reinforced by rhyme (*c<u>at</u> / r<u>at</u>*) and alliteration (*<u>gn</u>aw/ <u>n</u>ibble*) as well as semantic similarities (*cat / rat; gnaw / nibble*).

10.4.2 Iconicity and bathos

In examining the texture of an everyday, run-of-the-mill piece of writing, we are primarily concerned with how a writer makes a 'well behaved' text in terms of the three factors already mentioned: sequence, segmentation and salience. However, in a literary text, we expect to see reasons for interesting departures from the norm (for example in variation and repetition), and these phenomena may need explanation beyond the form of the text itself, on the planes of representation (ideational rhetoric) and discourse (interpersonal rhetoric). I have already offered some essentially iconic explanations for textual features such as the steady rhythmic repetition of *the steady film of yellow light upon the page* (ll. 3–4). To say that a text has iconic potential is to say that it invites interpretation of texture as in some way imitative of the representation – the unfolding world of reality constructed through the text. For the present text, on the ideational plane, it can be recognized that these features of the text invite iconic 'enactment' of the meaning in our minds; but, on the discourse plane, these typically literary iconic effects turn out to be undercut by the ironic or humorous tenor of the work as a discourse. Among the textual features lending themselves to this treatment are a number of examples of what may be called 'bathos', a form of irony which results from build-up (towards a climax) followed by let-down (or anticlimax):

[38] Opals and emeralds, they lie about the roots of turnips. (l. 46)

In this simple, epigrammatic sentence, the ordering is crucial: from the opulently poetic *opals and emeralds* we move to that most prosaic and bathetic of root vegetables, the *turnip*.

Turning once more to the first sentence and to the last two sentences of the text, we see bathos in action again. The first sentence, as already noted, places 'the mark on the wall' in the climactic position of end focus: but to appreciate this as an example of bathos, it is best to quote the sentence once again, omitting this key phrase:

Perhaps it was the middle of January in the present year that I first looked up and saw . . .

Let us imagine our first encounter with this text, experiencing it linearly from left to right, in the order basic to our way of experiencing any sentence. The sentence is remarkable for the way it builds up expectation. This is done by the delaying effect of syntax: partly by the cleft sentence construction, and also by the use of two introductory adverbials, one a complex prepositional phrase. Prose tradition leads the unprepared reader to expect something fairly momentous: an opening sentence, particularly one constructed so climactically at the beginning of a story, should evoke suspense and excitement. So it is (from this point of view) disappointing that the object of the verb *saw* is not, for example, 'the man who was to change my life' or 'a flying saucer circling around the United Nations building', but something so trivially domestic as a mark on a wall!

As the culmination of the whole story, the bathos of the last two sentences (*Ah, the mark on the wall! It was a snail*) is easier to grasp if we have read all the way through the text. We will have experienced the expansive reveries which have led the narrative through one imaginative adventure after another. A myriad of topics have been explored, moving now to the trifling everyday impedimenta of life and now to profound issues of historic, philosophical or religious truth. It seems that the narrator's mental odyssey, unfolding under its own momentum, will continue for ever, as she shows no inclination to use direct action to solve the problem she has set herself:

[39] No, no, nothing is proved, nothing is known. And if I were to get up at this very moment and ascertain that the mark on the wall is really – what shall we say? < . . . > what should I gain? – Knowledge? < . . . > and what is knowledge? [< . . . > signals omissions from the text.]

In this extract (from part of the text not previously quoted), the narrator rather comically contemplates direct physical intervention to solve the riddle of the mark, but nothing comes of it: the reverie launches into yet another imaginative digression. And so, at last, the only way the quest manages to reach a conclusion is by the brusque masculine intrusion already quoted. The bathos here lies in the fact that the mark, which has been the object of such concentrated speculation, turns out to be, if anything, even less worthy of attention than previously thought. (Is it accidental that *snail* and *nail* rhyme – that, indeed, the *nail* is, as it were, phonologically and orthographically enveloped in the *snail*?) At least the nail would have a human history, giving room for imaginative reconstructions of how it came to be there. But the snail is nothing but a palpable reproach to the narrator who describes herself as 'not being a very vigilant housekeeper', a description ironically illustrated by her apparent inactivity through the whole length of the text.

10.5 The ideational function: representation of (mock) reality

On the representation plane, we consider 'The Mark on the Wall' as an ongoing fictional or non-fictional reality – as a story. (We are not sure if the text describes real goings-on or imaginary ones, and it seems not to matter which. In this respect, 'The Mark on the Wall' shows a typical characteristic of lyric poetry.) At this simplistic level, the story begins, as any traditional story should, with an enigma: what is the mark on the wall? And the quest is for the identity of the mark on the wall, the revelation of which is absurdly postponed time after time. Finally the enigma is solved, and closure is reached. Although in Extracts A and B I have presented only a page or two from the beginning and ending of the story, these extracts are representative of the whole story in the following respect: it continues a cyclic pattern, digressing and returning to the 'mark' again and again, until the narrator's reverie is finally shattered, and she is confronted by a matter-of-fact truth. Some periodic reappearances of the mark on the wall are these (each '< . . . >' standing for a major episode of digression):

[40] In certain lights that mark on the wall seems actually to project from the wall.
< . . . >
[41] And if I were to get up at this very moment and ascertain that the mark on the wall is really –
< . . . >
[42] I must jump and see for myself what that mark on the wall really is –
< . . . >
[43] Still, there's no harm in putting a full stop to one's disagreeable thoughts by looking at a mark on the wall.
< . . . >

Text is the vehicle for the representation. So one aspect of the reader's interpretation process is the recovery of the representation from the text. To some extent, this is just a matter of decoding the meanings of words, phrases and sentences. But it is also a matter of discovering the reference of referring expressions such as pronouns and full noun phrases, and of filling in gaps which the text leaves in its representation of reality. This is the domain of what is sometimes called 'referential pragmatics' (Leech 1983: 11), or what I here call, following Halliday's terminology, IDEATIONAL pragmatics. It is where the implicatures of Grice's Cooperative Principle operate (see Chapter 9, p. 120), or more generally, where inferential strategies do their work in teasing out meaning and reference.

Woolf's text is somewhat problematic from this point of view, in a way which is not unusual in twentieth-century fictional prose, in its exploration of subjectively experienced reality. She sprinkles the text with many information gaps, for which readers have to construct 'bridging assumptions'. This particularly arises with items of definite reference, such as the definite article *the*, demonstratives like *that*, and personal pronouns like *he*. Such items normally imply a common ground of knowledge of context shared between addresser and addressee, but the common ground here is often left for the reader to reconstruct. Returning yet again to the opening sentence, we note that the phrase *the mark on the wall* is introduced by the definite article, suggesting prior knowledge of the identity of the mark in question – something which we as readers obviously do not yet share. This device of 'in medias res', a common feature of modern fiction, suggests that the narrator is drawing upon a past history of familiar things and events that we, as readers, are fictionally assumed to know about. (Notice the difference if we were to substitute *a mark on the wall* for *the mark on the wall* in the first sentence.) The effect is taken further in the subsequent sentence – for example (in ll. 4–5):

[44] the three chrysanthemums in the round glass bowl on the mantelpiece

This shows more furnishings of the domestic scene of which the narrator assumes prior familiarity. Further down, in lines 10–12, the information gaps become more daring and challenging to the reader:

[45] that old fancy of the crimson flag flapping from the castle tower came
      into my mind, and I thought of the cavalcade of red knights riding up
      the side of the black rock.

To make sense of these definite references, we have to reconstruct something much more familiar to Virginia Woolf's generation than our own: the traditional British parlour with its open coal fire, and the traditional children's fantasy (typically encouraged by adults) of seeing pictures in the fire. Presumably, the flames licking around the coal would suggest 'crimson flags', or 'red knights' climbing the side of a 'black rock'. At this point there has been a transition from the familiar furniture of the room to the familiar furniture of the imagination, hingeing on another definite reference: *that old fancy*.

The information gaps are of various kinds, and definite reference is only their most usual trigger. For example, lower down, in lines 19–22, there appears to be the beginning of a logical argument, signalled by an *if*-clause and a conditional sentence:

[46] If that mark was made by a nail, it can't have been for a picture, it must
      have been for a miniature – a miniature of a lady with white powdered
      curls, powder-dusted cheeks, and lips like red carnations.

As the sentence proceeds, it becomes a total *non sequitur*; yet, again, as we readers make the effort to bridge the gaps, we try to unravel an implicit argument, perhaps as follows. The mark (as it says in lines 14–16) is only a few inches above the projecting mantelpiece; therefore the nail – if such it is – would be only high enough on the wall to permit the hanging of a miniature picture. This leads to a further unsignalled transition from the assumed world of reality to the world of what is unreal, yet somehow real as a stereotype,[12] as the narrator summons up a picture (of *a lady with white powdered curls*) which might have hung there. Moving on, we find yet further missing links:

[47] A fraud, of course, for the people who had this house before would
      have chosen pictures in that way – an old picture for an old room.
      (ll. 22–24)

A fraud, of course is puzzling: why is the imaginary miniature a fraud? Presumably, as the narrator goes on to hint, because the previous owners, who must have hung the hypothetical picture there, were not people who would own real antique family heirlooms. They were able only to give a false impression of family lineage by buying an *old picture for an old room*. And, incidentally, why is the miniature considered to be antique? I suppose, because the imagined lady with 'white powdered curls' is in the fashion of the eighteenth century – a period sufficiently remote from the early-twentieth century to give the right genteel feeling of wealth and antiquity.

Once again, gaps are signalled (but not explained) by another definite expression, here, in the repeated and emphasized use of *that*:

[48] would have chosen pictures in *that* way (l. 23)
[49] *That* is the sort of people they were   (l. 24)

This recurrence of unreferenced definiteness in the text could be pursued further, but I will mention only one more particularly striking example, this time an unreferenced use of the pronouns *he* and *she,* as well as *the*, in the episode in lines 28–32:

[50] . . . so <u>he</u> said, and <u>he</u> was in process of saying that in his opinion art should have ideas behind it when we were torn asunder, as one is torn from <u>the</u> old lady about to pour tea and <u>the</u> young man about to hit <u>the</u> tennis ball in <u>the</u> back garden of <u>the</u> suburban villa as one rushes past in the train.

Here the repeated *the* suggests the generic use of the definite article, indicating a single 'typical' instance of a category held up as an instance of the whole class. This use of *the* seems to tell us 'Of course, we all know what that experience is like – it's an inescapable fact of railway travel' – yet, the scene is highly particularized. It appears that the narrator's mind contains images peculiar to her own experience, like the 'cavalcade of red knights' and 'the lady with white powdered curls' already mentioned. Yet these are presented as somehow typical and general.

From the interpreting reader's point of view, this 'problematic' inexplicitness of the text in reflecting the representation ultimately invites explanation on the discourse plane. I will merely return, at this point, to the obvious observation that this discourse is a kind of *interior monologue*, representing the sequence of unverbalized or semi-verbalized impressions which (our common experience tells us) largely takes place in the stream of consciousness. At the same time as Virginia Woolf was experimenting with her interior monologue technique, James Joyce was experimenting along very different lines in *Ulysses*.[13] Yet both experiments, interestingly enough, involved the liberal use of information gaps. If writing is to give a realistic experience of the largely subconscious or semiconscious inner flow of the mind, it seems that much of what is thought must remain implicit, below the level of conscious verbalization. Another feature of interior monologue is the sudden switch to a new topic, observed in:

[51] look at the dust on the mantelpiece, for example, the dust which, they say, buried Troy three times over (ll. 71–2)

The first use of *the dust* here refers to the tiny amount of dust on the mantelpiece, whereas the second refers to a vast quantity of dust accumulating across the millennia. The syntactic linkage of a relative clause (beginning with *which*) brings together an immense disparity of physical scale, place and time, within the same sentence.[14]

On the representation plane itself – as a kind of story – the work appears both remarkably simple and, yet again, incongruous. First, as already noted, the story line is apparently of the utmost triviality. Secondly, it consists almost entirely of digressions. If the main 'plot' is the search for the mark's identity, there is no serious plot development at all, and, as in Lawrence Sterne's *Tristram Shandy*, the work's *raison d'être* appears to lie in the virtuosity of its digressions. The story, in fact, is built on a periodic structure resembling that of a rondo (in music) or a rondel (in poetry): a cyclic pattern whereby the main theme, the mark itself, after its initial statement, is repeated again and again between successive detours: *a b a c a d a e a . . . a*. However, in Extract A, we note how the mental digressions develop into excursions further and further away from the starting point. The first excursus (lines 2–16) tracks the immediate domestic history of the 'mark' – when it was first noticed. The second excursus (lines 17–32) explores a more distant and conjectural history relating to the previous owners of the house. The third excursus (lines 33–56) takes us yet further afield, to the generally uncertain and haphazard nature of life, and this leads directly on to a fourth excursus indulging in fanciful speculations about life after death (lines 57–67). In summary:

Digression 1: the immediate past
Digression 2: the more distant hypothetical past
Digression 3: the imaginary present
Digression 4: the imaginary future
. . .

And so on, this recursive structure continues through nine pages – until we reach the conclusion in Extract B. Thus, although it is nominally about 'the mark on the wall', in practice the story immerses us in the inner life of the mind, from which we briefly emerge from time to time as the 'mark' comes back to notice yet again.

A further unusual aspect of the representation is its merging of the vague or fanciful with the meticulously factual. This merger has already cropped up in the first sentence, where we have observed a sequence of modality (*perhaps* – uncertainty), time (*the middle of January in the present year*), event (*I looked up and saw . . .*) and an observed object (*the mark on the wall*). The narrator seems to be painstakingly trying to recover the exact set of circumstances which originally brought the mark to notice. A similar set of circumstantial details is spelt out in the following definite noun phrases, loaded with adjectival or other modifiers: *the three chrysanthemums* in *the round glass bowl*, and *the small round mark, black upon the white wall, about six or seven inches above the mantelpiece*. Later, in lines 42–6, after lamenting the 'mystery of life' and 'the inaccuracy of thought', the narrator gives us a highly specific, though oddly ill-assorted, list of things lost: *three pale blue canisters of book-binding tools, the bird cages, the iron hoops, the steel skates, the Queen Anne coal scuttle, the bagatelle board, the hand organ*. She is keen to demonstrate, it seems, that despite a sense of overwhelming impenetrable confusion, the mind can still pin down the minutiae of factual reality.

The impression, however, is that certainty is overwhelmed by uncertainty, imprecision by vagueness. Imprecision or uncertainty is conveyed by many different linguistic devices. First, there is the overt exclamation, the *cri de cœur*:

[52] Oh! dear me, the mystery of life; the inaccuracy of thought! The ignorance of humanity! (ll. 37–8)

Secondly, there are modal adverbs and modal auxiliaries. The first word of the text, *perhaps*, occurs more than once in Extract A, and six times in the whole text. Modals are often epistemic, expressing varying degrees of uncertainty:

[53] Yes, it <u>must</u> have been the winter time (ll. 5–6)
[54] it <u>can't</u> have been for a picture (ll. 19–20)
[55] the people who had this house before us <u>would</u> have chosen pictures in that way (ll. 22–3)
[56] ten to one I <u>shouldn't</u> be able to say for certain (ll. 35–6)

Other devices of uncertainty are the combining of words like *certain* and *sure* with negatives; the hypothetical use of the past tense; the use of question marks: *three pale blue canisters of book-binding tools?*, and the non-completion of sentences. The following clause, which ends one of the digressions, grasps at precision, but then peters out into vague uncertainty:

[57] which will, as time goes on, become more definite, become – I don't know what . . . (ll. 66–7)

In different episodes, happenstance and uncertainty are explored, in relation to the past (roughly ll. 1–46), in relation to the imaginary present (roughly ll. 1–46–56; 68–73; also in Extract B), and in relation to the future (ll. 57–67), progressively widening the story's world of reference, and taking it further away from the reality of the present moment.

In all, examination of the mind style, on the representation plane, suggests that the interior monologue brings together apparent contradictions: between

FACT and FANTASY (e.g. *the round glass bowl* . . . *the crimson flag*, ll. 5, 10)

the PARTICULAR and the GENERAL (e.g. *the young man about to hit the tennis ball*, l. 31)

the PRECISE and the IMPRECISE (e.g. *become more definite* < . . . > *I don't know what*, l. 67)

the TRIVIAL and the GRAND, the NON-TRIVIAL (e.g. *the dust on the mantelpiece,* < . . . > *the dust which* < . . . > *buried Troy*, ll. 71–3)

ORDERLINESS and DISORDERLINESS

OUTER REALITY OF 'FACT' and INNER REALITY OF IMAGINATION

(The last two pairs of opposition need no further illustration.) In this merging of opposites, 'The Mark on the Wall' is an exploration of 'modern consciousness' which Woolf elsewhere attributes to the 'ordinary person' as follows:

> . . . He follows every thought careless where it may lead him. He discusses openly what used never to be mentioned even privately. And this very freedom and curiosity are perhaps the cause of what appears to be his most marked characteristic – the strange way in which things that have no apparent connection are associated in his mind. Feelings which used to come single and separate do so no longer. Beauty is part ugliness; amusement part disgust; pleasure part pain. Emotions which used to enter the mind whole are now broken up on the threshold.
>
> ('The narrow bridge of art', *Collected Essays* II: 222)[15]

10.6 The interpersonal function

The discourse plane is where, if anywhere, the whole interpretation of a text is brought together, by taking account of the overarching stance of the implied author (or narrator), subsuming the world-view represented in its ideational representation. But let us first consider the interpersonal character of 'The Mark on the Wall' in a more direct way. What kind of relationship between speaker/writer and addressee does the work presuppose? Ostensibly the work is an interior monologue – representing a single narrator and the 'voice of her mind'.

It is worth reminding ourselves that at the time of 'The Mark on the Wall's' writing, the interior-monologue technique it represents was a considerable innovation. The normal expectation, with a written text, is that there is a difference between the 'author' and the 'readership', as writer and recipient of the work. There is also a long narrative tradition whereby the author maintains a distinctly different identity from characters in the fictional reality of the work, using, for example, clear devices of direct and indirect speech reporting to maintain the difference. But, in Woolf's interior monologue, there appears to be no such distance, either between writer and reader or between writer and fictional character. The distinctions which are generally considered basic to speaker–hearer or writer–reader communication do not seem to exist, since all is merged into the omnipresent 'voice' of the narrator.

This leads to a reflection on the function of the 'conversational style' already noted in the section on lexigrammar (10.2.2). Many features of conversational style bring into focus the spontaneity of the unfolding monologue. But 'monologue' refers normally to a speech by one person addressing one or more others. There is no sign that anyone is listening to the 'voice', or reading over the shoulder of the supposed writer. If there is any genre of writing whose style this resembles it is the style of a diary (and Virginia Woolf was, of course, a notable diarist).[16] However, even the writer of a personal diary can be expected to show some awareness of a readership. There is no detectable sign of such an envisaged readership in 'The Mark on the Wall'. Even the features which I described in 10.2.2 as 'interactive', and therefore implying a dialogue situation involving two or more speakers, lack the characteristics normally associated with conversational exchange. Thus questions in 'The Mark' either tend to be rhetorical and expressive of an individual's strong emotional and intellectual involvement, not unlike exclamations:

[58] Why, after all, should one not be born there as one is born here . . . ?
   (ll. 59–60)

or, they tend to be expressive of doubt, puzzlement, or uncertainty:

[59] Where was I? What has it all been about? (Extract B)

Exclamations also reflect the internal 'voice' of mental soliloquy, in expressing emotive involvement:

[60] Oh! dear me, the mystery of life . . . (l. 37)

Imperatives are self-urgings, directed at the narrator herself: . . . *let me just count over a few of the things lost in one lifetime,* . . . Elsewhere the 'voice' can provide answers to implicit, unspoken questions: *Yes, it must have been the winter time . . .*

Thus Woolf has applied the characteristics of the language of dialogue to the dialogic impulses going on in one person's being. In this way the many-sidedness of consciousness which Bakhtin (1981) saw in the many-voiced, dialogic character of literature can actually be manifested in a single mind. The comic humour or irony we have noted are also part of this many-voicedness. A double awareness – both in favour of the subject, and opposed to it, is the essence of irony. For example:

[61] Tumbling head over heels in the asphodel meadows like brown paper parcels pitched down a shoot in the post office! (ll. 52–4)

The delightful associations of life after death in the Elysian fields are severely undercut by the comically unfavourable vision of human beings being thrown down the chute like parcels.

10.7 Conclusion

Woolf's achievement in this story is to create a style for such an inner voice, in which key dichotomies (e.g. between the particular and the general, the imaginary and the real) are capable of coalescence. The experienced life of the individual, as represented through this style, is full of vigour, colour and intensity. And through this style, Woolf is able to show the interconnected-ness of apparently irreconcilable opposites, the 'contradictories' mentioned above that the fully conscious mind has to distinguish.

Amid this merging of opposites, we need to recognize further mergers. This chapter began with the distinction between the textual, ideational and interpersonal functions of language, but in 'The Mark on the Wall', these three appear to coalesce in a single function, the *expressive* function – or what Jakobson (1960 – see Chapter 8, p. 105) called the *emotive* function, expressive of the addresser's subjective world of feelings, impressions, thoughts. The merger of the textual and ideational functions is evident in the impossibility of distinguishing what is represented to be in the 'world out there' and the mind style of the narrator. In Woolf's interior monologue, these cannot be separated, as nothing can be deemed with certainty to exist apart from the narrator's subjective world. (One possible interpretation of the text, for example, is that the mark on the wall does not exist in objective reality, but is a figment of the narrator's imagination.) A merger of the ideational and interpersonal functions is also plausible. The distance implied by the separation of ideational and interpersonal planes – the distance of the fictional 'reality' expressed through the 'tone' or 'point of view' of the narrator – cannot really be maintained in a text where no reality can be shown to exist apart from the inner impressions of the narrator.

This merging or combining of functions of language is a characteristic of much poetry: in Jakobson's terms (1960: 357 – see Chapter 8, pp. 105–6) the dominant poetic function is combined with the emotive (i.e. expressive) function in lyric poetry. In this connection, it is interesting to note that I.A. Richards sees the dominant function of poetry as the expression of feeling (Richards 1929: 354–5). In Chapter 8, however, I contrasted Richards's view of literature and that of Jakobson, who identified a specific poetic function of language. Jakobson's characterization of the poetic function as the 'set towards the message' (or, as I would prefer to say, the 'set towards the text') is equivalent to the characterization of literature (see Chapter 8, pp. 114–16) as *autotelic* – that is, as being communicatively self-motivating and self-justifying. The reason for mentioning Jakobson and autotelism here is to bring together the 'expressive' (Richards) and 'poetic' (Jakobson) concepts of the dominant language function in literature. 'The Mark on the Wall' is expressive of the narrator's consciousness – but who is the narrator? By treating 'The Mark on the Wall' as literature, we treat the narrator as a 'virtual' person. Whether she is to be identified with Virginia Woolf, the real-life author, is not our concern. Hence the expressive function of language as manifested in this work is a 'virtual' function, subordinated to the more dominant autotelism of a literary text. 'The Mark on the Wall', in addition to its expressive role in representing the subjective reality of the consciousness, has plentiful characteristics of literature in the form of foregrounding – as we have seen, for example, in such features as innovative metaphor, parallelism, snatches of metre, iconicity. 'The Mark on the Wall', we can conclude, is a lyrical poem written in prose.

Notes

1. Cited in Mepham (1991: 54). I owe this quotation and the following one to Sara Heaton, whose dissertation at the University of Bangor I supervised in 2003.
2. Letter to Ethel Smythe, 29 December 1931.
3. From Vorobyova (2005), citing Baldwin (1989: 13). I am grateful to Olga Vorobyova for drawing my attention to her paper, and providing references to earlier discussions of 'The Mark on the Wall'.
4. Wales (1992: 71–103) explores the dialogic nature of Joyce's interior monologue in *Ulysses*.
5. Detailed treatments of conversational syntax, including its relation to the unplanned nature of conversation, can be found in Biber et al. (1999: 1038–125) and Carter and McCarthy (2006: 164–240).
6. Asphodel is a flower which, according to Homer, grew on the Elysian plains of the dead.
7. For the ideas in this section, I am indebted to the inspiration given by an unpublished paper by Elena Semino: 'Figurative language and the representation of consciousness in fiction' (2004).
8. As David Lodge points out, 'there are lyrical descriptions of qualia in prose fiction as well as verse' (2002: 12–13). By 'qualia' is meant subjective experiences of a very specific, irreducible, ineffable character.

9. Here I am borrowing Halliday's and Hasan's convenient term 'texture' to refer to the characteristics of texts – see Halliday and Hasan (1976); Halliday (1978: 113, 133); Halliday and Hasan (1989: 70–96).

10. For pragmaticists, this implication is a case of Gricean implicature, due to the Maxim of Quantity (Grice 1975) (see pp. 91–2). That is, if the mark had only been noticed once, it would have been unnecessary to mention that it was 'for the first time'.

11. Compare similar effects in the 'Ode to the West Wind', Chapter 5, pp. 63–4.

12. I confess to omitting much of the detail needed in describing how the mind makes sense of seeming nonsense. One valuable tool for such explanations is the concept of cognitive 'worlds' (possible worlds, text worlds, fictional worlds) constructed in the course of interpreting a text (see, for example, Ryan 1991, Semino 1997, Werth 1999). Perhaps more pertinent here, as a cognitive tool of interpretation, is the theory of mental spaces and conceptual blending (see, for example, Fauconnier and Turner 2002, Dancygier 2006). The lady of the miniature, portrayed in this text, gives a neat illustration of conceptual blending, inhabiting as she does two different imaginary mental spaces – that of the physical miniature painting on the wall, and that of an eighteenth(?) century ancestress long dead.

13. See Wales (1992: 68–104) for the styles of interior monologue in *Ulysses*; Joyce develops a set of different styles: not only the monologue of Leopold Bloom, but also those of Stephen Dedalus and Molly Bloom.

14. As in the case discussed in note 12, here conceptual blending theory provides a way of resolving the apparent illogicality of the dust on the mantelpiece and the dust that buried Troy being 'the same dust'. Two mental spaces totally different in topographical terms except for a small conceptual overlap are blended together.

15. Quoted by McNichol (1990: 94–5).

16. Woolf's diaries – like her letters – sometimes show a close resemblance to the style of 'The Mark on the Wall'. Consider, for example, the following passage:

> *Wednesday 10 August* [1927]
> Yes, the motor is turning out the joy of our lives, an additional life, free & mobile & airy to live alongside our usual stationary industry. We spin off to Falmer, ride over the Downs, drop into Rottingdean, then sweep over to Seaford, call, in pouring rain at Charleston, pass the time of day with Clive – Nessa is at Bodiam – return for tea, all as light & easy as a hawk in the air. Soon we shall look back at our pre-motor days as we do now at our days in the caves.

> This shows, like 'The Mark', oral features of style such as listing, parenthetical sentences like 'Nessa is at Bodiam', imitating the spontaneity of the mind in full flow, metaphorical use of verbs of motion (e.g. 'sweep over to Seaford'), simile ('as light & easy as a hawk in the air') and comic exaggerated leaps of the imagination ('. . . as we do now at our days in the caves' – another interesting case for conceptual blending theory).

CHAPTER 11

Work in progress in corpus stylistics: a method of finding 'deviant' or 'key' features of texts, and its application to 'The Mark on the Wall'

This chapter takes up a theme already discussed over forty years ago, when I was writing the paper reprinted here as Chapter 2: the assumption that literary foregrounding is manifested in deviation from some kind of general norm of the language. Back in the 1960s, the idea that one could measure such deviation statistically seemed fanciful, but since then computers and computer corpora have begun to bring it to fruition.

More immediately, this chapter is best seen as a sequel to Chapter 10, in which Virginia Woolf's 'The Mark on the Wall' was the object of study. It reports a small experiment in what has become known as *corpus stylistics* (see section 11.1), using 'The Mark on the Wall' as a case study, to see whether the empirical basis of stylistic analysis could be put on a sounder footing by using an objective, empirical method of text analysis. In this experiment, I made use of a corpus comparison tool developed by Paul Rayson, entitled Wmatrix (see the website at http://ucrel.lancs.ac.uk/wmatrix.html).[1] Recently this tool has been used for stylistic analysis, and results have been promising, although the application of Wmatrix to literary texts is still in its infancy. For example, at the PALA (Poetics and Linguistics Association) Conference at Hirakata, Japan, July–August 2007, papers were presented by Mick Short, Brian Walker and Yufang Ho on the results of using this software with literary texts. The findings of the present experiment provide only indirect support for the theory of foregrounding based on deviation, but I suggest they are successful enough to encourage further studies of a similar nature.[2]

11.1 A method in corpus stylistics: Wmatrix

First, let me try to clarify the nature of this software, and why it seems to be useful for the stylistic analysis of literature. In treatments of style, particularly in this book, it has been common to identify what is interesting and significant in a piece of writing with those features of the text that are found to be in some way 'deviant' or 'exceptional'. (After all, a text which was utterly normal, and totally in line with readers' expectations, would not be interesting from the literary point of view.) Indeed, the concept of foregrounding, which is central to the way literary style has been characterized in this book, depends on identifying what is *deviant*, what draws attention to itself, in the author's use of language in a text.

Objectively speaking, the idea here is a statistical one: linguistic features that are *deviant* (i.e. significantly more frequent than normal, in a text) will tend to come to the attention of a sensitive and observant reader attuned to the use of the language. But as soon as we talk about the impact on the reader – the recognition of prominent or salient features in a text – we move away from the text as an objective linguistic phenomenon to its psychological impact on the mind of the reader. Furthermore, 'prominence' as observed by the reader (which might be due to a spelling or typographical error, for example) does not guarantee the *literary* relevance, or the *foregrounding*, of a textual phenomenon. Here we have to deal with something more subjective still – the reader's evaluation of the impact of prominence in terms of his or her appreciation of its contribution to the text as a literary work.[3] This relation between deviation, prominence and foregrounding is represented in the following diagram, taken from the discussion of style in Leech and Short's *Style in Fiction* (2nd edn 2007: 41).

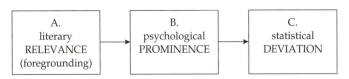

Figure 11.1 A model of the dependency of foregrounding on deviation

As we said in that book, 'We interpret the arrow in X → Y to mean "all instances of X are instances of Y"'. But in the opposite direction, the relation does not hold' (ibid.). According to this formulation, all cases of fore-grounding should be cases of statistical deviation, but not all cases of statis-tical deviation are cases of foregrounding.

Let us suppose, then, that a computer program will tell us which are the significantly deviant features of a text, and how deviant they are. It will not tell us which features are foregrounded, but it could well be a very useful guide. As a heuristic strategy, it will be possible to run the program auto-matically over the text, and arrive at a set of linguistic features which are empirically derived 'good bets' to follow up in undertaking a subsequent stylistic analysis in terms of foregrounding. To test this was the nature of my experiment.

In the present instance, I did not use Wmatrix as a preliminary to 'human' stylistic analysis, as the above paragraph suggests. My analysis of 'The Mark on the Wall' in the last chapter preceded in all essentials the development of Wmatrix. In fact, that chapter was written before I learned (with Paul Rayson's valuable help) how to use Wmatrix. So the aim of the provisional experi-ment reported in this chapter is to examine Wmatrix's automatic analysis of deviation in 'The Mark' *post hoc*, as it were, to see how far, if at all, it con-firms the features I chose to emphasize as foregrounded, in my *subjective* (albeit textually based) analysis of its style. If Wmatrix was successful in picking out features that I found noteworthy in my analysis, this would be in principle an important support for a framework of stylistic analysis depending on textual evidence for foregrounding, as presented in this book.[4]

I say 'in principle' above, because in practice there are a number of prob-lems in treating a Wmatrix analysis of 'The Mark on the Wall' as a reliable testing ground for a stylistic analysis of the text. One major impediment is the degree to which I (or whoever else does the stylistic analysis) can be relied upon to be a competent stylistician. Can Geoffrey Leech make stylist-ically relevant and well-founded observations about the text? If he cannot, then this effort is wasted, and there is no more to be said.[5] Another major impediment (or rather set of impediments) consists of the limitations regarding what Wmatrix, in the present state of computational and corpus linguistics, can do. Thirdly, if Wmatrix provides a statistical profile of a whole text, sources of foregrounding located in particular parts of the text will probably be overlooked. All this will become clearer as I explain (avoid-ing technicalities as much as possible) how Wmatrix works, and what are the limitations, at least in the present experiment, to its use as a 'deviation discovery tool'.

To proceed further, it is necessary to define (in ways that a computer program can understand and implement) (a) what can be regarded as deviant (and therefore what is regarded as 'normal'; (b) what is the range of linguistic *features* Wmatrix can recognize and deal with.

Wmatrix, as a tool for text comparison, works as follows. The investigator chooses two texts (or collections of texts) to compare statistically, in terms of frequency of observed features. (I am using 'feature' very broadly, to refer to any linguistic phenomenon in a text which can be reliably identified and counted.) Let us call these texts (or corpora) for comparison Ta and Tb.

Next consider the simplest case, where the features are orthographically identified words. The different words – technically known as word types – are counted in the two texts, and frequency lists of the words are automatically compiled. For example, as the most frequent word in English, the word *the* will almost invariably be at the top of each frequency list. The frequency lists are then compared statistically, to arrive at words listed in order of **keyness**. This term 'keyness' has recently become rather popular in corpus linguistics, because of the use of the term 'keywords' by the creator of the popular corpus search and retrieval package Wordsmith Tools, Mike Scott,[6] to name one of the programs bundled together in Wordsmith Tools. This program does the same kind of thing as Wmatrix, in comparing two (collections of) texts, and listing words in order of keyness.

But what does 'keyness' mean? It means 'distinctiveness value', in the sense that the words most 'over-represented' in Ta (when compared with Tb) will be at the top of the list – with a high positive value – whereas any words equally common in both texts will appear in the middle of the list (with a value of zero), and the words 'under-represented' in Ta – and therefore most 'over-represented' in Tb – will appear at the bottom of the list with a high negative value. The use of 'over-represent' and 'under-represent' here, by the way, is devoid of any value judgment: these terms simply refer to the relative frequency of a word in Ta versus Tb.

For example, in comparing 'The Mark on the Wall' with other texts, it is not surprising that the word *mark* itself appears at the very top of the list, as the word with the highest 'keyness'. That is, the word *mark* stands out as the word most frequently used in 'The Mark on the Wall' as contrasted with the other textual material used for comparison. The words in the keyness list are ordered according to their keyness value, calculated as a positive score of *log likelihood*, a measure of significance not unlike the chi-square measure familiar to social scientists. Any score at or above 3.8 is significant to the level of $p < 0.05$ in chi-square terms; any score at or above 6.6 is significant to the level of $p < 0.01$. Other critical values are: $p < 0.001 = 10.83$; $p < 0.0001 = 15.13$. In any comparison, many words tend to have more highly significant scores than these. In one of the comparisons I made for 'The Mark', the keyness score for the word *mark* was as high as 157.64.

Predictable though this example may be in general terms, this result gives some insight into how the frequency measure of keyness may be related to foregrounded effects. From the discussion in Chapter 10 it is clear that *mark* is a key word in the text, not only in frequency terms, but in its central thematic role in 'The Mark' as a literary work.

How does the statistical notion of keyness relate to deviation? To explain this, we have to take a further step: instead of comparing Ta with Tb, we compare it with a corpus – a collection of texts which can be called a *reference corpus* (and symbolized Tr), because it is intended to represent a norm for comparison. One of the virtues of a program like Wmatrix is that the textual materials to be compared as 'Ta' and 'Tr' do not have to be of the same size. In fact, Tr can be a corpus hundreds of times larger than Ta, containing a whole range of different types of text. The formula that calculates keyness solves the problem of size discrepancy by normalizing the frequency data to a standard measure. All raw frequency counts can be normalized, for example, by being expressed as a percentage of all the word occurrences (i.e. word tokens) in the text.

However, the concept of deviation has often faced objections on the grounds that deviation implies a norm – and what can be considered a norm? 'The language as a whole' was an earlier answer (Bloch 1953: 40–44); but the task of quantifying the frequency of features of the 'language as a whole' has seemed an impossibility, even an absurdity. (Would one have somehow to collect and quantify all the texts ever written in English; or all twentieth century texts; or all utterances ever uttered in English? These are ridiculously impossible tasks to fulfil, and in any case, how would one choose between them?)

More recently, however, the idea of quantifying a general textual norm has seemed less absurd. Since the 1980s, advances in the power of computers have brought great progress in the compilation of large corpora of a language, and it can be maintained that such large and textually diverse corpora as the British National Corpus[7] (BNC), containing about 100,000,000 running words and over 4,000 texts, mostly originating in the 1990s, provide a broadly representative and balanced cross-section of 'the use of the English language as a whole'. This would be challenged by some, however, for various reasons – for example, the BNC contains far more written texts than spoken material. In any case, even if it is granted that the BNC represents the English language (or more precisely the British variant of the language) in the 1990s, there are no corpora like the BNC for earlier periods. It seems clear, for example, that if we were to compare 'The Mark on the Wall' with the BNC, or to some part of it, the 'key' values we would observe could represent historical differences in the language between the 1990s and 1917, when 'The Mark on the Wall' was written, rather than differences of style entirely attributable to texts or their authors. To conclude, a reference corpus should not be chosen from an epoch different from that of the text for comparison.

In fact, determining an appropriate norm for comparison, that is, an appropriate reference corpus, is not a straightforward matter. It will generally be agreed that the reference corpus should be of the same period as the text being examined, permitting synchronic comparison. But what about genre? Should a novel's style be compared only with other works by the same author; with other novels; with written texts in general; with the most diverse collection of texts one can make, including transcriptions of spoken data? There is again no easy answer. If possible, it is better, I would argue, to take a 'scatter-gun approach', that is, to undertake a series of comparisons with different relevant norms, preferably with reference corpora of different level generality.

But is this feasible? Up to recently, technical limitations combined with legal limitations (in the form of copyright law) have prevented easy access to the necessarily very large and preferably varied bodies of electronic textual materials that we would need for a reference corpus. However, in the last ten years or so, the variety, size and amount of texts of different periods available on the Web or on storage media have increased enormously, and at last the possibility of assembling a range of suitable reference corpora for particular texts of particular historical periods looks like being realized.

Fortunately, Wmatrix makes it very easy to undertake such multiple comparisons, using different reference corpora. This is the approach that I tried out, in a limited way, for my Wmatrix experiment with 'The Mark'. Initially I had a problem in that the period of 1917 when 'The Mark' was written was difficult to match.[8] The best 'reference corpora' obtainable in electronic form I could find were (a) three novels written in the 1890s by female novelists;[9] and (b) the 'General Fiction' section of the Lanc-31 corpus[10], containing twenty-nine 2,000-word samples from narrative texts written in the late 1920s or early 1930s. Neither of these reference corpora was strictly contemporaneous, but I hoped that the time distances between them and 'The Mark' were small enough to preserve their usefulness as a norm of comparison. The results, indeed, were better than I thought, in that with the different reference corpora, the key word lists showed a remarkable similarity – as will be seen in section 11.2. The same similarity existed when, as a further experiment, I used each of the three 1890s' novels individually as a reference corpus. The conclusion I came to is that the findings regarding what makes a text distinctive are robust enough to be replicated in all essentials when somewhat different reference corpora are used. This strengthens the argument for multiple comparisons with different reference corpora, and suggests that slight differences of period, genre and so on among alternative reference corpora are unlikely to make substantive differences to the results. That is, what is unusual, or deviant, about a text tends to show up in a keyness analysis even though somewhat different reference corpora are used as norms.

To clarify, deviation, with regard to a linguistic feature, can be defined in practice as a positive significant score on the scale of keyness, when the text under scrutiny is compared with a suitable reference corpus or a group of reference corpora. This means that the feature is significantly more frequent in Ta than in Tr.

My next task is to elucidate the notion of 'linguistic features' for the purposes of this comparison. In Wmatrix as constituted at present, three types of linguistic features can be quantified: (a) individual words; (b) part-of-speech (POS) categories; (c) semantic categories of words. All these features are word-based.[11] The first is lexical, the second grammatical, and the third semantic. The second and third – (b) and (c) – are available because the software is available to undertake automatic *POS-tagging* and *semantic tagging* of texts or corpora, using the CLAWS and USAS tagging software developed at Lancaster.[12] Roughly speaking, POS-tagging (part-of-speech tagging) means assigning a grammatical category (such as singular common noun, interjection, modal verb) to each word in the corpus; while 'semantic tagging' means assigning a semantic marker to each word. Although the achievement of these programs is impressive, there is an error rate of approximately 3 per cent in the case of POS-tagging and of 8 per cent in the case of USAS – so the identification of features is not perfect. Another drawback is that the categories used for the analysis are debatable: other researchers, devising a set of tags for this purpose, might well arrive at a different way of categorizing the grammatical form and meaning of words. There is room for plenty of disagreement, in particular, about what semantic categories are appropriate.[13]

Further, it is fairly obvious that what can be done automatically in linguistic analysis by computer program is severely limited in complexity and detail, compared with what trained human beings can recognize in text samples. Of the types of linguistic observations made in Chapter 10 regarding 'The Mark on the Wall', most are too subtle or abstract to be automatically replicated by a computer program. For example, no computer can reliably recognize patterns of alliteration, rhythmic regularities, metaphors and similes, referential gaps, syntactic parallelisms, to mention a few of the prominent characteristics dwelt on in that chapter, and even the syntactic irregularities such as left-dislocation, anacoluthon, parentheticals highlighted in Chapter 10 are very difficult to recognize with a computer program. My reluctant conclusion is that, at least for the present, the range of linguistic features recognizable by Wmatrix is a limited one, and even those features (especially in the case of semantic categories) cannot always be trusted.[14] In spite of this, Wmatrix produces interesting as well as solidly factual results, as the following outline of its most significant output will show.

11.2 The results

With these preliminaries over, then, we look at some of the actual analysis by Wmatrix. We will have space for examining only the most significantly deviant features – those with log likelihood scores well over the $p < 0.001$ level. One way to interpret this is to say that the deviation of the features noted is highly likely to be due to the intentions of the author at some level, rather than being the result of random or haphazard linguistic behaviour. By no means does this indicate, however, that the author (Virginia Woolf in this case) was consciously aware of choosing such features.

Table 11.1   KEYWORDS: WORDS OF ABNORMALLY HIGH FREQUENCY IN 'THE MARK ON THE WALL'

Most 'over-represented' keywords in 'The Mark on the Wall' (with numbers of occurrences in the text in brackets)			
compared with three 1890s novels		compared with 1931 general fiction	
1. mark (15)	7. is (44)	1. mark (15)	7. *of* *(130)*
2. wall (14)	8. thoughts (4)	2. is (44)	8. nail (4)
3. Whitaker (6)	9. *Precedency* *(3)*	3. wall (14)	9. *reality* *(4)*
4. one (31)	10. tree (6)	4. thoughts (9)	10. tablecloths (4)
5. tablecloths (4)	11. nail (4)	5. Whitaker (6)	11. worshipping (4)
6. worshipping (4)	12. *phantoms* *(3)*	6. one (31)	12. tree (6)

11.2.1 Words

To give a small taste of the results, I give in Table 11.1 the top eleven words, measured in keyness, of 'The Mark on the Wall', calculated by comparing this text with the two reference corpora already mentioned: (a) the three novels written by female novelists in the 1890s and (b) the 'General Fiction' section of the Lanc-31 corpus.

Nine of the eleven top 'over-represented' words occur in both lists (those not shared by both lists in italics), confirming the point just made in section 11.1: the choice of reference corpora produces less variable results than one might think. One can think of plausible reasons why quite a few of the words occur on the lists, although finding a reason does not necessarily imply foregrounding. The presence of the words *mark* and *wall* at the top of the lists needs no further discussion. They are key words in the text by any criterion.

Nail is another concrete noun which, although it occurs only four times in the text, has considerable thematic importance. This brings to mind, incidentally, a peculiarity that may be thought a disadvantage of relatively short texts such as 'The Mark' when processed by Wmatrix: some words can show up with a high keyword rating, even though their use is limited to a few occurrences. For example, *nail*, a relatively rare word in general English, was, as one would expect, rare in the two reference corpora, with the result that its four occurrences in 'The Mark' scored a particularly high keyword rating.

A similar observation can be made about other items in the list – rare words that happen to make their appearance in 'The Mark' several times:

Whitaker (6), *tablecloths* (4), *worshipping* (4), *Precedency* (3). An additional point to make with these items is that their few occurrences tend to cluster together: they occur in a 'clump' in a particular part of the text. *Whitaker* is a word the narrator seizes on in one of her digressions as it represents to her the inexorable power of futile, factual reality which the mind must resist, and which, she hopes, will be *laughed into the dustbin . . . : for who will ever be able to lift a finger against Whitaker's Table of Precedency?* (Whitaker's *Almanack* is a well-known British reference work, published every year, containing vast quantities of detailed facts about the current state of the country and of the world – lists of Members of Parliament, tables of Precedency, and the like.)

Similarly, *worshipping*, like *thoughts* and *tablecloths*, turns up with unusual frequency in 'The Mark' simply because of its repetition in a structure of parallelism: *worshipping the chest of drawers, worshipping solidity, worshipping reality, worshipping the impersonal world*. In these cases, we can see how the word contributes to a foregrounded effect – not only by the parallelistic repetition of the same patterns *worshipping* + Noun, but the oddity of combining the verb with an assortment of concrete and abstract nouns. Such clumps of rare words, although they occur only a handful of times, are, I would argue, 'good bets' to follow up in the search for foregrounding effects.

Of the other items of abnormally high frequency in Table 11.1, I will mention just the pronoun *one*, which occurs in the Ta as many as 31 times, 26 of its occurrences being examples of the non-specific personal pronoun *one* ('a person' or 'people in general'). This may be a generally favoured word in Woolf's vocabulary, but its particular function here seems to be to emphasize the combination of the *general* and the *specific*. This pronoun *one* seems to refer to the narrator herself, but also seems to objectify her as a generalized third-person experiencer. It is thus close in function to the generic uses of *the* discussed in the last chapter (section 10.5). Notice the recurrence of both generic *the* and generic *one* (both italicized) in the following passage:

> because *one* will never see them again, never know what happened next
> . . . as *one* is torn from *the* old lady about to pour out tea and *the* young man
> about to hit *the* tennis ball in *the* back garden of *the* suburban villa as *one*
> rushes past in the train.
>
> (p. 138, Extract A, lines 26–32)

In my Chapter 10 analysis, I did not mention this use of *one*; although I did notice it, it did not seem a particularly important style marker. Here, the statistical analysis brought forcefully to my attention something which I can now see fits well into the foregrounding analysis of Chapter 10.

Other words in the lists in Table 11.1 have less intriguing explanations. *Is*, as the most common present-tense verb in English, presumably owes its keyword status in 'The Mark' to the tendency for the reference corpora to reflect the conventional use of the narrative past tense in English fiction. 'The Mark', focusing on immediate experience of what is in the narrator's mind, uses the present tense much more than the past, and is to this extent deviant from the fictional norm. *Thoughts*, similarly, reflects the stream-of-consciousness focus of 'The Mark': narrative events tend to reflect what is happening in the mind. All the keywords I have commented on in this section can be seen to contribute, in one way or another, to the literary foregrounding in this text.

At this point we briefly look at 'negative keywords' – as one might reasonably call them – that is, words which are of abnormally low frequency in 'The Mark'. While it is highly unlikely that the absence of such words impacts in any way on the consciousness of the casual reader, for us they can reveal significant aspects of style that might be easily overlooked. Table 11.2 lists the 'top negative keywords' for both of the reference corpora, as in Table 11.1.

Table 11.2

Most 'under-represented' keywords in 'The Mark on the Wall' (with numbers of occurrences in the text in brackets)							
compared with three 1890s novels				compared with 1931 general fiction			
1. her	(2)	6. his	(5)	1. she	(1)	6. you	(6)
2. he	(6)	7. was	(12)	2. had	(2)	7. his	(5)
3. she	(1)	8. you	(6)	3. her	(2)	8. him	(1)
4. had	(2)	9. said	(3)	4. he	(6)	9. said	(3)
5. him	(1)			5. was	(12)		

It is remarkable that the top nine keywords are identical for the two rather different reference corpora, again strengthening the conviction that variation resulting from the choice of reference corpus can be overemphasised. The words most distinguished for their rarity in Woolf's narrative are the singular pronouns *he* and *she* and their variants. These are among the most common words in third-person narrative generally, as are the past tense verbs *was*, *had* and *said*. Third-person pronouns and the past tense are both key manifestations of the conventional distancing of third-person narrative – which tells of 'other people' of 'another time'. Woolf's text is exceptional in avoiding third-person reference to people, and also in avoiding the past tense, for reasons made clear in Chapter 10: the text focuses on the immediate subjective life of the addresser's mind, and hence the first-person pronoun (see section 11.2.2) and the present tense are strongly favoured at the expense of the third person and the past tense. To this may be added the second person (*you*), which is also avoided, in a text that, as we noted in Chapter 10, lacks any addressee.

Table 11.3

Most 'over-represented' parts of speech in 'The Mark on the Wall' (with numbers of occurrences in the text in brackets)			
compared with three 1890s novels		**compared with 1931 general fiction**	
1. VVZ (49)	6. DDQ (40)	1. VVZ (49)	6. DDQ (40)
2. NN2 (187)	7. VV0 (58)	2. NN2 (187)	7. VV0 (58)
3. PN1 (41)	8. PNX1 (2)	3. PN1 (41)	8. *AT* (219)
4. VBZ (50)	9. RGQ (6)	4. VBZ (50)	9. PNX1 (2)
5. IO (130)	10. *RPK* (2)	5. IO (130)	10. RGQ (6)

Key: AT – article neutral for number; chiefly the definite article *the*
DDQ – *wh*-determiner or *wh*-pronoun (e.g. *what, which*)
IO – the preposition *of*
NN2 – plural common noun (e.g. *tables, women, thoughts*)
PN1 – singular indefinite pronouns (e.g. *one, anything, nobody*)
PNX1 – indefinite reflexive pronoun (i.e. *oneself*)
RGQ – *wh*-adverb of degree (*how* when modifying another word)
RPK – *about* used in the expression *be about to*
VBZ – present tense –*s* form of the verb *to be* (i.e. *is*)
VVZ – present tense lexical verb ending in –*s* (e.g. *says, wishes*)
VV0 – present tense lexical verb not ending in –*s* (e.g. *say, find*)

11.2.2 Parts of speech: grammar

Turning now to the level of grammar, we take a cursory look at the list of 'key parts of speech' – the exceptionally favoured grammatical word classes in 'The Mark'.

Some of the keyword classes are easily explicable, considering our earlier discussion in section 11.2.1. VBZ, VVZ, and VV0 are forms of the present tense – and we have already noted Woolf's preference for the immediacy of the present tense over the more conventional past-tense presentation of the narrative in fiction writing. In contrast to these tags, which are normally very common, the tag PNX1 is normally rare, and is restricted to the single pronoun *oneself*, a variant of the impersonal pronoun *one* we have already noted as very characteristic of this text, with its merger of the generic and the specific. The keyness of PN1 is chiefly due to one word that takes this tag, the pronoun *one*, already commented on. The keyness of the article tag AT, on the other hand, is due to the exceptionally high frequency of the definite article *the* in this text – and in Chapter 10 I commented on article usages which are particularly prominent in 'The Mark':

[1] <u>the</u> three chrysanthemums in <u>the</u> round glass bowl on <u>the</u> mantelpiece

(ll. 4–5)

[2] we were torn asunder, as one is torn from <u>the</u> old lady about to pour tea
      and <u>the</u> young man about to hit <u>the</u> tennis ball in <u>the</u> back garden of <u>the</u>
      suburban villa as one rushes past in the train.

(ll. 30–32)

Example [1], repeating example [44] in Chapter 10, illustrates the first-mention use of *the* to refer to items already assumed to be part of the familiar context: a device of psychological immediacy. Example [2], repeating [50] in Chapter 10, illustrates the generic use of *the*: a stereotypic use which, like impersonal *one*, encompasses generic and specific meaning.

The high frequency of the tag RGQ, standing for a modifying use of *how*, is restricted to exclamatory structures of the form *How* (+ adjective/adverb) + Subject + Verb:

[3] How readily our thoughts swarm . . .   (l. 17)
[4] How shocking, and yet how wonderful it was to discover . . .
[5] How peaceful it is down here.

As illustrated on p. 141 (see example [6]), this is one of the interactional structures associated with impromptu speech, but more than this, it is a feature, I suspect, characteristic of Woolf's individual style: it expresses the thoughts and feelings of the narrator in a dramatic and emotionally charged way.

The key tags NN2 (for plural nouns) and IO (for the most common of English prepositions, *of*) are less easy to explain, and indeed I could think of no convincing way of linking them to the stylistic analysis of 'The Mark' in Chapter 10. But it occurred to me, on scanning through the examples of plural nouns, that they reflect the rich, bewildering variety of the world of experience portrayed by Woolf in this interior monologue. Here is a particular passage teeming with *of*s with plural nouns from the initial part of 'The Mark', quoted as Extract A in Chapter 10 (p. 141):

> let me just count over a few *of* the *things* lost in one lifetime, beginning, for that seems always the most mysterious *of losses* – what cat would gnaw, what rat would nibble – three pale blue *canisters of* book-binding *tools*? Then there were the bird *cages*, the iron *hoops*, the steel *skates*, the Queen Anne coal-scuttle, the bagatelle board, the hand organ – all gone, and *jewels*, too. *Opals* and *emeralds*, they lie about the *roots of turnips*.

Plurality in nouns is associated with generalization, and the piling up of plural nouns in a passage like this brings a mass of cumulative detail. But detail is not found just in lists of plural nouns, but also in the ways they are modified, and the relations between nouns, typically expressed by *of*. While it would be incredible to suggest that Woolf consciously chose to highlight

173

plural nouns and *ofs*, it is arguable that the exuberance of her style here and elsewhere in the text manifests itself in the superabundant use of such words.

11.2.3 Semantics

We move now to the third and last kind of linguistic feature that Wmatrix can count: semantic features from the USAS semantic tagging software.[15] The comparison between 'The Mark' and the two reference corpora in this case can be best represented as two lists in which the features are described and listed in order of keyness, and exemplified by one or two individual words:

Table 11.4

Most 'over-represented' semantic tags/features in 'The Mark on the Wall' (numbers of occurrences in the text in brackets)	
compared with three 1890s novels	**compared with 1931 general fiction**
1. Evaluation: authentic (*real, reality, really*) (16)	1. General and abstract (*thing, things*) (15)
2. Plants (*tree, roots, stalk, flower*) (29)	2. Evaluation: authentic (*real, reality, really*) (16)
3. Solid materials (*coals, glass, iron, emeralds*) (18)	3. Colour and colour patterns (*blue, light, pale*) (39)
4. Colours and colour patterns (*blue, light, colour*) (39)	4. *Life and living things (life, lives)* (8)
5. General appearance and physical properties (*mark*) (18)	5. Mental object, conceptual (*thought, idea, ideas*) (20)
6. General and abstract (*thing, things*) (15)	6. Plants (*tree, roots, stalk, flower*) (29)
7. Mental object, conceptual (*thought, idea, ideas*) (20)	7. General appearance and physical properties (*mark*) (18)
8. Living creatures: animals, birds (*cat, snail*) (20)	8. *No kin (illegitimate)* (2)
9. *Objects generally (bowl, rock, hoops)* (15)	9. *Large, tall, long (higher, deeper)* (3)
10. *Strong obligation and necessity (must, should)* (17)	10. Living creatures: animals, birds (*cat, snail*) (20)
11. *Smoking and non-medical drugs (cigarette(s))* (3)	11. *Universe (world, moon)* (10)
12. *Furniture and household fittings (chair, table)* (9)	12. Solid materials (*coals, glass, iron, emeralds*) (18)

Note: One feature, picturesquely named the 'grammatical bin', has been omitted from the left-hand list (where it occurred in seventh position), because it has no semantic value: it applies to words which have primarily a grammatical rather than semantic function, and whose meaning cannot be easily categorized, such as *the, it, be, was, of*.

Here, as before, items which are not shared by both lists are italicised, so that we can note, as in the previous tables, the strong resemblance between the two lists derived from comparison with different reference corpora. Also, the features in this case, being based on meaning, are more informative and lead more directly towards interpretation. Whereas *reality* did not show up so prominently in the individual word list (Table 11.1), it teams up in Table 11.3 with similar words such as *real* and *really*, achieving the top position in one list and the second position in the other list under the semantic rubric 'Evaluation: authentic'. This feature naturally associates with the feature 'General appearance and physical properties', underlining the thematic pre-occupation of 'The Mark' with appearance and reality.

On the other hand, the comparison of these lists does show greater discrepancies than that of the earlier lists, and in part this must be due to the greater amount of 'noise in the system': there is a larger proportion of error in the assignment of tags to words, and the labels can be too general or too specific for their purpose in a given textual comparison.

Now for some more positive observations. The 'Evaluation: authentic' feature, as I have said, reflects the repeated use of *real, reality* and *really*. This philosophical enigma – the nature of reality: is it something internal or external to the human consciousness; is it the specific or the general; physical or mental? – is a theme that recurs, and lies at the heart of the interplay of opposites discussed towards the end of Chapter 10 (section 10.5). The prominence of colour terms noted in Chapter 10 (section 10.2.3) is also confirmed by the very high position of the feature 'Colour and colour patterns' on both keyness lists. Likewise, prominent are words referring to 'Life and living things' and 'Living creatures': two different features belonging to a more general semantic field, and to them we may add 'Plants' as another feature manifestly connecting to the natural world, to which the narrator's imagination frequently resorts (see, for example, the paragraph beginning 'But after life' in Extract A on p. 139). This is also a topic given thematic prominence frequently through simile and metaphor. Whereas the sense of rapid movement prominent in 'The Mark' is not reflected in Table 11.4, in a general sense the 'liveliness' of the passage is represented in these features. One last key semantic feature deserving special notice is 'Mental object, conceptual', referring to the psychological reality we experience through the whole narrative. This ties up with the prominence of psychological verbs *think, look*, etc. noted in section 10.2.3, p. 143.

We can see how the above key semantic features serve to situate 'The Mark' in its own domain of mental experience, confronting the existential paradoxes of life, confronting a world of colour, of animate beings and inanimate objects, through sensory perception, memory and imagination. The innovative nature of this stream-of-consciousness writing was more than a little at odds with the prevailing themes and techniques of fiction of the age, and this we see reflected in the exceptional frequency Wmatrix assigns to these features associating the internal with the external world. If it is felt that these semantic themes correspond only in a rather generalized way to the foregrounded phenomena I discussed in Chapter 10, it is worth reflecting that the semantic level of statistical analysis captures only the 'aboutness' of the text, and even this is at a somewhat abstract level. The other thing to note here is that the key semantic feature list derives from the whole text, tending to smooth out the meanings achieving prominence only in a part of the whole text.

11.3 Conclusion

It is worthwhile summarizing here both the negative and positive aspects of this experiment in relating the objectively measured 'deviant' characteristics of a text with foregrounding as an indicator of literary qualities. I acknowledged from the start that not all deviation can be explicable in terms of foregrounding. But I hoped that the statistical profile of deviant or key features – keywords, keyword classes, key semantic features – would provide a quantity of 'good bets', stylistic markers that could be expected to contribute to the literary function of the text.

Most of the negative aspects of the experiment were emphasized from the beginning in section 11.1: that the choice of reference corpora could be difficult to justify; that the range of linguistic features capable of being recognized by Wmatrix would be a limited word-based subset of those identified and commented on in Chapter 10; that the tool, at least as used to analyse a whole text, in the case of Virginia Woolf's 'The Mark on the Wall', would not be able to identify features locally foregrounded through internal deviation, but only features foregrounded in terms of the whole text.

In spite of these drawbacks, there is a considerable satisfaction in noting that the software highlighted as 'key' many features that were easy to link directly with the foregrounded elements discussed in Chapter 10 – for example, Wmatrix identified as supremely 'key' the words *mark*, *wall* and (to a lesser extent) *nail*, obviously salient in the narrative. Examples like *worshipping*, singled out as key in spite of their rarity, acted as pointers to local repetition, especially in parallel structures. The exceptional frequency of the definite article POS-tag highlighted Woolf's special usages of *the* in this text. The high frequency of *how* as an adverb of degree was found to be due to its use in exclamations beginning *How . . .* – a feature of conversational spontaneity brought into the discussion of conversational syntax in section 10.2.2. The high frequency of 'colour' words, as well as words relating to 'life, living creatures', related to the conspicuous thematic salience of colour and vitality in 'The Mark'.

Another class of high-frequency features was less directly connected with the interpretation of the text in Chapter 10, but could nevertheless be seen as 'good bets', suggestive of foregrounded effects of which I was not aware before I conducted the experiment. An example is the pronoun *one*, which clearly ties up with the generic-specific tension in the text, as noted with respect to generic use of *the*.

A third category consisted of features that were found to be deviant in statistical terms, but were not in any obvious way explicable as foregrounding. I have not spent time discussing these, but it seems that keywords like *Whitaker* and *tablecloths* have only a limited significance in the context of the work as a whole. The most that can be said is that these are peculiar details of the world outside the mind, concrete realia, on which the narrator's mind fastens in its ongoing confrontation with reality. It is clear, too, that there is little of artistic significance in the semantic categories 'Smoking and non-medical drugs', 'No kin'. It is not unexpected that deliberate haphazardness of the text could be expected to throw up anomalies such as these, and in any case, as I have stressed in section 11.1, there is no necessary expectation that deviation implies foregrounding.

My conclusion, therefore, is that this experiment has led to productive results (as well as a few unhelpful ones), and merits being followed up by further investigations of a similar kind. It is worth remembering, in conclusion, that no stylistic analysis by an individual is complete. A text of the richness and depth of 'The Mark on the Wall' will not be exhausted by one analysis, but will benefit from a number of alternative analyses. If I were to rewrite Chapter 10, now, having gone through the procedures described in this chapter, I believe that my analysis of foregrounding in 'The Mark' would be improved: I would have noticed more relevant features, and would be less influenced by personal preferences or as to which features of style to highlight.

Notes

1. The more advanced version of the program, Wmatrix2, was used.
2. It should be made clear that Wmatrix can be used for other purposes than comparing a text with a general external norm. It can be used, for example, in comparing the speech of different characters or narrators in a single work, or comparing a revised version of a work with its original version. The papers given at the PALA 2007, mentioned above, were of these kinds.
3. This is not to say that such subjective impressions of a text are incapable of being empirically investigated. Psychological testing methods have be applied to the responses of a sample of readers, for example, to investigate prominence and foregrounding. For studies of this kind, see van Peer (1986), Emmott et al. (2007) and contributions to the special issue of *Language and Literature* edited by van Peer (**16** (2), May 2007).
4. This would also be a defence of stylistics against the influential attack by Stanley Fish (1980) which dismissed stylistic analysis as arbitrary and (viciously) circular. On this attack, known as the 'fish hook', and corpus stylistics as a possible answer to it, see O'Halloran (2007).

5. But it would be possible to set up a more ambitious and time-consuming experiment where the results would be independent of the individual stylistician's analysis. This would be the case if responses were elicited from a sufficient number of informants (equivalent to the subjects in a psychological test) to obtain an overall score for the kinds and/or degrees of foregrounding found in a particular textual passage (see van Peer 1986 for experiments of this kind). These results, when compared with the output from Wmatrix, would be a more soundly based validation of foregrounding theory.

6. See 'WordSmith Tools, version 4 – A short users guide' http://www.pala.ac.uk/sigs/corpus-style/practical1.pdf.

7. See the British National Corpus website at http://www.natcorp.ox.ac.uk.

8. Most novels written in or around 1917 are still in copyright.

9. The three novels were *The Story of Bessie Costrell* by Mrs Humphry Ward, *The Real Charlotte* by Edith Somerville, and *The King with Two Faces* by Mary Coleridge.

10. This corpus, compiled at Lancaster University in a project funded by the Leverhulme Trust, has recently been completed in a provisional form (see Leech and Smith 2005). The corpus is designed to match as closely as possible the LOB and FLOB corpora (sampled from written British English of the years 1961 and 1991 respectively). The text category K 'General Fiction' provided a suitable reference corpus.

11. However, plans are underway to extend the range of linguistic features to be used for comparison to include syntactic and collocational patterns.

12. For further details of these tagging tools, see the UCREL website at Lancaster University: http://www.comp.lancs.ac.uk/ucrel/.

13. The USAS semantic categories, on the other hand, are reasonably comprehensive and well-founded, being based on the categories of Tom McArthur's *Longman Lexicon*.

14. Wmatrix is a state-of-the-art piece of software still undergoing development to increase its functionality. What I describe as 'limitations' generally come from sources other than the tool itself. Rayson's webpages on Wmatrix at http://ucrel.lancs.ac.uk/wmatrix/#ref can be consulted for more technical accounts. The tool (in its earlier version) is fully explained in the PhD thesis (now online), Rayson (2003). More recent papers dealing with Wmatrix are also available at the same website.

15. An early experiment used a prototype version of this software to compare semantic features in different episodes in Joyce's *A Portrait of the Artist as a Young Man*. The results were published in Wilson and Leech (1993).

CHAPTER 12

Closing statement: text, interpretation, history and education

12.1 The book's relation to other work

The aim of this last chapter is 'theoretical' – or perhaps 'philosophical'. It is to put the framework of stylistic analysis, as presented in this book, in the context of other people's thinking, and to draw a few simple conclusions about the text, interpretation, history and linguistic–literary education. To many readers this may seem like a reversion to the 'bad' old days of New Criticism and Jakobsonian formalism. However, I maintain that a balance needs to be struck between the analysis of texts and the understanding of processes and sources of interpretation. In the 1950s, the emphasis was too much on the text as a linguistic object, a 'verbal icon'. Since that time, there has been a movement to the other extreme of seeking enlightenment and purpose from what is outside the text. Consequently, the virtues of close engagement with the text have been too often forgotten. If this book serves to restore this balance, from the theoretical viewpoint it will have served its main purpose.

12.1.1 In linguistics and stylistics

Let us look first at developments in linguistic theory. Methods which have expanded the domain of stylistics since the 1960s have been strongly informed by text linguistics and discourse analysis. The literary work has been consequently treated not as a linguistic artefact in a narrow sense of the 'verbal icon' (Wimsatt 1954) of the New Critics, but as a discourse placed in a broad context of social function and social action.[1]

There has been a movement to interpret literature in INTERTEXTUAL or CRITICAL DISCOURSE frameworks, as a social, cultural, ideological and historical construction.[2] This movement 'outwards' from the text not merely to its literary context but to its context in society reverses the orthodoxy of a previous generation. Whereas the strictest creed of the era of New Criticism and formalism was that nothing beyond the text on the page was needed for its exegesis and evaluation,[3] the creed of more recent times has been the opposite: that the 'words on the page' are of little or no account, compared with what constructions are put on the text from outside it, particularly from the viewpoint of the reader.[4] This *flight from the text* has been accompanied, from time to time, by anti-formalist sentiments, targeting particularly the once-revered figure of Roman Jakobson.[5]

There is no reason why the newer orientation of DISCOURSE STYLISTICS should neglect the formal analysis of texts which was brought to a high degree of finesse by Jakobson and his associates in the 1960s (see Chapter 8), and in its best manifestations it does not. But too often, discourse stylistics can lead to a concentration of attention on discoursal techniques, and on the cultural, social or political resonances of the discourse. This can lead to the neglect of the close examination of a text, and a hands-off approach to its formal characteristics. In this, I would argue, discourse stylistics has sometimes yielded to the negative effects of dichotomies: as in some other fields, FUNCTIONALISM and FORMALISM have been treated as polarized opposites. The separation of the functional from the formal study of a literary text has led to an easy assumption, alongside a similar trend of post-structuralist literary theory, that the form–meaning relation is unstable, that all observations are ideologically slanted, and that there can be no such thing as agreement on what a literary work means. Literary interpretation can easily degenerate into subjectivism, but we do not have to go the whole hog with this belief in the 'essential slipperiness' of meaning. Rather, in keeping with the prototype theory of Rosch (see Rosch and Lloyd 1978), it can be recognized that meanings have a firm, invariable core, along with a variable or 'fuzzy' periphery.

In contrast to the above trends, my own view throughout the past forty years has remained one which may be called FORMALIST FUNCTIONALISM (see especially Chapter 8; also Leech 1980: 26–9). As the first sentence of Chapter 3 (p. 28) makes clear, I never went along with formalism in believing that the nature of a literary work can be expounded, in all its complexity, by a detailed examination of its formal linguistic features (as in e.g. Jakobson and Jones 1970). Similarly, as Chapter 1 (pp. 6–8) made clear, I have never adopted the supposedly formalist view[6] that the definition of what is or is not literature can be determined by formal means – e.g. by saying that a literary text can be detected, as by a litmus test, through formal features such as deviation or parallelism.

At the same time, I have persisted in taking the concepts of DEVIATION and FOREGROUNDING, concepts which gained popularity in the early era of formalist stylistics, as keys to the stylistic explication of literature. It is true that the first of these terms, in particular, has had a bad press in stylistics and literary theory: it conveys a rather negative message, that literature thrives on its 'departures' from a norm – whatever that norm may be. But I have continually regarded these concepts of deviation and foregrounding as bound together in a FORMAL–FUNCTIONAL nexus: the 'differentness' of literary language requires not only formal identification qua *deviation* but functional explanation (as *foregrounding*), in terms of the new significances that it brings – see Chapter 5 on the various kinds and degrees of deviation, and their relation to foregrounding.

The use of the first-person pronoun 'I' above is not to be taken as a sign that my approach has been unique. On the contrary, many of those working in stylistics have observed this balance between form and function, and have worked along similar lines (I could mention, for example, Fowler 1975b, Short 1996, van Peer 1986, Verdonk 1988, Wales 1992).

I welcome the widening scope of stylistics in dealing with all types of text, literary and non-literary, and seeing them in a broad discoursal context rather than a narrower, purely textual one. I also recognize that literature is open to examination from many different points of view, and from many different ideological starting points. At the same time, I maintain that the study of literature as a thing in itself, without any ulterior explanatory goals, is itself a valid activity. My approach remains one which does not give any methodological or theoretical precedence to function over form, or to form over function. As a stylistician, one can work from form (studying the linguistic characteristics of texts) to function (studying the significance or effect of such features in their communicative context), or from function to form. But long-sighted focusing on function at the expense of form is just as biasing as its opposite – the supposed myopia of formalism. The methodology of stylistics (as Spitzer saw long ago[7]) may be seen as cyclic in the same way as the methodology of science is (see Leech and Short 2007 [1981]: 12). Science works from observation to hypothesis formation (inductively), and from hypothesis to observation (deductively), progressively refining theory by cyclic re-engagement with the data. This iterative model also works well for stylistics, if one substitutes 'textual evidence' for 'observation', and 'interpretation' for 'hypothesis': stylistic analysis is a matter of alternating induction and deduction. Those who find the scientific analogy jarring may wish to reflect that the world of C.P. Snow's[8] 'Two Cultures', arts and sciences, which seemed to fit Cambridge in the 1950s, has a very dated ring today. In the modern academic world, a growing range of disciplines (including linguistics) and 'interdisciplines' (including stylistics) are used to combining humanistic with scientific methods.

In the late 1980s, Carter and Simpson (1989: 3–20) traced the history of stylistics in terms of a sequence of dominant trends, which, simplified, can be presented as follows:

1960s	formalism
1970s	functionalism (and generative grammar)
1980s	broadening contextual orientation: pragmatics and discourse

If one were to depict a continuation of this broadening pattern, it might be:

1990s	?socio-culturo-political–historical–discoursal–cognitive orientation.

The progression from a narrower to an ever broader and vaguely defined view of the subject was disturbing here. Like Yeats's 'widening gyre', one wondered if, for stylistics, 'the centre cannot hold'. Could we preserve the empirical strength of stylistics – its close attention to and careful description of the linguistic features of the text itself and the responses of readers – while ranging so widely across the humanities and social sciences in order to place it in its setting?

One manifestation of this widening gyre is the argument that the study of discourse, far from being an attempt to elucidate literary texts for their own sakes, is essentially a sociological, political or ideological activity. This argument, associated with critical discourse analysis (CDA) and its close relative critical discourse stylistics, is often accompanied by the claim that there is no such thing as a politically or ideologically unmotivated study of literature, since literature itself is born out of political and ideological settings.[9] In contrast, there is a counterargument (cf. Widdowson 1995, 1996) that such preoccupations bring partiality to the work of the discourse analyst or stylistician, which should avoid commitment to a particular ideology, in order to avoid placing the interpretation of the literary text within the shadow of ideas extraneous to it. The only 'bias' to be countenanced in stylistics, in my own way of thinking, is the bias in favour of the textual work itself. Similarly, the only 'ideology' stylistics needs is the ideology that the integrity of the text itself outweighs everything: for the text, its interpretation and the relations between them are the explicanda of stylistics. Surely our purpose, in using the techniques of stylistic analysis, should be to take a reasoned and unprejudiced approach to the interpretation of literature on the basis of analytical engagement with literature, together with what knowledge and insight can be obtained, whether from linguistics or other disciplines.

As I see it, to argue otherwise would be to give up the claim for stylistics as a discipline answerable to reason, observation and scholarly standards.

(Whether such disciplines are called 'science', 'social science' or 'humanistic scholarship' is irrelevant.) If a given writer is committed to a particular ideology, creed or philosophy, then there is good reason for the analyst to see things from that point of view, in order to understand the motivating forces behind the text. But to insist on ideological construction as basic to the understanding of a text is to give up the goal of unprejudiced investigation. To those who argue there is no escape from ideological *parti pris*, the reply must be to argue that, if this is true, our aim should be not to cultivate such bias, but to minimize it.

The *flight from the text* has taken something of a turn for the better recently: what has been called a 'cognitive turn'. The trend known as COGNITIVE STYLISTICS, under the influence of cognitive linguistics and cognitive science generally, has brought a welcome concentration on the mechanisms of psychological processing and representation of meaning. This leads to an appreciation of how common mental structures and processes lead readers to 'make meaning' in similar ways on the basis of textual material.[10] On the other hand, it has once more channelled the mind of the stylistician in directions where the text tends to be given less detailed attention, as a keener focus is placed on the unobservable cognitive structures and operations in the mind of the reader.

Nevertheless, this account should not be read as a plea to avoid focus on the reader, and to revert to a narrower formalism. After all, when we talk of the difference between the text and the interpretation, the interpretation is something that seems to lie outside the text, in the mind of the reader, or perhaps more generally, in the minds of a collectivity of readers. This is equally important. One hopeful sign, going against the *flight-from-the-text* tendency, is the growth of significant findings in the field of EMPIRICAL STYLISTICS: a movement which sees the relation between literature and its interpretation as capable of empirical investigation, for example, through the study of elicited reports of readers' responses in relation to the characteristics of the text.[11]

12.1.2 In literary theory and literary criticism

Turning now to literary theory, there appears to be an even greater gulf between the view presented, in one form or another, throughout this book, and the dominant influences on recent thinking.

Stylistics was born in an age when the influential schools of critical thought advocated close reading and explication of the literary text. The British movement of PRACTICAL CRITICISM and the American school of NEW CRITICISM had both been emphasizing the autonomy of the poetic text, sometimes going so far as to exclude extra-textual matters from the business of literary criticism.[12] Although this often led to too narrow a concentration on the 'words on the page', it was nevertheless salutary in focusing on the literary work itself as the main object of study, rather than on extrinsic factors such as its historical and biographical background, or the personal subjective response of the reader. Now all influential schools of criticism seem to agree on one thing: the inadequacy of the New Critics – for reasons that resemble the arguments, in linguistic stylistics, for rejecting the legacy of formalism.

It is problematic to state, in this case, what has replaced the discarded frameworks. Nothing in the way of a stable 'consensus' theory has arisen, and fragmentation and pluralism seem to be the ruling spirits of literary critical thought. One sign of this has been the lack of any new 'authoritative overview' of literary theory to replace Wellek and Warren (1949 [1956]). As de Beaugrande (1988: 417–8) put it:

> the most trusted precepts [of criticism] have undergone such a violent shaking that none of them seems secure enough to provide an absolute foundation for the literary enterprise . . . Recently, . . . the whole arena has suffered tremors and shocks that enforce a ceremonious debate upon what remains or will become of the ancestral performance called 'criticism' . . . The very acts of writing and reading, formerly treated as facts of life, come to look diffuse, evasive, exitless, utopian.

If there is any dominant trend, it can be broadly circumscribed by a general use of the labels 'post-structuralist' and 'post-modern'. In literary studies, as in stylistics, the rejection of the text-oriented criticism might be described as a 'flight from the text'. After reading among recent schools of critical thought, one may be excused for concluding that critical attention focuses on anything except what is the nature of the text itself, and what it is saying, as a piece of language. However, this *flight from the text* (as I would characterize it) is achieved by a radical redefinition of the notion of 'text' itself. For example:

> Theories of reading demonstrate the impossibility of establishing well-grounded distinctions between what can be read and what is read, between text and reader.
>
> (Culler, *On Deconstruction*, 1983: 75)

In other words, the text can encompass not just the language it comprises, but anything the reader finds in it. Reader response criticism, as developed severally by Fish (1970), Iser (1978), and others, sees the text as existing only with the active participation of the readers: it needs 'concretization' through the creative act of interpretation. The logical end point of this kind of thinking is met in Jacques Derrida's maxim that 'there is nothing outside of texts'.[13] Perhaps this should be more excusably interpreted to mean that everything we experience in our universe has to be made sense of through the mediation of some cultural–linguistic code. But if we take this claim literally to mean that we cannot experience any kind of reality except through the mediation of texts, it is demonstrably absurd. My response to it inclines towards Samuel Johnson's famous rejection of Berkeley's proof of the non-existence of matter: in Boswell's words:

> BOSWELL: It is impossible to refute it . . .
> Johnson, striking his foot with mighty force against a large stone, till he rebounded from it, answered, 'I refute it *thus*.'
>> (Boswell's *Life of Johnson*, 6 August, 1763)

Yes, it is possible to experience reality without the mediation of texts – especially through perception and physical interaction with one's environment. (Anyone who believes otherwise should try cycling at full tilt into a brick wall.) But this does not release the stylistician from the genuinely important task of explaining how texts mean what they mean: a task which is not facilitated by expanding the meaning of *text* to cover everything that exists or is experienced in the world.

Other attacks on the autonomous existence of texts as linguistic phenomena have come from the directions of DECONSTRUCTION (Derrida 1967a) and INTERTEXTUALITY (Kristeva 1980, 1986), both proffering, in their more extreme forms, an infinite regression of text elucidation – or text subversion. Deconstruction, as a process of interpreting or expounding a text by subverting its meanings, can never be complete, since the text through which deconstruction takes place must then be open to further deconstruction – and so on ad infinitum. Equally, the intertextual procedure of expounding one text by relating or reducing it to other texts to which it refers or alludes can never become complete if each of these 'other texts' is assumed to presuppose a further set of texts from which it derives its significance.[14] The notion of TEXT itself has become so divorced from its primary linguistic denotation that it is seen (in Culler's eyes, 1975, 1983) as 'the "possibility of endless replication" that "is constitutive" of the "structure" of the "sign".' This (quoting Barthes 1977: 146) makes the 'text' a 'multidimensional space in which a variety of writings . . . blend and clash', 'a tissue of quotations drawn from innumerable centres of culture', 'a machine with multiple reading heads from other texts' – 'a weaving . . . produced only through the transformation of another text' (Derrida 1981 [1972]: 26).[15] It is true that etymologically the word *text* originates in a metaphor of 'weaving' – the weaving of linguistic material together in a larger whole. But one wonders, when critical vocabulary in the definition of basic terms is so highly coloured with metaphor and hyperbole, whether the connection with texts as linguistic phenomena is not in danger of being lost altogether.

Those who have appeared to become enchanted with the subtlety and novelty of this thinking have lost touch with basic realities. By pushing a will-o'-the-wisp conception of *text* and *text meaning* into a fantastic *reductio ad absurdum* world of infinite regression, these tendencies appear to have led theorists to lose sight of the existence of texts in a very obvious and concrete form. Let me try to clarify this by quoting the first six definitions of *text* in a standard dictionary:

(1) the main body of a printed or written work as distinct from commentary, notes, illustrations, etc.
(2) the words of something printed or written.
(3) (*often plural*) a book prescribed as part of a course of study.
(4) *Computer technol.* the words printed, written, or displayed on a visual display unit.
(5) the original exact wording of a work, esp. the Bible, as distinct from a revision or translation.
(6) a short passage of the Bible used as a starting point for a sermon or adduced as proof of a doctrine.

It is clear enough from these, and from the everyday use of the term, that a text is an object consisting of linguistic material. This is the sense in which a literary work (say, a novel) exists independently of its author, or of any given reader.[16] A novel or a poem is one example of a text. This humdrum sense of the existence of a text enables us, for example, to ask someone 'Which Brontë novels have you read?' or 'How many Keats poems do you know by heart?', and to receive a clear and simple answer. This is the sense of a text's existence presumed by any literature syllabus which names particular works (texts), and is indeed the irrefutable, dull, common-sense basis on which literary scholars identify what their subject matter is. And of course, as a linguist, it makes sense for me to define a text simply as a linguistic object – something consisting of linguistic material. I will try to elucidate what kind of 'linguistic object' it is in the next section of this chapter.

12.2 What is a text?

As a necessary step before going on to more theoretical and educational issues, I would like to deal further with this foundation stone of stylistics – that is, the nature of text. This is because if we do not understand the nature of a text, we cannot understand the nature of textual interpretation.[17] To begin with, I will want to dispose of the myth that, if one rejects the extremely broad understanding of *text* just discussed, one has to go to the other extreme and say that a text is a purely physical thing: 'just marks on paper'.

The position I take on the ontology of text is, I believe, a fairly standard one in linguistics. There is nothing innovative or daring about defining a text as a linguistic object – a manifestation of the use of language – although it may seem so, simply because over the last generation the term *text* has been used fancifully in many senses apart from this basic one. The view I take on text can be caricatured as positivist or empiricist by those for whom these terms are irredeemably negative; or there will be those who will also tend to exaggerate it as the view that a 'text' is simply 'marks on paper'. But in what follows, I will clarify a superficial set of ambiguities in the way 'text' is used in linguistics and in everyday usage: for there are three levels of abstraction at which the notion of text can be defined. But at the same time this will build up a more securely founded view of 'text' as 'linguistic object' than has often been assumed.

First of all, there *is* a sense in which *text* refers to some marks on paper. It is possible, without departing from normal usage, to pick up a piece of paper on which is written, for example, a poem or an advertisement, to point to it and to say 'This is a text'. It is similarly possible to pick up a piece of paper on which is printed Shakespeare's *Sonnet 116* and say 'This is (or 'Here is') Shakespeare's *Sonnet 116*'. However, in general the term *text* (like related hyponymic terms such as 'poem', 'play', 'novel') is used in a more abstract way than this: as an abstraction that could be made more explicit by the rewording, 'This is a *copy* of a poem (or advertisement)'. Here we encounter the idea that a text may be instantiated in different copies, or (to use the linguistic term) a text as a TYPE may be instantiated in many different text TOKENS. Imagine two students following the same course in English literature, both going into a bookshop to buy (a copy of) a set *text* – say, *The Mill on the Floss*. Notice that the words in brackets – 'a copy of' – can be omitted in ordinary parlance. This is a standard unnoticed case of metonymy, and one which would only come to light if one student jokingly said to the other: 'My text is on the syllabus, but yours isn't' (referring to the two copies of *The Mill on the Floss*). Already, in thinking of texts as text *types*, of which there can be many physical instances, we are one level removed from the equation of a text with a purely physical phenomenon – a set of marks on paper. And at least one further level of abstraction may be made: from seeing a text as an abstraction over many tokens, to seeing it as an abstraction over many types. This further abstraction from physical substance will take place, for instance, if we say that a number of different *editions* of a classic are *editions* or *versions* of the '*same*' text, poem, play or other work of literature. This is of course a familiar phenomenon: different editions may differ in minor or major ways from one another – e.g. in terms of layout, pagination, spelling, even grammatical or lexical detail. (Compare the quarto with the folio versions of *Othello*. A syllabus may or may not specify if a 'set text' is to be read in a particular edition.) And yet – although the distinction between 'same text' and 'different texts' may become blurred here – we can still refer to the editions as manifestations or realizations of the same text, i.e. instances of the same linguistic object. There may be further levels of abstraction over which a single *text*, in ordinary parlance, may range – for example, the 'same' edition (say the Folio Edition of *Hamlet*) may be reprinted or may be reproduced in a facsimile edition. The whole thing may be represented as a kind of hierarchical tree, with $text_1$, $text_2$ and $text_3$ representing different levels of abstraction in defining 'text':

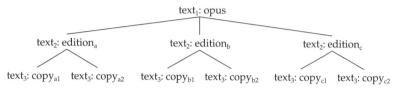

Figure 12.1 Three different senses of 'text'

Clearly there are limits to this abstraction of the notion of 'text' from physical substance, and we reach them rather quickly if we allow wholesale changes of wording: for example, a modernized version of a medieval poem such as *Sir Gawain and the Green Knight*, in which words and sentence structure are rather freely replaced by modern equivalents, could scarcely be called the 'same text' as the original.[18] What this exploration of the ambiguities of abstraction of the ordinary English word *text* shows is that *text*, like other words, is a term whose meaning has some fuzzy boundaries. But, in a fairly strict sense, as long as two instantiations consist of (approximately) the same words (and punctuation?) in the same order, we are happy to call them (examples of) the same text, using *text* in the sense of 'text: opus' in Figure 12.1.[19] Hence it seems acceptable, as a first major approximation, to say that there is an important level of abstraction at which the term *text* may be defined as a complete PUNCTUATED WORD STRING. What this means is that so long as we reproduce the same words in the same order, with punctuation in the original positions, we are reproducing the SAME TEXT.[20] Agreed, this definition is likely to become hazy when we consider borderline cases; but it is not surprising to find that the concept of *text*, like that of *literature* discussed earlier (see p. 7), has prototype characteristics.

Thus, for certain poems of e. e. cummings, the requirement of reproducing the same words in the same order is not sufficient: the two-dimensional arrangement of words on the page is a very important feature of the text, and must be reproduced. For most other texts, especially prose texts, this feature is unimportant and can be variable in different editions. There is a case, though, for claiming that a poetic text needs to be reproduced not only in terms of its verbatim content, but also in terms of its graphological structure, that is, in terms of verse lines and stanzas. If we include these aspects of the written form of a text under the term 'lineation', then this notion of lineation can also apply to the paragraphing of a prose text, and the definition of *text* (in the sense of text₁: opus) can be slightly tightened to 'a punctuated and lineated word string'. (Note that lineation does not include the division of a printed text into justified lines on the page, which is arbitrary and insignificant as far as a prose text is concerned, and is comparable to other normally non-significant features of a printed text such as pagination, font and type size.)[21]

Defining a text such as *The Mill on the Floss* as 'a punctuated, lineated word string' does not obviously say anything interesting about it, and might be taken as a demeaning description of a great novel. But patience! We are building up the definition of *text* gradually, and have not yet reached the important part. On further consideration we discover that 'a punctuated, lineated word string' is an inadequate definition: it could refer to a magic incantation in no language at all, such as *magi maki mika pika oo walai!*, or a sequence of nonsense words or word strings, such as might occur in a psychologist's memory test. Would such a word string be a text? Decidedly not: the requirement that a text is a linguistic object or message is missing. 'Linguistic' here means that a text must be in a particular language such as Swahili, Korean or English. Also, a word string is not a text unless it is found to have structure and coherence of the kind associated with the use of a language. It is important, then, that to be a text, a word string has to be redefined as 'a punctuated lineated word string *in a particular language*'.

This qualification 'in a particular language' is crucial. An elementary linguistics textbook will inform us that a *language* is a multilevel coding system, that is, a system which is used to encode and decode messages, enabling the human user to convert sounds (or visual marks) into meanings, and meanings into sounds (or visual marks). This means that a text, as a word string, cannot be disassociated from the meanings which such words express, and the sounds and visual marks by which such words can be transmitted to others who know the same language. The word *chair* in English means something quite different from the word *chair* ('flesh') in French; it is also pronounced differently. Thus a word written down as part of a text is inevitably associated with the meanings(s) and pronunciation(s) it conventionally has in *the language that the text is in*. Moreover, the occurrence of a set of words, punctuated, and in a particular sequence, will bring an associated (set of) grammatical structure(s), together with its/their meaning(s) and pronunciation(s). Note that all the bracketed elements of the last two sentences indicate the possibility, in any language, for there to be multiple meanings, multiple pronunciations and multiple structures associated with each word string. This amounts to saying that a language, as a multilevel coding system, is subject to ambiguity and multiple realization – that is, one-to-many and many-to-one coding relations. But the crucial thing to note, in this context, is that a text, as a punctuated, lineated word string, is not merely a word string, but has a phonology, a lexis, a grammar and a semantics associated with it. For example, if a poetic text did not have a phonology associated with it, we would not be able to make such claims as 'This poem is written in heroic couplets', or 'This poem contains assonance'. Similarly, if a text had no syntax or semantics, we could not make observations, as I did in Chapter 10 (pp. 140–2), about Woolf's 'The Mark on the Wall', as a text in the English language, containing speech-like syntax or a multitude of colour terms.

12.3 Ambiguity and interpretation

It is common, in literary studies, to overestimate the extent to which texts are ambiguous, and hence to overstate the extent to which different readers (or one reader on different occasions) can vary in the way they make sense of the text. At one extreme, it is sometimes suggested that readers can read what meanings they like into a text. This is surely as great an error as the opposite extreme view (often held by the 'everyday reader') that a text is unambiguous, and conveys a single invariable message to anyone who reads it. But the latter view (the 'everyday reader's' view) has some basis in the experience of reading non-literary texts. Outside literature, in practice, ambiguities are rarely noticed in a text, and it is quite difficult to find examples when one is looking for them. As an example, let us consider a simple English question out of context: *Who's taking the chair?* There are two word-level ambiguities here:

(a) *Chair* could refer to a piece of furniture or to the presiding role at a meeting;
(b) *Taking* could denote a physical action (*take* the chair, in the sense of picking it up taking it to another position); or else it could denote a social action (*take* the chair in the sense of assuming the role of chairperson).

There is also a third ambiguity at the syntactic level: the progressive or continuous construction *is taking* could refer to something going on at the PRESENT time, or to something that will take place in the FUTURE. However, ambiguities (a) and (b) cannot be multiplied out: as a whole, there is only the possibility of *taking the chair* being read either in the physical action sense, or in the social action sense. Thus four meanings are possible:

(a′) *is taking the chair* = physical action in the present
(a″) *is taking the chair* = physical action in the future
(b′) *is taking the chair* = social action in the present
(b″) *is taking the chair* = social action in the future.

It is important to observe that other facets of the sentence are semantically stable: e.g. its status as a question; its syntactic structure as subject–verb–object; the definite referent of *the chair*; the fact that the interrogative word *who* refers to a person whose identity is sought by the speaker. Moreover, it is unlikely that *Who's taking the chair?* would constitute a text in itself. It would typically be embedded in a larger text (most likely, a transcription of a dialogue) with co-text to the left and/or right of it, and it is highly probable that in that case the ambiguities, or at least most of them, would be resolved. For example, if the sentence were preceded by another question by the same speaker, *What's happening tomorrow?*, the future reading would be assured. It is true that from a theoretical perspective, a text may be semantically underdetermined, because of the presence of lexical or grammatical ambiguities. But in practice, a reader often has little or no choice but to resolve an ambiguity in one particular way, so that the meaning is very largely determined by what is in the text, rather than by the reader's selection of one meaning rather than another. If this is true of ordinary everyday texts, surely it must be at least partially true of literary works such as poems and plays. For example, in the following well-known couplet of Pope,

> Here thou, great Anna! whom three realms obey,
> Dost sometimes counsel take – and sometimes tea.
>
> *(The Rape of the Lock,* III)

the final word *tea* is unambiguous, and refers to the same beverage as is referred to by *tea* in the everyday utterance: *Do you want a cup of tea?*

The Pope couplet, as far as I can tell, is no more susceptible to ambiguous readings than the everyday utterance *Do you want a cup of tea?*. It is true that the reader, to understand what the whole couplet is about, needs to catch the reference to Queen Anne, the British monarch (1702–14) at the time of Pope's composition of the poem, and to the 'three realms' that she ruled (England + Wales, Scotland and Ireland). But this is a matter of the reader's interpretation on the basis of background knowledge and reference, not of the meaning of the words and structures of the couplet. There is a 'division of labour', in making sense of any kind of text, between decoding the linguistic message, and interpreting it in terms of real-world knowledge, pragmatics, sociocultural significance, and so on. This 'division of labour' is crucial – for one task we use linguistic knowledge, and for the other we use cognitive capabilities not specific to language, such as inference and real-world knowledge – although the decoding and interpreting are closely interrelated activities. But we should not overestimate what the reader has to bring to the linguistic text, as contrasted with the meaning potential that is inherent in the text, by virtue of being in a particular language.

But wait: this argument is running a little ahead of itself. I want to consider two questions a sceptic might raise as objections at this point. **Question (a):** Can one really argue that linguistic content, as well as form, is inherent in the text as a linguistic object? After all, if someone does not know the language the text is in, they cannot read (and make sense of) the text. So the meaning must lie outside the text.

One answer to this challenge is to recall that a text is defined as being *in a language* (otherwise this question does not make sense since a text could consist of nonsense strings) – and a language has not only words, but phonology, lexis, grammar and semantics. This definition takes us a long way from texts as just 'marks on paper', since a text, so defined, has both an abstract (cognitive and social) as well as a concrete aspect. Like many terms (e.g. social terms such as 'ownership' and 'marriage'), linguistic terms such as 'text' refer to something which exists socially and psychologically, as well as physically.

Another answer is to invite the objector to undertake a thought experiment as follows. Suppose archaeologists discover some inscriptions left by a vanished civilization using some mysterious set of written symbols. Suppose the archaeologists cannot decipher the inscriptions, and end up by dismissing them as pictorial concoctions for purposes of magic. Later, a genius discovers how to decipher the inscriptions and reconstructs the language and the culture of the people who wrote the inscriptions. Someone might claim that the inscriptions were not texts – but just some kind of mumbo-jumbo, until the decipherment was achieved. But when they were deciphered and the language reinvented, they 'became' texts again, as they had been for their original authors.

The point is, this is a very strange way of describing what happened. Did the texts cease to be texts, and become mumbo-jumbo, and then revert to being texts when they were deciphered? It is nonsensical to suppose that these inscriptions underwent transformation in this way, when what changed was not the texts themselves but the human understanding (or lack of understanding) of them. Therefore a sounder conclusion would be that they had been texts all along – they were still texts invested with meaning, even when there was no single living person who knew the language they were in. And the lost language was not reinvented, but *rediscovered*. From this thought experiment, the conclusion is that texts do have form and meaning, as linguistic objects, independent of the existence of any (living) writers or readers of them. In fact, this conclusion accords with common-sense understanding of what a text is. And what I called a 'thought experiment', or something very similar to it, is in fact what has actually happened, historically speaking, in the decipherment of the scripts of dead languages, such as the Minoan Linear B, and the Mayan glyphs.

The second question is:

Question (b): Can one really reduce the interpretative role of the reader to nothing but resolving occasional textual ambiguities?

The answer is a resounding 'No'. I am using the word *ambiguity* here to refer to a lack of unresolved semantic choice in the text itself, at the level of linguistic semantics that applies, for example, to meanings as defined in a dictionary. In this restricted sense, ambiguity is a property of the text itself, without considering the role of the reader. In resolving such ambiguities, a reader resolves some of the uncertainties in the textual message. But of course, reading a text is typically a much more active affair than this suggests. There are other levels of interpretation – for example, at the interpersonal level, or at the level of contextual implications – to be considered. It is arguable that these levels of interpretation are not found in the text itself (although they arise from the reader's interaction with the text), but are more in the mind of the reader who interprets it. Again an example may be taken from the simple sentence *Who's taking the chair?*, this time in the physical sense of 'Who's picking up the chair and taking it somewhere?'. The question to consider is: how do we identify the referent of the definite description *the chair*? Well, it will typically be clear, from the situation or from a previous part of the text, *which* chair is being referred to. This information will not be *actually* found in the text, although it may well be inferred clearly enough from the physical situation or from previous mention. Even on the pragmatic level, where the reference of expressions like *the chair* is determined, the text may give very little choice to the reader but to infer that a particular referent is intended. But the mind has to arrive at this interpretation by inference – by drawing conclusions from the text *plus* the context – for reference does not reside just in the text itself. In other words, by saying that a text exists *in a particular language*, I do not mean to suggest that the whole significance of the text resides in, or is derivable from, the text as a linguistic object. Rather, the whole meaning (or significance) of the text can only be derived from the interaction of the text with particular readers. It is necessary in this way to strike a careful balance between the view that the interpretation of the text lies solely in the text itself, and the view that the interpretation of the text lies solely in the reader's mind.

The reader's share of the task is especially great in attempting to comprehend a literary work, or just part of it. My assumption, running through various chapters of this book, is that interpretation is particularly multivalent and open-ended *in literature*, and perhaps more particularly *in poetry*.[22] This can largely be explained by the phenomenon of foregrounding, which invites interpretations over and above the commonplace meanings which word strings have in typical non-literary texts. Hence I want to make clear that my aim here is not to play down the importance of the active role taken by readers in using inference, perception and imagination to seek interpretations. It is rather to emphasize, as a foundation for this interpretative activity, that the text as a linguistic object is itself meaningful, without reference to this or that reader, before considering the particular significances individual readers may add to it. The meaning in the text is something independent of readers, a common ground which different readers share by virtue of speaking the language. Moreover, different readers also share to a considerable extent the cognitive machinery, and the same non-linguistic background (e.g., rationality, imagery, schematic modelling, knowledge and assumptions about the world). It is becoming clear from empirical studies (see van Peer 1986, 2007) that even foregrounded features that are somehow 'deviant' from normal language use rely for their interpretation on a great deal of cognitive and cultural common ground between the interpretative processes of different readers.

To sum up: in this framework, the term *text* refers to a punctuated, lineated word string in a particular language. The fact that a text is 'in a particular language' invests it not only with formal but also with semantic characteristics, including ambiguities and semantic gaps. The term *interpretation* refers to the readers' contribution, which may be sought collectively or individually, as the making-sense or significance of the text, including resolving ambiguities.

The importance of this commonality of interpretation should not be underestimated. In non-literary discourse, it is the common ground between different interpretations which makes everyday communication possible. Without it, language would not perform its largely successful social and practical communicative functions that we rely on day by day for a multitude of purposes, even for our survival (think, for example, of the largely successful broadcast of warnings of floods, hurricanes and other natural disasters). In literary discourse, this common ground may be less evident because of the superabundance of interpretations available. But it is still sufficient to ensure that the interpretation and appreciation of a literary text can go forward on the basis of what is in the text itself – what is open to inspection and to cooperative sense-making, independently of the mind of its writer or of any individual reader. Shared responses between readers are far more substantial than has been thought, and rely on the *meanings and formal characteristics which reside in the text*.

To conclude this section, Figure 12.2 pictures the relation between writer, text and reader.

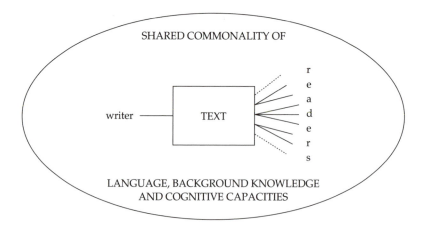

Figure 12.2 The communicative situation in literature

12.4 Historical and educational viewpoints

Building on the above conclusions, it is possible to construct an argument for the educational role of stylistics.[23]

The value of stylistics in literary education is, firstly, to help give access to the understanding and appreciation of literature. It is important, in my view, that that access does not rely on acceptance of this or that theory or ideology: it is open to all who know the language, or who know something of how the language works. This is a liberating conclusion for many native speakers of English who find literary theory a complex and baffling field which interposes unnecessarily between the student and the text. It is also liberating for non-native speakers, many of whom are well used to consulting English grammars and dictionaries, and have an analytic, metalinguistic knowledge of the language far superior to that of most native speakers. They will find their knowledge of *how* the language works a big aid to discussion of the text: it will compensate, to some extent, for the lack of contextual and cultural background knowledge, which in many cases native speakers will have in greater measure. This helpful levelling of the playing field between native speakers and non-native speakers is my first reason for arguing the educational value of stylistics.

Secondly, in small group teaching, the kind of activity that takes place in a well-conducted stylistics seminar particularly lends itself to educational goals. This is a kind of interactive discussion activity where the class *addresses* a text (which students have preferably looked at in advance) and explores its significance, impact and value. The teacher invites students' individual responses, while drawing the group's attention to factors of evidence, literary sensitivity, and historical and biographical background, but where, above all, reference is made to the text in arguing for or against given positions. This is a valuable discipline, as well as stimulating training in the appreciation of literature. It can be added that such seminars tend to be socially as well as educationally rich in benefits, as students are sharing their varied insights in an area where individual responses are valued.

Thirdly, the method of stylistic analysis is reliant on, and encourages, linguistic analytic knowledge of a relatively theory-neutral kind. No particularly specialist knowledge is needed. I would argue that for stylistics, linguistics proper provides a useful methodological 'toolbox' rather than any all-embracing theory.[24] This kind of practical knowledge of how language works is useful for many kinds of application.

Fourthly, the heuristic explanatory cycle of induction and deduction (comparable to the hypothetico-deductive method of science according to Popper 1979) is common to stylistics and to many other disciplines, and is a valuable and versatile intellectual activity to cultivate. It applies in many other fields: for example, natural science, social science, and the investigation of the past through history, archaeology and palaeontology. It also encourages an informed and sensitive response to language, and to texts in all their variety. Its goal is to arrive at (a) an evidentially warranted inter- pretation and appreciation of the text, and (b) an understanding of how that interpretation/appreciation is supported by the way the text works as a lin- guistic and communicative phenomenon.

Fifthly, stylistics understood as above rehabilitates the important role of background (knowledge) in the understanding of literature. The traditional basis of literary education – literary history in a broad sense – has often been sidelined in recent times. Instead, emphasis on the reader's end of the com- municative process has caused the text to be seen as something that changes with changes in context, including historical change. But acquisition and application of background (intellectual, social, political, biographical, his- torical) is an undeniable enrichment of an educational programme rooted in texts and their significance.

Let us consider a little further why this is. The stylistic method, as expounded here, is a method of approach to literature which aims to be independent of ideologies and value judgments as far as possible. The one value judgment that is made, initially, is that the literary work (or some part of it) is worth studying, and that it is worth searching for its richest and most rewarding interpretative result, building on *how* a text conveys what it conveys. But this focus on interpretation does not necessarily release us, as readers, from the constraint of trying to reconstruct what the author *meant* by it. According to Grice's framework for pragmatics (Grice 1957, 1969)[25], which in a broad sense I espouse here, the meaning of any piece of lin- guistic communication is to be equated with the communicative *intentions* of the speaker or writer. Grice's well-known seminal formula for speaker meaning was:

> '[S] meant something by x' is (roughly) equivalent to '[S] intended the utterance of x to produce some effect in an audience by means of the recognition of this intention'. (where [S] = *speaker*)
>
> (Grice 1957: 58)

Hence, interpreting a text involves reconstructing what were its author's most likely communicative intentions. This association of meaning with intention is further developed by Sperber and Wilson (1995 [1986]: 29), who recast Grice's formulation by breaking down the speaker's or writer's meaning into two intentional components:

Informative intention: to inform the audience of something
Communicative intention: to inform the audience of one's informative intention.

Whether the emphasis on information is justified here is something to be questioned. Certainly the 'something' of which the audience or reader is 'informed' is to be understood in a very broad sense, to include whatever is meant to be conveyed by a text. But the association of meaning with 'speaker's or writer's intentions' is well established in pragmatics, and is indeed founded on an everyday meaning of *mean*: 'What did you *mean* by that?' can be reasonably paraphrased as 'What did you intend to communicate?'. The major problem, of course, is that we have no direct access to what the author's intentions were: a problem I now address.

This focus on intentions as the source of meaning apparently clashes with the New Critic's well-known rejection of intention in the interpretation of literature (see Wimsatt and Beardsley 1954 [1946] on the 'Intentional fallacy'). However, it is crucial to see that the role of the reader, in interpreting, is *not* to find out what the author's intention *was*. (Clearly this is in general not possible, since in the understanding of literary works or, for that matter, any kind of linguistic communication, there is no direct access to the author's intention.) Rather, the reader's role is to *reconstruct* the communicative intentions of the author, so far as is possible from the evidence available – especially the evidence provided by the text. If we think of a written text as a linguistic communication preserved through time, available for any reader to interpret, the kind of evidence most obviously available to the reader, in interpreting the text, is first and foremost the linguistic content of the text itself, including lexical and grammatical meaning. But there are also other kinds of evidence, which should surely not be denied to any reader who wishes to use them in making a reasonable reconstruction of the author's most likely communicative intentions. These include what the author may have communicated to others about his or her authorial intentions (e.g. by writing a preface, adding notes to the text, etc.), and what may be more indirectly inferred about the author's intentions, from what we know about the background of the work, its author and its audience, and hence what might have been in the author's mind at the time of writing. These three sorts of evidence may be summarized as:

(1) Evidence from the TEXT
(2) Evidence from what the author said or wrote ABOUT the text
(3) Evidence from the assumed BACKGROUND of author and text

So, to emphasize the point, we do not know what the author's intentions were, but we can do our best to reconstruct them from evidence – which is precisely what human listeners and readers (consciously or unconsciously) do in trying to make sense of any linguistic communication, whether in a literary work or not.

This notion of BACKGROUND is of course very broad. I have not used the popular term 'background *knowledge*' because this is more restrictive. 'Background' includes familiarity with situational factors such as:

- the place and time of composition
- the biography of the author
- the cultural value systems available to the author
- the assumptions and beliefs about the world available to the author both as an individual and a member of a particular social milieu
- assumptions about conventions and traditions (especially literary conventions and traditions) available to the author.

But we should also not forget the *linguistic* background. To reconstruct the author's probable intentions, we also need to know about the language of the time and place of composition: this includes whatever historical and dialectal information about the language may be relevant.

Interpreting a text, according to the above recipe, is beginning to seem a Herculean task. Naturally a complete availability of relevant background is impossible. We all have to attempt to reconstruct meaning on the basis of partial and uncertain knowledge of background, and to some readers, background may be more important than to others. However, the 'perfect literary reader'[26] would be a person who was aware of all relevant background available in terms of current sources of knowledge and understanding. The fact that we cannot possibly become 'perfect readers' should not deter us from becoming 'better readers' – which is where education comes in.

When earlier I mentioned the *common ground* between different readers' interpretations, I principally had in mind on the one hand *linguistic* common ground, in that readers share the same language which they use in interpreting the same text, and on the other hand the common ground of *shared assumptions about background* which guide their interpretation of the text (I use the term 'assumptions' here, following Sperber and Wilson (1995), as a more flexible and accommodating alternative to 'knowledge'). Sperber and Wilson point out that communication between addresser and addressee takes place on the basis of mutual assumptions, and this common ground between them makes relatively stable communication possible. There is a similar assumption of common ground which different readers share, on the basis of their awareness of the mutual assumptions they have both with the author, and with each other. There is therefore here a triangle of mutual assumptions which achieves a certain degree of stability for communication and interpretation even in respect to literary texts, and which ensures that reasoned and evidence-based discussion of literature can take place. As Figure 12.3 shows, literary appreciation need not be, and should not be, a free-for-all:

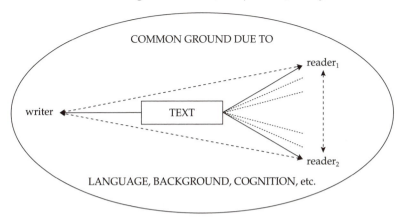

Figure 12.3 Common ground between author and two or more different readers

It is time to draw to a conclusion about the historical and educational function of stylistics. I have argued, on the basis of Gricean intentionality, that reconstruction *as far as possible* of the author's communicative intentions is a reasonable goal of literary interpretation and appreciation. For this purpose we need as much as we can get of awareness and understanding of background, and also of awareness of the language and the way in which it works to achieve meanings and effects in literature. The second of these requirements has both a synchronic and a historical dimension. From the synchronic point of view, it is scarcely controversial that non-native speakers of a language benefit from learning as much of that language as possible, if they want to appreciate the literature written in that language. From a historical point of view, it can hardly be denied, on the same basis, that we need to have a good understanding of the language of a particular period, in order to appreciate the literature of that period (e.g. we need to understand the language of the Elizabethan era in order to understand the literature of the Elizabethan stage).

In summary, referring back to the three kinds of evidence mentioned above, I see literary–linguistic education as based on the three goals of becoming familiar and knowledgeable about (1) the text, (2) anything the author may have communicated about the text, and (3) the assumed background of the text.

Perhaps the preceding two paragraphs will strike many readers as setting up too high a goal – as a counsel of perfection, in fact. Do we really have to become philologists and antiquarians in order to appreciate the works of Shakespeare, for instance? My argument (based on the objective of reconstructing communicative intentions) is that we would indeed need to pursue literary–linguistic–historical courses of study in order to become 'optimal readers' of Shakespeare. In practice, although no one is an 'optimal reader' of Shakespeare, students will progress to some extent along that road by virtue of listening to, watching, and studying Shakespeare's works. The goal of literary–linguistic education is surely worth pursuing in terms of a broadening and deepening of this grasp of what the author might have meant. We can think of it as progressively attempting to close the 'communicative gap' between reader and author.[27]

There is, however, another way of construing the purpose of literary education with stylistics as a support. This is more in tune with literary theoretical positions in the post-structuralist or post-modern age – for example, with reader response theory and the new historicism. This method is to cut away the author's corner of the triangle in Figure 12.3. We give up the quest for the communicative intention of the author, and concentrate instead on our own community of readers, and their interpretation of the text. By abandoning 'what the author might have meant', we lay ourselves open to simple error – e.g. misconstruing the meanings of words – but we save the directness of impact and meaningfulness of the work for audiences of different periods, different cultures and different societies.

It is frequently claimed that a work of art changes in the course of historical and cultural transmission: that Dante's *Divina commedia*, for instance, is a different work for the thirteenth century, for the eighteenth century or for the twenty-first century. This is manifestly true if we accept that *Divina commedia* as a literary work includes the responses that *Divina commedia* has evoked over the centuries. However, I have already argued that this is stretching the definition of a work too far: *Divina commedia* is essentially a text, as defined in section 12.2. The view that the text itself has changed over the centuries is, on this understanding, quite invalid, except in so far as editors may have changed the linguistic form of the text (for example) in order to revive a historically more authentic version, or (more controversially) to achieve a version more acceptable in one's own age. However, it can still be claimed (in tune with the reader response approach) that the significances of the text (and responses to the text) have changed over the centuries, and that a validity can be attributed to the changing significances of the text, even if they are remote from what was intended when it was first written. This justification relies on the assumption that a work of art is not just for its own age, but all time.

It is no doubt true that, using stylistic techniques, and referring to a community of readers of, say, the early twenty-first century we could arrive at a range of 'early twenty-first century interpretations' of Dante, which may contain some features which would be alien to Dante's own understanding of his own masterpiece. I do not deny that stylistics can be helpful to this viewpoint – since stylistics concerns the systematic study and interpretation of texts, but does not require its practitioners to be literary historians. This 'author-free' standpoint is potentially rewarding as well as unavoidable in the case of texts whose author is unknown and for which the communicative intentions and background of the author(s) are unknown – for example, much oral literature, and ancient texts of obscure origin such as the Biblical *Song of Solomon* (which can be interpreted as a love poem, a religious allegory, a drama, etc.). Moreover, there is an argument that, once a poem is created, its author gives up the privileged position of being an 'authority' on what it means: that he or she simply becomes one reader and interpreter of the poem. However, against this, I argue the superiority of the 'author-intention' view of interpretation rather than the 'author-free' view for two intellectual reasons.

First, the 'author-free' view has no way of eliminating errors due to ignorance of the language. For example, the word *politician*, in Shakespeare's sense of 'plotter, schemer', would never occur to a modern audience without knowledge of Shakespearean English, and hence when Lear says . . . *like a scurvy politician . . . (King Lear* IV vi 172) thoughts of modern party politics and spin doctoring are likely to intrude! Likewise, in *Blow, blow thou winter wind / Thou art not so unkind / as man's ingratitude (As You Like it* II vii 175) a modern audience is likely to understand *unkind* in the weakened modern sense, rather than in Shakespeare's sense of 'cruel, unnatural'. Secondly, the 'author-free' view appears to have no criterion for establishing the superiority of one reading over another. This could come dangerously close to the 'anything goes' philosophy of interpretation.

In summary, I present the following two diagrams, to show the two views of how to interpret a literary work where the writing and the reading of the text are (widely) separated in time.

In Figure 12.4, the aim of the reader is to 'close the communication gap' between author and reader. In attempting this, the reader can be said to try, in an interpretative sense, to become a reader of the writer's own period. In Figure 12.5, the gap is bridged by, in effect, abandoning the writer's participation in the communicative situation.

Although I argue the superiority of one viewpoint (Figure 12.4), my view is that both viewpoints can be adopted for literary–linguistic education. The viewpoint in Figure 12.4 is necessary if we are to come closer to the author's meaning and to avoid misconstruing what the language 'says'. The viewpoint in Figure 12.5 is desirable if we are to explore what the text means for the present time and for present readers. It can be maintained that each new age adds to the significance of a literary work: for example, feminist criticism of the last generation may have added interpretations which were unavailable to the author and readers of the author's time, but are nevertheless relevant for our own time. In pursuing these two different notions of significance, we acknowledge that a literary work is both (a) of its own time, and (b) for all time. According to Gadamer's theory of hermeneutics (1972, 1976) these two apparently contradictory *horizons* are reconcilable.[28] By reaching back to the author's own time we do not need to sacrifice the viewpoint which sees its particular relevance and significance for the present age.

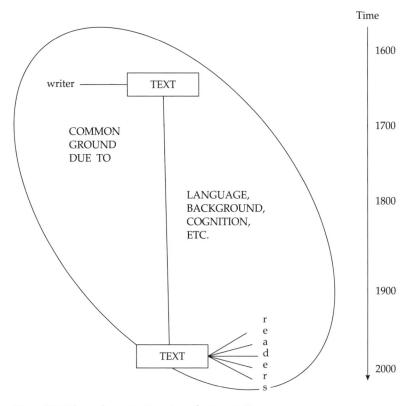

Figure 12.4 The author-intention view of interpretation

Although I have argued that a 'readerly' view and an 'authorly' view of a text are both educationally viable, my concluding preference is to say that scholarly integrity belongs to the second view, which has been too much neglected in the intellectual climate of recent times.

12.5 Conclusion

I have argued that there is a 'division of labour', for a reader, between the decoding of the language of a text and the interpretation of the text, using what the reader brings to it.[29] This corresponds to a 'division of labour', in stylistics, between the task of linguistic description and literary interpretation (that is, between identifying the relevant features of the text, and showing how they contribute to the interpretation). Of these two tasks, linguistic description is to a large extent a matter of presenting linguistic evidence observable in the text, and there is correspondingly little opportunity for

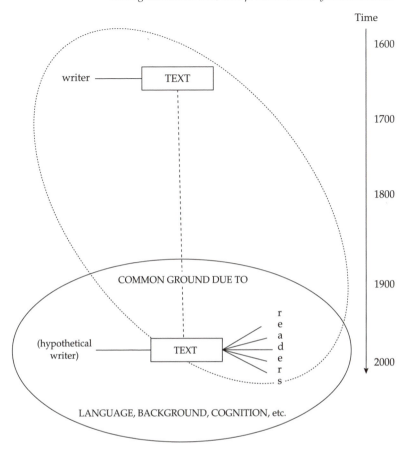

Figure 12.5 The author-free view of interpretation
Note: In this case the common ground is shared by the readers only: there is no link to the original author.

variable responses from individual to individual. Interpretation, on the other hand, gives more scope for variability of response, including literary background. I contend, further, that the 'division of labour' maintains a balance between commonality and variability of reader response, a balance which explains why people's understandings (even when constrained by evidence, reasonable argument, and so on) substantively agree, but also interestingly differ, in the interpretation of a work of literature.

I have also argued that this 'division of labour' has been misconstrued through previous intellectual influences on stylistics. In the era of formalism and structuralism, the emphasis was often too much on the formally

Language in Literature

identifiable linguistic characteristics. Little attention was given to the mechanisms and the variability of interpretation. In the post-structuralist, postmodern era, on the other hand, emphasis has been heavily placed on the variability of response, and the lack of any stable understanding of what a text means. This has been partly due, in my opinion, to a misuse of the term *text* in a way that can include almost anything that can enter into a text's interpretation.

I hope that this book will have led to a greater understanding that 'linguistic text' and 'literary interpretation' are not opposing sides in a tug-of-war, but two cooperative endeavours of comparable value.

Notes

1. These developments are traced in surveys of stylistics and recent schools of thought: see Carter and Simpson (1989: 1–20), and – with particular reference to fiction writing – Leech and Short (2007: 282–304). Wales (2001) is invaluable in providing brief stimulating and informative synopses of school of thought, critical concepts, linguistic concepts, etc.
2. See Fowler (1996), Birch (1991), Burton (1982), Jean Jacques Weber (1992) for Critical Discourse approaches to literature and other texts. It should be noted that the 'critical' in the collocation 'critical discourse' has overtones of examining texts from the viewpoint of ideology and power. This is different from the association of the older collocations 'literary critical' and 'literary criticism' with the study and evaluation of the qualities of literary works.
3. Perhaps the best example of formalism applied to an English text is Jakobson and Jones (1970) on Shakespeare's *Sonnet 129*.
4. See Barthes (1977) on the 'death of the author'; the affective stylistics of Fish (1970); the intertextuality theory of criticism of Kristeva (1980, 1986) and a number of other influential trends referred to later in this chapter.
5. Attridge (1987) provides a respectful but critical retrospective view of Jakobson's work on linguistics and poetics, as reflected in his famous 'Closing Statement' at the *Style in Language* conference (Jakobson 1960). For earlier critiques of Jakobson, see Fowler (1975b: 2–3, 82–8) and Werth (1976).
6. In the 1920s, the heyday of Russian formalism, such claims were made by leaders of the movement. Later other scholars, such as Levin (1962), made similar claims. However, Jakobson (1960) avoided a formalist definition of literature, by claiming that his formal principle (see Chapter 8, pp. 104–05) defined not poetry, but the *poetic function*, which could be found in non-literary as well as literary texts. The attempt to define the boundary between literature and non-literature in terms of some 'recipe' – formal or otherwise – is traced historically by Pratt (1977: 3–37), who calls it 'the Poetic Fallacy'.
7. Spitzer (1948) termed this cyclic movement the 'philological circle'. His discussion of it in *Linguistics and Literary History* is reprinted in Freeman (1970: 21–39).
8. 'The two cultures' was the theme of Snow's Rede Lecture at Cambridge University in 1959.
9. As Fairclough, a leading practitioner of CDA, sees it (1996: 50): 'CDA has given particular focus to explanatory relations between texts and social relations of power, and therefore to questions of ideology. . . . this emphasis comes out of the particular political conjuncture within which CDA emerged . . . and reflects the

political commitments of its practitioners'. See also Burton's (1982), Birch's (1989) and Weber's (1992: 1) ideologically committed stylistics. Burton's (1982: 196) rather exaggerated view is: '*All* observation, let alone description, *must* take place within an already constructed theoretical framework of socially, ideologically and linguistically constructed reality, whether the observer/describer of observation is articulately aware of that framework or not'. At its most extreme, this kind of determinist *parti pris* thinking takes the form that Sell (2000: 288–9) calls 'the historicist assumption': 'The assumption that human beings are so fully determined by sociocultural factors that they lack any real personal autonomy'. Sell adds (ibid.) 'It is important to note that many scholars describing their work as historicist would reject such a determinist view'. This is not to deny the validity of CDA's critique of texts influential in the body politic, such as various types of political and media discourse.

10. See Stockwell (2002) and Tsur (2003) on cognitive poetics; Semino and Culpeper (2002) on cognitive stylistics.

11. Empirical study of literature is illustrated by van Peer (1986), Short (1989a), Steen (1994).

12. These trends are pre-eminently illustrated by the methods of 'practical criticism' in Richards (1929), and the New Critical writings in Wimsatt (1954), especially the essays on the 'Intentional fallacy' and the 'Affective fallacy' written by Wimsatt and Beardsley.

13. The source and original form of Derrida's quote is: 'Il n'y a pas de hors-texte' (from *Of Grammatology*, Derrida (1967b) – see Wright (1995: 533).

14. This is not to deny the value of intertextual reference as *one* aspect of the expounding of a text. The trouble is that intertextuality, as a concept of critical theory, confounds a number of different relations between texts: among them genre membership, allusion, quotation, speech and thought presentation, register borrowing.

15. These quotes via de Beaugrande (1988: 246–7).

16. It would be unfair to convey the impression that all prominent literary theorizing of the past generation has been inimical to text-oriented analysis. One critical movement which has much in common with stylistics, and which gives fuller significance to it, is that of HERMENEUTICS associated (for example) with the writings of Gadamer (1972, 1976). His notion of the 'hermeneutic circle' of interpretation is highly relevant to the analogy with scientific method I gave above, as is Spitzer's older notion of the 'philological circle' which leads the literary exegist cyclically from the external linguistic features to the 'inward life-centre' of a work – see Spitzer (1948: 27). Gadamer's idea of the cyclic interaction between interpreter and text, or of whole context and individual parts, is close to the recurrent interplay of form and function which I had in mind in talking of a formal–functional approach to stylistics. There is recursion here too, but the role of cyclic recursion is similar to that of the recurrent testing of scientific hypotheses – it leads to a greater precision, understanding and insight in the explanation of the textual object.

17. The English language is the enemy of stylistics in two respects: it prefers to treat both *text* and *interpretation* to be countable nouns, rather than mass nouns. We talk about *a text* and *an interpretation* of it, or alternatively about *texts* and *interpretations* in the plural, as if it is natural and unavoidable to recognize discrete lumps of text and discrete interpretations of them. But from many points of view this is simplification. I will occasionally want to ignore this limitation, and use *text* and *interpretation* as mass nouns.

18. It would be even more dubious to call an original novel and its translation into another language as the 'same text'. Here, incidentally, there begins to be a divergence between 'text' and words like 'novel' which otherwise seem to belong to the same level of abstraction: it seems rather natural to refer to *The Mill on the Floss* and its translation into Japanese as 'the same novel'.

19. Of course, this notion of 'text' is heavily dependent on the written language, as is traditional. If we wanted to extend the term 'text' to include spoken text (e.g. as in oral poetry), this definition would have to be reformulated in terms of abstractions from the spoken rendering of the text. Another potential problem of the meaning of *text* relates to the combination of words with music, or words with visual content. I believe that the ordinary use of the word *text* justifies here limiting its reference to the linguistic content of multimodal works.

20. Note that, rightly, this provisional definition says nothing about the length of a text: the fact that some texts (like lengthy novels) are extremely long punctuated word strings should not bar us from recognizing that some other texts (such as the Eisenhower electioneering slogan *I like Ike*, famously analysed by Jakobson 1960: 357), are extremely short.

21. In this connection, a useful distinction has sometimes been made between graphology and graphetics, the written equivalents of phonology and phonetics in the spoken language. In each pair, the former refers to features systematically and significantly deployed in the language, whereas the latter refers to features of physical substance which are not necessarily of linguistic significance. It seems a reasonable generalization to say that two versions or copies of the same text (in the sense of text$_1$: opus), should be alike in their graphological form and structure, but that they do not need to be alike in graphetic detail.

22. There is no implication here, however, that ascribing interpretations to poems is a kind of free-for-all in which ignorant or idiosyncratic readings are as good as any other. I am reminded here of the interpretative weaknesses that I.A. Richards (1929: 13–18) labelled the 'ten difficulties of criticism': he included among them 'mnemonic irrelevancies', 'stock responses', 'doctrinal adhesions' and 'general critical preconceptions'. Whereas these faults of reading may intrude into a reader's interpretation *in spite of* the text, in my view, a *relevant* component of interpretation should be capable of substantiation with reference to the text.

23. On approaches to the teaching of stylistics, see McIntyre (2003), Short and Archer (2003), and other contributions to the special issue of *Style* **37** (1) (2003).

24. This assumption lies behind the provision by Short (1996: xiii and *passim*) and Leech and Short (2007: 61–6) of non-theory-laden linguistic checklists or checksheets, as an aid to stylistic analysis. Fowler (1986: 7), on the contrary, argues that stylistics should use a well-articulated theoretical model such as the functional model of Halliday.

25. Although H.P. Grice himself did not use the term 'pragmatics', the branch of linguistics that goes under that name was initially founded on the work of Grice and other philosophers (such as J.R. Searle).

26. To prevent confusion, let me say that this 'perfect reader' cannot be equated with other examples of idealized or generalized readership emanating from various versions of reader-oriented theory or criticism: Riffaterre's (1959) average reader, Fish's (1970) informed reader, Culler's (1975) ideal reader. The 'perfect reader' I mention is an unattainable ideal, but to the extent that we move towards this ideal, we become better readers, or at least better-informed readers, more in tune with the author's intentions.

27. See Sell (2000: 1–4 and *passim*) on the communicative relation between author and reader.

28. In fact, Gadamer (1972, 1976) argued that an understanding of a text is based on a fusion of (or a dialogue between) the two *horizons* of the text's period and one's own period.

29. Such a 'division of labour' is widely maintained and accepted in pragmatics – cf. Grice's (1975: 43–4) distinction between what is said and what is implicated; Sperber and Wilson's (1995: 9–15) distinction between decoding and inference; and a well-established tradition of Neo-Gricean thought – see e.g. Jaszczolt (2005) – based on the semantics/pragmatics distinction.

References

ABERCROMBIE, DAVID (1973 [1964]) 'A Phonetician's view of verse structure', in *Studies in Phonetics and Linguistics*, London: Longman, 17–25.

ADAMSON, SYLVIA (2003) 'Text, context and the interpretive community', unpublished paper presented at the Modern Language Association, San Diego, 2003.

ATKINS, J.W.H. (1934) *Literary Criticism in Antiquity*, vol. ii, Cambridge: Cambridge University Press.

ATTRIDGE, DEREK (1982) *The Rhythms of English Poetry*, London: Longman.

ATTRIDGE, DEREK (1987) 'Closing statement: linguistics and poetics in retrospect', in Fabb et al. (1987), 15–32.

ATTRIDGE, DEREK (2004a [1988]) *Peculiar Language: Literature as Difference from the Renaissance to James Joyce*, London: Routledge (1st edition published at Ithaca, NY: Cornell University Press, 1988).

ATTRIDGE, DEREK (2004b) *The Singularity of Literature*, London: Routledge.

AUSTIN, J.L. (1962) *How to Do Things with Words*, Oxford: Clarendon Press.

BACH, K. AND R.M. HARNISH (1979) *Linguistic Communication and Speech Acts*, Cambridge, MA: MIT Press.

BAIN, ALEXANDER (1887) *English Composition and Rhetoric*, enlarged edition, Part I London, etc.: Longmans Green & Co.

BAKHTIN, MIKHAIL (1981) *The Dialogic Imagination: Four Essays*. Austin: University of Texas Press.

BALDWIN, DEAN R. (1989) *Virginia Woolf: A Study of the Short Fiction*, Boston: Twayne.

BARCELONA, ANTONIO (ed.) (2000) *Metaphor and Metonymy at the Crossroads: A Cognitive Perspective*, Berlin and New York: Mouton de Gruyter.

BARTHES, ROLAND (1977) 'The death of the author', in Heath, S. (ed.) *Image – Music – Text*, London: Fontana.

BATESON, F.W. (1968) 'Language and literature', *Essays in Criticism*, **18**, 164–82.

BIBER, DOUGLAS, STIG JOHANSSON, GEOFFREY LEECH, SUSAN CONRAD AND ED FINEGAN (1999) *Longman Grammar of Spoken and Written English*, London: Longman.

BIERWISCH, MANFRED (1970) 'Poetics and linguistics', in Freeman, D.C. (ed.) *Linguistics and Literary Style*, 96–115.

BIRCH, DAVID (1989) *Language, Literature and Critical Practice*, London: Routledge.

BIRCH, DAVID (1991) *The Language of Drama*, London: MaCmillan.

BLOCH, BERNARD (1953) 'Linguistic structure and linguistic analysis', in Hill, A.A. (ed.) *Report of the Fourth Annual Round Table Meeting on Linguistics and Language Study*, Washington DC: Georgetown University Press.

BOOTH, WAYNE C. (1961) *The Rhetoric of Fiction*, Chicago: University of Chicago Press.

BROWN, PENELOPE AND STEPHEN LEVINSON (1987 [1978]) *Politeness: Some Universals in Language Usage*, 2nd edn, Cambridge: Cambridge University Press.

BÜHLER, KARL (1965 [1934]) *Sprachtheorie*, Stuttgart: Fischer.

BURTON, DEIRDRE (1982) 'Through glass darkly: through dark glasses', in Carter, R. (1982), 195–214.

CARTER, RONALD (ed.) (1982) *Language and Literature: An Introductory Reader in Stylistics*, London: Unwin Hyman.

CARTER, RONALD (2004) *Language and Creativity: The Art of Common Talk*, London: Routledge, Oxford: Oxford University Press.

CARTER, RONALD AND MICHAEL MCCARTHY (2006) *Cambridge Grammar of English: A Comprehensive Guide*, Cambridge: Cambridge University Press.

CARTER, RONALD AND PAUL SIMPSON (1989) *Language, Discourse and Literature: An Introductory Reader in Discourse Stylistics*, London: Unwin Hyman.

COHN, DORRIT (1978) *Transparent Minds: Narrative Modes for Presenting Consciousness in Fiction*, Princeton, NJ: Princeton University Press.

COOK, GUY (1994) *Discourse and Literature: The Interplay of Form and Mind*, Oxford: Oxford University Press.

COULTHARD, MALCOLM AND DAVID BRAZIL (1979) *Exchange Structure*, Birmingham: ELR.

CRYSTAL, DAVID AND DEREK DAVY (1969) *Investigating English Style*, London: Longman.

CULLER, JONATHAN (1975) *Structuralist Poetics*, London: Routledge and Kegan Paul.

CULLER, JONATHAN (1983) *On Deconstruction: Theory and Criticism after Structuralism*, London: Routledge and Kegan Paul.

CURETON, RICHARD D. (1992) *The Rhythmic Phrasing in English Verse*, London: Longman.

DANCYGIER, BARBARA (2006) 'What can blending do for you?' *Language and Literature* **15** (1), 5–15.

DE BEAUGRANDE, ROBERT (1988) *Critical Discourse: A Survey of Literary Theorists*, Norwood, NJ: Ablex.

DE BEAUGRANDE, R. AND W. DRESSLER (1981) *Introduction to Text Linguistics*, London: Longman.

DERRIDA, JACQUES (1967a) *L'Écriture et la différence*, Paris: Seuil (translated 1978 as *Writing and Difference*, London: Routledge).

DERRIDA, JACQUES (1967b) *De la grammatologie*, Paris: Minuit (translated 1974 as *Of Grammatology*, Baltimore, MD: Johns Hopkins University Press).

DERRIDA, JACQUES (1981 [1972]) *Positions*, Paris: Minuit (translated 1981 as *Positions*, Chicago: University of Chicago Press).

DOUTHWAITE, JOHN (2000) *Towards a Linguistic Theory of Foregrounding*, Alessandria: Edizioni dell'Orso.

EDMONDSON, WILLIS (1981) *Spoken Discourse: A Model for Analysis*, London: Longman.

EMMOTT, CATHERINE, ANTHONY J. SANFORD AND EUGENE J. DAWYDIAK, (2007) 'Stylistics meets cognitive science: studying style in fiction and readers' attention from an inter-disciplinary perspective', *Style*, **41** (2), 204–24.

EPSTEIN, E.L. (1975) 'The self-reflexive artefact: the function of mimesis in an approach to a theory of value for literature', in Fowler, R. (1975b), 40–78.

ERLICH, VICTOR (1965 [1955]) *Russian Formalism: History and Doctrine*, The Hague: Mouton.

ERVIN-TRIPP, SUSAN M. (1972) 'Sociolinguistic rules of address', in Pride, J.B. and Holmes, J. (eds) *Sociolinguistics*, Harmondsworth: Penguin, 225–40.

FABB, NIGEL, DEREK ATTRIDGE, ALAN DURANT AND COLIN MCCABE (eds) (1987) *The Linguistics of Writing: Arguments between Language and Literature*, Manchester: University of Manchester Press.

FAIRCLOUGH, NORMAN (1996) 'A reply to Henry Widdowson's "Discourse analysis: a critical view" ', *Language and Literature*, **5** (1), 49–56.

FAUCONNIER, GILLES AND MARK TURNER (2002) *The Way we Think: Conceptual Blending and the Mind's Hidden Complexities*, New York: Basic Books.

FIRTH, J.R. (1957) *Papers in Linguistics 1934–51*, Oxford: Oxford University Press.

FISH, STANLEY E. (1970) 'Literature in the reader: affective stylistics', *New Literary History* **2**, 123–62.

FISH, STANLEY E. (1980) 'What is stylistics and why are they saying such terrible things about it?', in *Is there a Text in this Class?: The Authority of Interpretative Communities*, Cambridge, MA: Harvard University Press, 68–96.

FORSTER, E.M. (1951) *Two Cheers for Democracy*, London: Edward Arnold.

FOWLER, H.W. (1965 [1926]) *A Dictionary of Modern English Usage*, Oxford: Oxford University Press.

FOWLER, ROGER (1966a) (ed.) *Essays on Style and Language*, London: Routledge.

FOWLER, ROGER (1966b) 'Prose rhythm and metre', in Fowler, R. (1966a), 82–99.

FOWLER, ROGER (1971) *The Languages of Literature*, London: Routledge.

FOWLER, ROGER (1975a) 'Language and the reader: Shakespeare's sonnet 73', in Fowler, R. (1975b), 79–122.

FOWLER, ROGER (1975b) (ed.) *Style and Structure in Literature: Essays in the New Stylistics*, Oxford: Blackwell.

FOWLER, ROGER (1977) *Linguistics and the Novel*, London: Methuen.

FOWLER, ROGER (1996 [1986]) *Linguistic Criticism*, 2nd edn, Oxford and New York: Oxford University Press.

FREEMAN, DONALD C. (ed.) (1970) *Linguistics and Literary Style*, New York: Holt, Rinehart and Winston.

GADAMER, HANS-GEORG (1972) *Wahrheit und Methode*, Mohr: Tübingen (translated 1975 [2nd revised edn 2004] as *Truth and Method*, New York: Continuum).

GADAMER, HANS-GEORG (1976) *Philosophical Hermeneutics*, trans. and ed. David E. Linge, Berkeley: University of California Press.

GARDNER, W.H. (1949) *Gerard Manley Hopkins (1844–1889): A Study of Poetic Idiosyncrasy in Relation to Poetic Tradition*, London: Secker & Warburg.

GARDNER, W.H. (1953) (ed.) *Gerard Manley Hopkins: Poems and Prose*, Harmondsworth: Penguin.

GARVIN, P.L. (ed. and trans.) (1958) *A Prague School Reader on Esthetics, Literary Structure and Style*, Washington, Georgetown: Georgetown University Press.

GIMSON, A.C. (1980 [1962]) *An Introduction to the Pronunciation of English*, London: Arnold.

GRICE, H.P. (1957) 'Meaning', *Philosophical Review*, **66**, 377–88. [Reprinted in Steinberg, D.D. and Jakobovits, L.A. (eds), *Semantics: An Interdisciplinary Reader in Philosophy, Linguistics and Psychology*, Cambridge, Cambridge University Press, 1971, 53–9.]

GRICE, H.P. (1969) 'Utterer's meaning and intention', *The Philosophical Review*, **78** (2), 147–77.

GRICE, H.P. (1975) 'Logic and conversation', in Cole, P. and Morgan, Jerry L. (eds), *Syntax and Semantics*, Vol. 3, *Speech Acts*, New York, 41–58.

HALLIDAY, M.A.K. (1961) 'Categories of the theory of grammar', *Word*, **17** (3), 241–92.

HALLIDAY, M.A.K. (1964) 'The linguistic study of literary texts', in Lunt, H.G. (ed.) *Proceedings of the IXth International Congress of Linguists*, 302–7.

HALLIDAY, M.A.K. (1967) *Intonation and Grammar in British English*, The Hague: Mouton.

HALLIDAY, M.A.K. (1970a) *A Course in Spoken English: Intonation*, Oxford: Oxford University Press.

HALLIDAY, M.A.K. (1970b) 'Clause types and structural functions', in Lyons, J. (ed.), *New Horizons in Linguistics*, Harmondsworth: Penguin, 140–65.

HALLIDAY, M.A.K. (1971) 'Linguistic function and literary style: an inquiry into the language of William Golding's *The Inheritors*', in Chatman, S. (ed.), *Literary Style: A Symposium*, New York: Oxford University Press, 330–65.

HALLIDAY, M.A.K. (1973) *Explorations in the Functions of Language*, London: Edward Arnold.

HALLIDAY, M.A.K. (1978) *Language as Social Semiotic*, London: Edward Arnold.

HALLIDAY, M.A.K. (1979) 'Modes of meaning and modes of expression: types of grammatical structure, and their determination by different semantic functions', in Allerton, D.J., Carney, E. and Holdcroft, D. (eds) *Function and Context in Linguistic Analysis*, Cambridge: Cambridge University Press, 57–79.

HALLIDAY, M.A.K. AND RUQAIYA HASAN (1976) *Cohesion in English*, London: Longman.

HALLIDAY, M.A.K. AND RUQAIYA HASAN (1989 [1985]) *Language, Context and Text: Aspects of Language in a Social-Semiotic Perspective*, Oxford: Oxford University Press.

HAYDN, H. AND E. FULLER (compilers) (1978) *Thesaurus of Book Digests*, New York: Avenel Books.

HILL, TREVOR (1958) 'Institutional linguistics', *Orbis*, 7, 441–55.

HOOVER, DAVID L. (2004) 'Altered texts, altered worlds, altered styles', *Language and Literature* 13 (2), 99–118.

ISER, WOLFGANG (1978) *The Act of Reading: A Theory of Aesthetic Response*, Baltimore, MD: Johns Hopkins University Press.

JAKOBSON, ROMAN (1960) 'Closing statement: linguistics and poetics', in Sebeok, Thomas A. (ed.), *Style in Language*, MIT Press: Cambridge, Massachusetts, 350–77.

JAKOBSON, ROMAN (1966) 'Grammatical parallelism and its Russian facet', *Language* 42 (2), 399–429.

JAKOBSON, ROMAN AND LAWRENCE JONES (1970) *Shakespeare's Verbal Art in 'Th'Expense of Spirit'*, The Hague: Mouton.

JASZCZOLT, K.M. (2005) *Default Semantics: Foundations of a Compositional Theory of Acts of Communication*, Oxford: Oxford University Press.

KÖVECSES, ZOLTAN (2002) *Metaphor: A Practical Introduction*, Oxford and New York: Oxford University Press.

KRISTEVA, JULIA (1980 [1969]) *Semiotikè: recherches pour une sémanalyse*, Paris: Seuil (trans. as *Desire in Language: A Semiotic Approach to Literature and Art*, Oxford: Blackwell).

KRISTEVA, JULIA (1986) 'Word, dialogue, and the novel', in Moi, T. (ed.) *The Kristeva Reader*, New York: Columbia University Press, 35–61.

LABOV, WILLIAM AND DAVID FANSHEL (1977) *Therapeutic Discourse*, New York: Academic Press.

LAKOFF, GEORGE AND MARK JOHNSON (1980) *Metaphors we Live by*, Chicago: University of Chicago Press.

LAKOFF, GEORGE AND MARK TURNER (1989) *More than Cool Reason: A Field Guide to Poetic Metaphor*, Chicago: Chicago University Press.

LANIER, SIDNEY (1880) *The Science of English Verse*, New York: Scribner.

LEAVIS, F.R. (1936) *Revaluation*, London: Chatto & Windus.

LEAVIS, F.R. (1948) *Education and the University*, London: Chatto and Windus.

LEECH, GEOFFREY N. (1969) *A Linguistic Guide to English Poetry*, London: Longman.

LEECH, GEOFFREY N. (1980) 'Grammar and rhetoric within a functional view of language', in *Explorations in Semantics and Pragmatics*, Amsterdam: Benjamins, 9–29.

LEECH, GEOFFREY N. (1983) *Principles of Pragmatics*, London: Longman.

LEECH, GEOFFREY N. AND MICK SHORT (2007 [1981]) *Style in Fiction: A Linguistic Introduction to English Fictional Prose*, London & New York: Longman.

LEECH, GEOFFREY N. AND NICHOLAS SMITH (2005) 'Extending the possibilities of corpus-based research on English in the twentieth century: a prequel to LOB and FLOB', *ICAME Journal* **29**, 83–98.

LEVIN, SAMUEL R. (1962) *Linguistic Structures in Poetry*, The Hague: Mouton.

LEVIN, SAMUEL R. (1963) 'Deviation – statistical and determinate', *Lingua* **12**, 276–90.

LEVIN, SAMUEL R. (1964) 'Poetry and grammaticalness', in Lunt, H.G. (ed.), *Proceedings of the IXth International Congress of Linguists* 308–14.

LEVIN, SAMUEL R. (1965) 'Internal and external deviation in poetry', *Word* **21**, 225–37.

LÉVI-STRAUSS, CLAUDE (1963 [1958]) *Structural Anthropology*, trans. Claire Jacobson and Brooke Gundfest Schoepf, New York and London: Basic Books.

LIPSKI, J.M. (1977) 'Poetic deviance and generative grammars', *PTL* **2** (2), 241–56.

LODGE, DAVID (2002) *Consciousness and the Novel*, London: Secker and Warburg.

MARTIN, ROBERT B. (1991), *Gerard Manley Hopkins: A Very Private Life*, London: HarperCollins.

MCINTYRE, DAN (2003) 'Using foregrounding theory as a teaching methodology in a stylistics course', *Style* **37** (1), 1–11.

MCNICHOL, STELLA (1990) *Virginia Woolf and the Poetry of Fiction*, London and New York: Routledge.

MEDD, HAZEL AND INA BIERMANN (compilers) (1998) *PALA Stylistics Bibliography 1990–1998*, Poetics and Linguistics Assocation.

MEPHAM, J. (1991) *Virginia Woolf: A Literary Life*, New York: St. Martin's Press.

MUKAŘOVSKÝ, JAN (1964 [1958]) 'Standard language and poetic language', in Garvin, P. L. (ed. and trans.) *A Prague School Reader on Esthetics, Literary Structure and Style*, Washington: Georgetown University Press, 17–30.

NEWELL, A. (1973) 'Artificial intelligence and concept of mind', in Shank, R.C. and Colby, K.M. (eds) *Computer Models of Thought and Language*, San Francisco: W.H. Freeman, 1–60.

NEWTON-DE MOLINA, D. (1976) *On Literary Intentions*, Edinburgh: Edinburgh University Press.

OGDEN, C.K. AND I.A. RICHARDS (1923) *The Meaning of Meaning*, London: Routledge & Kegan Paul.

O'HALLORAN, KIERAN (2007) 'The subconscious in James Joyce's "Eveline": a corpus stylistic analysis that chews on the "Fish hook"', *Language and Literature*, **16** (3), 227–44.

OHMANN, RICHARD (1971) 'Speech acts and the definition of literature', *Philosophy and Rhetoric* **4**: 1–19.

PARISI, D. AND C. CASTELFRANCHI (1982) 'A goal analysis of some pragmatic aspects of language', in Parret, H., Sbisà, M. and Verschueren, J. (eds) *Possibilities and Limitations of Pragmatics*, Amsterdam: John Benjamins, 551–68.

POPE, J.C. (1942), *The Rhythm of Beowulf*, New Haven: Yale University Press.

POPPER, KARL R. (1979 [1972]) *Objective Knowledge: An Evolutionary Approach*, Oxford: Oxford University Press.

POUND, EZRA (1934) *Make it New: Essays*, London: Faber.

PRATT, MARY LOUISE (1977) *Towards a Speech Act Theory of Literary Discourse*, Bloomington, IN: Indiana University Press.

PUTTENHAM, GEORGE (1936 [1589]) *The Arte of English Poesie*, ed. Gladys D. Willcock and Alice Walker, Cambridge: Cambridge University Press.

QUIRK, RANDOLPH., SIDNEY GREENBAUM, GEOFFREY LEECH AND JAN SVARTVIK (1985) *A Comprehensive Grammar of the English Language*, London: Longman.

RAYSON, PAUL (2003) 'Matrix: a statistical method and software tool for linguistic analysis through corpus comparison', PhD thesis, Lancaster University.

REID, T.B.W. (1956) 'Linguistics, structuralism and philology', *Archivum Linguisticum*, **8**, 28–37.

RICHARDS, I.A. (1929) *Practical Criticism*, London: Routledge & Kegan Paul.

RICHARDS, I.A. (1936) *The Philosophy of Rhetoric*, Oxford: Oxford University Press.

RICHARDS, I.A. (1970) 'Jakobson's Shakespeare: the subliminal structure of a sonnet', *Times Literary Supplement*, 28 May, 589–90.

RIFFATERRE, MICHAEL (1959) 'Criteria for style analysis', *Word*, **15**, 154–75.

ROSCH, ELEANOR (1975) 'Cognitive representations of semantic categories', *Journal of Experimental Psychology: General* **104**, 193–233.

ROSCH, ELEANOR AND BARBARA B. LLOYD (eds) (1978) *Cognition and Categorization*, Hillsdale, NJ: Erlbaum.

RYAN, MARIE-LAURE (1991) *Possible Worlds, Artificial Intelligence, and Narrative Theory*, Bloomington, IN: Indiana University Press.

SACKS, HARVEY, EMANUEL SCHEGLOFF AND GAIL JEFFERSON (1974) 'A simplest systematics for the organization of turn-taking in conversation', *Language*, **50** (4), 696–735.

SANDELL, R. (1977) *Linguistic Style and Persuasion*, London: Academic Press.

SEARLE, J.R. (1969) *Speech Acts: An Essay in the Philosophy of Language*, Cambridge: Cambridge University Press.

SEARLE, J.R. (1975) 'A taxonomy of illocutionary acts', in Gunderson, K. (ed.) *Minnesota Studies in the Philosophy of Science*, vol. 7, *Language, Mind and Knowledge*, Minneapolis: University of Minnesota Press, 344–69.

SEBEOK, THOMAS A. (ed.) (1960) *Style in Language*, Cambridge, MA: MIT Press.

SELL, ROGER D. (ed.) (1991) *Literary Pragmatics*, London: Routledge.

SELL, ROGER D. (2000) *Literature and Communication*, Amsterdam: Benjamins.

SEMINO, ELENA (1997) *Language and World Creation in Poems and Other Texts*, London: Longman.

SEMINO, ELENA AND JONATHAN CULPEPER (eds) (2002) *Cognitive Stylistics: Language and Cognition in Text Analysis*, Amsterdam: Benjamins.

SHORT, MICK (ed.) (1989a) *Reading, Analysing and Teaching Literature*, London: Longman.

SHORT, MICK (1989b) 'Discourse analysis and the analysis of drama', in Carter, R. and Simpson, P., 139–70.

SHORT, MICK (1996) *Exploring the Language of Poems, Plays and Prose*, London: Longman.

SHORT, MICK AND DAWN ARCHER (2003) 'Designing a worldwide web-based stylistics course and investigating its effectiveness', *Style*, **37** (1), 27–46.

SIBLEY, F. (1959) 'Aesthetic concepts', *Philosophical Review*, **68**, 421–50.

SIBLEY, F. (1965) 'Aesthetic and nonaesthetic', *Philosophical Review*, **74**, 135–9.

SIBLEY, F. (1968) 'Objectivity and aesthetics', *Proceedings of the Aristotelian Society*, Supp. 42, 31–54.

SIMPSON, PAUL (1989) 'Politeness phenomena in Ionesco's *The Lesson*', in Carter, R. and Simpson, P., 171–94.

SINCLAIR, JOHN (1991) *Corpus, Concordance, Collocation*, Oxford: Oxford University Press.

SINCLAIR, JOHN MCH. (1966) 'Taking a poem to pieces', in Fowler, R. (ed.) (1966a), 68–81.

SINCLAIR, JOHN MCH. AND R. MALCOLM COULTHARD (1975) *Towards An Analysis of Discourse*, London: Oxford University Press.

SPERBER, DAN AND DEIRDRE WILSON (1995 [1986]), *Relevance: Communication and Cognition*, 2nd edn, Oxford: Blackwell.

SPITZER, LEO (1948) *Linguistics and Literary History*, Princeton, NJ: Princeton University Press.

STEEN, GERARD (1994) *Understanding Metaphor in Literature*, London: Longman.

STOCKWELL, PETER (2002) *Cognitive Poetics: An Introduction*, London: Routledge.

SVARTVIK, JAN (1982) 'The segmentation of impromptu speech', in Enkvist, Nils-Erik (ed.) *Impromptu Speech: A Symposium*, Åbo: Åbo Akademi, 131–45.

THOMAS, JENNY (1995) *Meaning in Interaction*, London: Longman.

TINDALL, W.Y. (1962) *A Reader's Guide to Dylan Thomas*, New York: Octagon.

TSUR, R. (2003) *On the Shore of Nothingness: A Study of Cognitive Poetics*, Exeter and Charlottesville, VA: Imprint Academic.

VAN DIJK, TEUN (1972) *Some Aspects of Text Grammars*, The Hague: Mouton.

VAN PEER, WILLIE (1986) *Stylistics and Psychology: Investigations in Foregrounding*, London: Croom Helm.

VAN PEER, WILLIE (2007) 'Introduction to foregrounding: a state of the art', *Language and Literature*, **16** (2), 99–104.

VAN PEER, W. AND J. HAKEMULDER (2006) 'Foregrounding', in Brown, K. (ed.) *Encyclopedia of Language and Linguistics*, 2nd edition, Vol. 4, Oxford: Elsevier, 546–51.

VERDONK, PETER (1988) *How Can We Know the Dancer from the Dance? Some Literary Stylistic Studies of English Poetry*, Amsterdam: Peter Verdonk.

VOEGELIN, C.F. (1960) 'Casual and non-casual utterances within unified structure', in Sebeok, T.A. (ed.) *Style in Language*, Cambridge MA: MIT Press, 57–68.

VOROBYOVA, OLGA (2005) ' "The Mark on the Wall" and literary fancy: a cognitive sketch', in Veivo, Harri, Pettersson, Bo and Polvinen, Merja (eds) *Cognition and Literary Interpretation of Texts*, Helsinki: Yliopistopaino, 201–17.

WALES, KATIE (1992) *The Language of James Joyce*, Basingstoke: Macmillan.

WALES, KATIE (2001 [1989]) *A Dictionary of Stylistics*, 2nd edn, London: Longman.

WEBER, JEAN JACQUES (1992) *Critical Analysis of Fiction: Essays in Discourse Stylistics*, Amsterdam and Atlanta, GA: Rodopi.

WELLEK, RENE AND AUSTIN WARREN (1949) *Theory of Literature*, New York: Harcourt, Brace and World.

WERTH, PAUL (1976) 'Roman Jakobson's verbal analysis of poetry', *Journal of Linguistics*, **12**, 21–73.

WERTH, PAUL (1999) *Text Worlds: Representing Conceptual Space in Discourse*, London: Longman.

WIDDOWSON, HENRY G. (1975) *Stylistics and the Teaching of Literature*, London: Longman.

WIDDOWSON, HENRY G. (1978) *Teaching Language as Communication*, Oxford: Oxford University Press.

WIDDOWSON, HENRY G. (1995) 'Discourse analysis: a critical view', *Language and Literature*, **4** (3), 157–72.

WIDDOWSON, HENRY G. (1996) 'Reply to Fairclough: discourse and interpretation: conjectures and refutations', *Language and Literature*, **5** (1), 57–69.

WILSON, ANDREW AND GEOFFREY, LEECH (1993) 'Automatic content analysis and the stylistic analysis of prose literature', *Revue Informatique et Statistique dans les Sciences humaines*, **29**, 219–34.

WIMSATT, W.K. (1954) *The Verbal Icon: Studies in the Meaning of Poetry*, Lexington, KY: University of Kentucky Press.

WIMSATT, W.K. AND MONROE C. BEARDSLEY (1954 [1946]) 'The intentional fallacy', in Wimsatt, W.K. (1954), 3–20.

WRIGHT, TERENCE R. (1995) 'Reader response under review: art, game or science?', *Style*, **29** (4).

YOUNGREN, WILLIAM H. (1972) *Semantics, Linguistics and Criticism*, New York: Random House.

Index

Index

paradox, 5, 61
parallelism, 20–3, 31, 61, 99, 100–101, 114, 149
parataxis, 142
parts of speech, 168, 172–4
passive voice, 99
past tense, 156, 171, 172
performance, **72–4**, 79, 82, 83
peripateia, 69
perlocutionary (act), 90–1
personification, 17, 67
philological circle, 42
phonemic (analysis/level), 44–7, 65
phonological patterning, 20–21, 26, 137, 139–40
plural nouns, 173–4
Poetics and Linguistics Association, 1, 163
Politeness Principle, the (in pragmatics), **91–3**, 96, 98, **118–35**
politeness, 111, 134
see Politeness Principle
Pope, Alexander, 22, 191
Popper, Karl, 108–9
POS
see part-of-speech categories
post-structuralist literary theory, 180
PP
see Politeness Principle
practical criticism, 5, 183
pragmatics, 2, **86–103**, 116, **118–35**, 182, 193
Pratt, Mary Louise, 106
present tense, 170–1, 172
principles of pragmatics
see Cooperative Principle, Politeness Principle
progressive structure, 141
prominence, 163
promotion (of stress), **71–2**, 82
pronouns, 152–4, 170, 171
prosodic foregrounding, 19
see also verse form
prototype concepts, prototype theory, **7**, 180
psychological verbs, 143, 175
punctuation, 188

questions, 140, 148, 158
Quintilian, 23

Rayson, Paul, 162, 164
reality, 175
reference corpus, 166–7, 169, 171
register, 13, 15
regulative goals, **89**, 91, 95, 98
reinforcement of schematic patterning, 24–6
repetition, 148–9, 176
see also parallelism, schematic patterning
representation, 110, 137, 151–5
response forms, 141
rhetoric, 11–12, 110, 111–112, 116, 117
rhetorical question, 118, 125
rhyme, 20, 65
rhythm (linguistic), **71–2**, 74, 79, 82, 83, 140
rhythmic compensation, 75
Richards, I. A., 37, 40, 107–8, 206
right dislocation, 141
rights (and obligations), 124–7, 128
Rossetti, Christina, 84
Russian formalists, 9

salience, 144
scansion, 70–2
see also musical scansion
schematic foregrounding, 19–23
schematic figures, 20–3
Scott, Mike, 165
Searle, John R., 90–5
segmentation, 144, 147–8
semantic(s), 22, 137, 142, 168, 174–6
sentence length, 147–8
sequence, 144
Shakespeare, William, 26, 37, 187, 201
Shaw, George Bernard, 8, **108–35**
Shelley, Percy B., 8, 56–69
Short, Mick, 163
Sibley, Frank, 38–40
significance, (statistical), 165
Sinclair and Coulthard, 95
Sitwell, Edith, 17
Sperber and Wilson, 196, 198
sound patterning, 5
see phonemic (analysis/level)
speech act, 93
sprung rhythm, 70
stream of consciousness, 137, **143–4**, 171, 175